International Journalism

Journalism Studies: Key Texts

Journalism Studies: Key Texts is a new textbook series that systematically maps the crucial connections between theory and practice in journalism. It provides the solid grounding students need in the history, theory, 'real-life' practice and future directions of journalism, while further engaging them in key critical debates. Drawing directly from how journalism is studied and understood today, the series is a full-service resource for students and lecturers alike.

Series Editors: Martin Conboy, David Finkelstein, Bob Franklin

Published Titles
Alternative Journalism Chris Atton and James Hamilton
Radio Journalism Guy Starkey and Andrew Crissell
Newspaper Journalism Peter Cole and Tony Harcup

International Journalism

Kevin Williams

Los Angeles | London | New Delhi
Singapore | Washington DC

SAGE Publications Ltd
1 Oliver's Yard
55 City Road
London EC1Y 1SP

SAGE Publications Inc.
2455 Teller Road
Thousand Oaks, California 91320

SAGE Publications India Pvt Ltd
B 1/I 1 Mohan Cooperative Industrial Area
Mathura Road
New Delhi 110 044

SAGE Publications Asia-Pacific Pte Ltd
33 Pekin Street #02-01
Far East Square
Singapore 048763

Library of Congress Control Number: 2010939221

British Library Cataloguing in Publication data

A catalogue record for this book is available from the British Library

ISBN 978-1-4129-4527-1
ISBN 978-1-4129-4528-8 (pbk)

Typeset by C&M Digitals (P) Ltd, Chennai, India
Printed by CPI Antony Rowe, Chippenham, Wiltshire
Printed on paper from sustainable resources

'To cover history from the front row', they had said. But nobody mentioned the reality that any time I turned up to witness history unfolding it would be from a hermetically sealed grandstand, a peripatetic 'press tent' in its many guises, with acolytes to supply pre-digested sound bites, statistics, internet connection, and pre-programmed access to the main players. All in time for deadline.

Paddy Smyth,
foreign correspondent,
The Irish Times.

CONTENTS

PREFACE

The origins of this book lie in the Masters programme in Journalism Studies at Cardiff University developed in the 1980s by Geoff Mungham and Don Rowlands. This brought students from all over the world to study in a multicultural environment the problems of reporting a rapidly changing world. Many of these students were mid-career journalists who took leave from their jobs to find the space and time – and money – to examine, discuss and debate their working practices and learn from each other about the best ways to report. The course combined theory and practice in the context of the then urgent debate around the establishment of a new international information order. A fair and balanced coverage of the so-called Third World was the demand that united most of the students on the programme. Improving intellectual and technical skills were part of the campaign to attain this objective. Close co-operation between the Masters scheme and the Thomson Foundation facilitated the programme. Several people played their part in delivering the teaching including Trevor Wade, Peter Twaites, Miranda Basner, Tor Ekevall, Paul Moorcraft, Mike Ungerma, Colin Larcombe, Bob Atkins and Brian Winston. But it was the students themselves who were crucial to the success of the programme including Zahera Harb, Bernadette Cole, Mala Jagmohan, Mackie Holder, Nixon Karithii, Linda Nassanga, David Ampofo, Salva Rweymamu, Ichakeli Maro, Manal Kabil and Louise Abbott to name but a few. Special thanks to Edita Nsubuga whose commitment to the programme went beyond the call of duty! They are among the many graduates of the Masters scheme who deserve thanks for the energy, insight and drive they gave to the programme in Cardiff, which helped to establish its international reputation. Sadly Geoff Mungham and Don Rowlands are no longer with us but what they left behind at Cardiff is a testament to their dedication, in particular the inspirational teaching of Geoff Mungham, which galvanised a generation of students from around the world and enabled them to make an improbable global–local connection between the district of Splott in Cardiff and the rest of the planet. The author would also like to thank Bob Franklin for asking him to write this book and his considerable patience in waiting for a manuscript. This was also shared by all those at Sage who also deserve thanks for deciding that it was worth waiting for. Thanks to Imogen Roome and Mila Steele. Several other people are also owed a debt of gratitude for their support of the Masters programme including John Underwood, Norman Cattanach, Jenny Palit, Maggie Griffiths, Aled Eurig, Val Williams and John Foscolo. I would like to thank Hans Henrik Holm for numerous stimulating discussions about the international media and journalism and the many insights he has provided. My colleagues on the Erasmus Mundus in Journalism within Globalization, in particular Monika Pater, Klaus Schoenbach, Peter Neijens, Neil Thurman and Roger Twose, have provided an invaluable reservoir of knowledge and insight. Thanks also to colleagues at Swansea, especially Chas Critcher and Yan Wu, for their willingness to listen to my ruminations about global journalism. Over the years conversations of both a fleeting and substantial nature with distinguished practitioners of foreign news reporting such as Lindsey Hilsum, Francesca Unsworth, Steve Evans and Jos Lemmers have put me back on the straight and narrow. Special thanks to Clare Hudson who has been supportive of all my efforts to make forays into the world of academia. Particular thanks are owed to her for letting me re-use ideas and material cited in her MSc(Econ) dissertation *Through Western Eyes: Newsgathering in the Third World* (Cardiff University, 1988) I would also like to thank the usual suspects, Marge, Ed, Alan, Frances, Griff, Rowley, Benny the Ball – who was unfortunately neglected in the acknowledgements in previous books – and last but not least Ie who has now left the BBC.

INTRODUCTION

THE CHANGING NATURE OF FOREIGN
CORRESPONDENCE

The revolution in information technology is ushering in new power relationships, new organizational structures, and new understandings of what constitutes journalism. (Livingston, 2007: 66)

The international journalism that is the focus of this book is the process by which men and women gather, handle and deliver news and information from around the world. At the heart of this activity is the foreign correspondent and the process of foreign correspondence. Foreign correspondence has a long history. News of what was happening abroad was a feature of Europe's earliest newspapers at the beginning of the seventeenth century. Today, the foreign correspondent enjoys prestige within the profession of journalism and is someone to be reckoned with by public policy makers (Hamilton and Jenner, 2002). He or she is the node of a system of international news gathering which provides media outlets around the world with a regular, reliable and rapid flow of information. However, this system is undergoing radical transformation. The capacity to learn more, more quickly about an ever increasing number of places and from a wide variety of sources is growing exponentially. Foreign news and its bearer, the foreign correspondent, is adapting to what has become an information rich world. The growing importance of commercial considerations and the arrival of new technology are among a number of factors that are altering the way in which international news is gathered, processed and disseminated (Hatchen, 2001: 126). Seasoned commentators question whether there is a future for foreign news (Hargreaves, 2000) and whether the journalism by which it is produced is represented as being in a 'state of crisis' (Campbell, 2004). The boundary that has traditionally separated foreign and domestic news has become more blurred and for many the category 'foreign' or 'international' news is 'inadequate to capture many of today's economic, political, cultural, and social interconnections that seem to overlook political borders' (Vargas and Paulin, 2007: 21).

The book seeks to explore the transformation that is taking place in foreign correspondence. This transformation is usually, if sometimes erroneously, associated with 'globalisation'. Global change can be seen in all aspects of human activity and there is a growing acceptance that globalisation is the best way to understand and unravel what is happening in contemporary international society. Globalisation is used to explain the developments that are taking place in international journalism and the changes in the capacity and ability of foreign correspondents to understand and interpret world events. It has diminished the role of the foreign correspondent within the international news system and broken down the 'us' and 'them' distinctions between nations and peoples that previously characterised foreign news. For some scholars and practitioners, the basic tenets of journalism as traditionally practised, including the defining concept of 'objectivity', are no longer fit for purpose in the emerging global age. What is required is a new form of international journalism. There have been calls for a more interventionist and committed journalism which 'serves as the persistent conscience of the new world order' (Seib, 2002: 121). Some argue that globalisation is bringing forth a new kind of journalism. The 'global journalism' that is emerging is seen as qualitatively different from foreign news reporting, which has been traditionally anchored within national parameters. It is 'deterritorialised' and represents a 'system of newsgathering, editing and distribution not based on national or regional boundaries – where it is not expected that shared national or community citizenship is the common reference uniting newsmakers, journalists and audience' (Reese, 2008: 240). The notion of 'global journalism' is controversial and, as we will see, a subject of debate, but what is not contested is that the complexities and contradictions of a rapidly changing international society present a challenge to the traditional process of foreign correspondence and the dominant values and ideals by which it has been practiced.

This introduction outlines in broad terms some of the changes that are occurring in modern international society. It describes the growing interconnectedness that characterises global change and the increased awareness that it offers. It outlines the growing complexities that embody contemporary international relations as well as the fundamental shifts that are taking place in the nature of international journalism and the debate this has generated about foreign news and journalism practices. It emphasises that global change poses a challenge to the capacity and ability of foreign correspondents to make sense of the world as well as the ways in which they report and represent international events. It begins, however, by drawing attention to a paradox; the opportunities to find out more about the world than ever before appear to be contradicted by a decline in the desire for such knowledge and information. We are continuously told by scholars, as well as those who work in the industry, that audiences in the world's remaining superpower, the United States, are less interested in what is happening outside their borders, other than at times of crisis. A headline in the *Los Angeles Times* sums this up: 'Foreign News Shrinks in Era of Globalization' (cited in Shaw, 2001).

The paradox of global change

Global change threatens to break down the geographical, national and cultural barriers that have traditionally hemmed in intellectual thought and communicative interaction. Interactions between peoples, consumers, governments and organisations at the global level are growing. It is possible to argue that we are on the verge of a 'great leap forward' in human consciousness and awareness, greater than at any other time since the Industrial Revolution. The signs of this growing awareness are seen at several levels. Air travel is taking more people to more places around the world and the tourist industry is facilitating the exchange, organising people's stays and encouraging their voyages. The number of international tourist trips increased from 25 million in 1950 to 760 million in 2004 (McGillivray, 2006: 174). Tourism is only one element of the huge growth recorded in the movement of people in the post-Second World War period. The number of refugees, asylum seekers, displaced persons and economic migrants has increased as a result of wars, famines and worsening economic and social conditions in many countries. Europe and America in the immediate wake of the 1939–45 war encouraged migrants – primarily from their former colonies or dependencies – to service their economies, which went through a period of boom in the 1950s and 1960s. The end of the Cold War increased the pressure to migrate, so that by the start of the twenty-first century one in every 255 people in the world was a forced migrant (Cohen and Kennedy, 2000: 144). Every day a large number of ordinary people, from students and au pairs to drug dealers and businessmen and women, are crossing national borders to make connections. The density of such connections has led the sociologist Manuel Castells (1996) to describe the society in which we live today as 'the network society'.

The mass media play a crucial role in furthering people's sense of interconnectedness. Twenty-four-hour news channels such as Cable Network News (CNN) and Al-Jazeera offer rolling international news continuously and often instantly, opening wider our window on the world. The internet and Twitter allow men and women across the world the opportunity to communicate directly with one another. Television affords access to information and images from other countries; the contemporary trade in international television is unprecedented, with people in all corners of the world accessing locally adapted versions of programmes such as *Big Brother*. Music from all over the planet seeps into homes and households through the CD and DVD, and television events as diverse as the World Cup and the murder trial of O.J. Simpson bring people together on all continents to share in a common viewing experience. As the then head of the world's largest media corporation, Steven Ross of Time-Warner, said in 1990:

> The competitive market place of ideas and experiences can only bring the world closer together. With new technologies, we can bring services and ideas that will draw even the most remote areas of the world into the international media community. (Ross, quoted in Robins, 1997: 16)

Foreign correspondents are the providers of much of the international news, information and analysis that flows across national borders. Technology is transforming the work of foreign correspondents. The frantic search for telephones that work and telex points from which to send dispatches that used to dominate the working lives of foreign reporters has ceased. Satellite technology enables reporters in the field to be in touch with their home office on a continuous basis. The cellular mobile phone not only makes it possible for reporters to talk directly to editors from wherever they are but also permits them to communicate breaking events and stories from on the spot. Similarly, lightweight portable cameras have made the most remote part of the world accessible to television. Electronic news gathering (ENG) equipment and satellites mean that stories can be edited in the field and sent back to be broadcast within hours of being filmed. With more rapid and plentiful airline connections, journalists can reach a story more quickly as well as file their reports faster than ever before. Correspondents criss-crossing the world, travelling from one country to another often thousands of miles apart, are providing their readers, viewers and listeners with a service more up-to-date than it has ever been. The casualty of this technological development has been the long stay reporter who settled down, developed roots and acquired an expertise on his or her 'beat' or part of the world.

There is, however, a paradox that confronts the growing interconnectedness. As more people go to more places, more quickly than ever before, and the news media enable far off events to encroach into people's everyday consciousness, the men and women who are charged with reporting what is happening in other places are disappearing. While people have a greater opportunity to know, learn and understand more about the world, foreign news is declining. This trend has been apparent since the end of the Second World War. For example, in 1945 there were over 2,500 US foreign correspondents based overseas; by the mid 1970s this had fallen to just over 430 (Dorman, 1986: 421). There was no full time correspondent for an African news outlet in Washington in the 1980s (Mowlana, 1997: 59). In the age of globalisation we are, according to Jonathan Dimbleby, getting:

> fewer and fewer people going to places for shorter and shorter periods, where satellites can instantly transmit their undigested, instant assessment … so as we're technically capable of being better and better informed, we are at risk of becoming less and less informed by fewer and fewer people. (Harrison, 1986: 76)

By the 1990s the decline in foreign news was seen as having reached a crisis point. The international news hole was described as 'an endangered species' and the foreign correspondent was declared as 'becoming extinct' (Hamilton and Jenner, 2002; Emery, 1989; Kalb, 1990). James Hoge (1997) could ask in the pages of America's leading journalism magazine, the *Columbia Journalism Review*, 'who gives a damn' about foreign news. A variety of interested parties were coming to the conclusion that international news coverage was 'inadequate' in the face of the rapid changes that were taking place across the planet. For example, the International Council on Human Rights Policy in the UK complained about the inadequacy and superficiality of international coverage of human rights, concluding that 'audiences that rely on the media to inform them are not always in a position to understand or judge properly the actions and policies of government and other authorities' (Sreberny and Paterson, 2004: 4). Concerns about the quality and quantity of international news are, as we shall see, not new but in the 1990s they were accompanied by technological, social, economic and cultural developments that threatened the very existence of the foreign correspondent.

The threat is most clearly articulated around the emergence of the internet, which is regarded as a direct challenge to the traditional means by which international news has been gathered, processed and reported. There are those who believe that the internet, together with a number of socio-economic changes, is rendering journalism obsolete. Vincent Campbell (2004: 1) concludes that news journalism is in 'its death throes, on the verge of losing the pivotal place in the transmission of information in societies all around the world'. According to Mike Bromley (1997), technological change, new business structures, the changing nature of news and the precarious status of the profession are interacting to bring about the 'end of journalism'. He emphasises how technology is changing journalism and increasingly making the journalist redundant as digital newsrooms and multi-skilling accelerate the breakdown of the demarcations between journalist and technicians, writers and camera operators, news gatherers and news processors

and between print, radio and television journalists (p. 341). In the words of
Jeremy Tunstall (1996), journalists are becoming 'technicians-with-words'.
If technology is making the profession of journalism redundant, we, the
ordinary members of the public, can today become actively involved in
gathering, reporting, interpreting and disseminating the news. According
to critics such as John Hartley, 'everyone is a journalist' (quoted in Weaver
and Loffelholz, 2008: 7).

We are living in an age in which the ordinary person can gather and
transmit foreign news. At the heart of this 'new' journalism are 'bloggers'.
The internet provides the opportunity for everyone, from the teenage dia-
rist, the professional journalist and established news organisations, to the
non-government organisation and terrorists and insurgents, to participate
in international communication (McNair, 2006: 133). The new medium,
according to Brian McNair (p. 151), 'goes way beyond the passivity of reclin-
ing in your easy chair to read the weekend book review' by allowing users
to 'have more control over content, access to a wider range of opinions, and
in many cases contribute themselves'. McNair endorses the view that 'this
is John Lennon's Power to the People, but turbo-charged and amplified. The
people want a voice, and now they really have it. Their own voice, unedited
and unfiltered' (p. 152). With every individual possessing the potential to
become a journalist, many believe that there is no future for the specialist
international news gatherer. According to the veteran American television
correspondent Garrick Utley (1997), today's communication technology
means that 'anyone sending information from one country to another is a
de facto foreign correspondent'.

An increasingly complex world

The world in which the contemporary foreign correspondent has to operate
has also been turned upside down. Political changes have come thick and
fast following the fall of the Berlin Wall in 1989. The end of the Cold War,
which had dominated the development of the post-war international system, has confronted editors, reporters and their audiences with considerable uncertainty and confusion. The ideological certainties within which
foreign correspondents could make sense of international events disappeared almost as quickly as the Wall was brought down. Between the end
of the Second World War and the 1980s the struggle between East and
West, capitalism and communism, America and the Soviet Union was the
frame – or 'meta-narrative' – through which policy makers, publics and the
media understood and interpreted world events. Edward Herman and Noam
Chomsky (1988: 29–31) identify anti-communism as one of the main filters
in explaining how the American mass media selected and reported news. The

extent to which this way of seeing the world exerted a hold over international society was manifest in the reluctance in the early days of the collapse of the Soviet Union to acknowledge that fundamental change was taking place. The international media struggled to shake off their cold war conditioning.

The end of the Cold War brought about a crisis in perception and understanding among the world's foreign press corps. Ethnic and civil wars in Europe and other parts of the world became more difficult to interpret and explain. Ethnic cleansing in the former Yugoslavia, genocide in Rwanda and Darfur, hatred in East Timor and the huge loss of life, nearly five million people killed, in the Democratic Republic of the Congo could no longer be accounted for by the clichés of the Cold War, the 'red menace', the 'global communist conspiracy' or the 'Russians are coming'. The *Washington Post* now had to struggle to represent international terrorism as sponsored, promoted and organised by the Soviet Union (Parenti, 1986). With the disappearance of Moscow's 'invisible hand', events around the world had to be seen, understood, reported and interpreted in their own terms. 'Soviet inspired' or 'pro-American' no longer made any geo-political sense (Seib, 2002: 20). Local knowledge became more important than ever as foreign correspondents grappled with the national, ethnic, community, civil, tribal and religious struggles that seemed to flare up everywhere in the 1990s. Using national policy and national policy makers to understand events was also problematic as the 'national interest' became more fluid in a rapidly changing world. The rhetorical certainties of 'good' and 'evil' crumbled away with the disappearance of the 'Evil Empire'. Delineating on moral grounds, in a period in which many governments subscribed to an 'ethical foreign policy', became a challenge for an international journalism used to the good guys/bad guys contrast of the Cold War frame. The zero-sum equation that shaped Cold War reporting was no longer fit for purpose.

The practice and priorities of international journalism changed in other ways with the passing of the US–USSR rivalry. The newsworthiness attached to countries and world leaders in the era of the Cold War was determined by their part in the superpower rivalry. According to Philip Seib (2002: 24), international reporting 'reinforced the conventional wisdom of the moment concerning the players in the superpower-dominated great game'. News organisations reorganised their news priorities and deployment of personnel in the post Cold War world. Countries that had been important sites of superpower struggle simply slipped off the news agenda. Nicaragua, Angola, Ethiopia, Indonesia and El Salvador could no longer gain coverage as a result of their status as proxy wars between East and West. Political orientation to one superpower or another could not guarantee the attention of international journalism. With international security issues lessening as a result of the decline of the threat of nuclear war, geo-politics ceased to be the primary story for foreign reporting. Other issues became more newsworthy as reporters explored different aspects of societies which had previously been locked away in the Cold War box. With the focus changing, foreign correspondents had to learn about new topics, acquire new information and cultivate new sources (Seib, 2002: 25). Globalisation brought with it broader issues including pandemics such as AIDS and SARS, climate change and the environment, and migration and human rights, which required international journalism to adopt a global rather than national perspective on the news of the day.

The uncertainties of the 1990s were temporarily swept away by the events of 9/11. The destruction of the Twin Towers by Al-Qaeda-inspired terrorists provided the world with a new enemy and a new ideological struggle with militant Islam. The shock of 9/11 brought about the only reversal in the downward trend in foreign news since 1945. Suddenly people, particularly in North America, were clamouring for more foreign news, shocked out of their complacency about events in the outside world. The desire to be informed, however, was short lived. Costly and unpopular wars in Iraq and Afghanistan instilled a sense of withdrawal from the rest of the world and its problems. The 'War on Terror' instigated by the US Administration under George Bush Junior in the wake of 9/11 failed to solve the 'crisis of meaning' created by the end of the Cold War (Laidi, 1998; Hammond, 2007).

Attempts to rebuild a 'grand narrative' that would embrace global politics and international reporting can be first identified with George Bush Senior's 'New World Order'. The clear and present disorder that proliferated at the time undermined the notion that the world was more peaceful, orderly and humane as presaged by those who believed in the 'end of history'. Rather it was a place in which you had to deal with 'rogue states', 'failed states', internal dissent, civil and ethnic conflict and virulent nationalism unleashed – according to some commentators – by the thawing of the Cold War. Who was fighting who was not always apparent. The conflict in the Balkans epitomised the confusion and uncertainty. 9/11 offered the opportunity to re-establish 'a world with meaning'. For a while, the American media suspended its critical faculties to come 'on team' in an all embracing war against an increasingly elusive enemy. The failure to find weapons of mass destruction, the growing alienation inside and outside America from George W Bush's foreign policy and inability to bring about the reconstruction of Iraq undermined the presentation of the threat posed. Passing the mantle of evil onto Al Qaeda, Saddam Hussein and international terrorism did not succeed. Despite the British Prime Minister Tony Blair touring the word asserting that the 'threat ... is not imagined' and the US government spending considerable sums to hire PR and advertising agencies to sell the Afghan and Iraqi conflicts, the 'war on terror' seemed to be nothing more than an 'expression of generalised and diffuse fearfulness' (Hammond, 2007: 73).

Fearfulness was reinforced by the sense or perceived sense of insecurity generated by global change. For some scholars global change furthers environmental, ecological, political and economic insecurity. Climate change, 'casino capitalism' and civil conflict are attributed to the unsettling forces unleashed by the new realities of a globalised world. Not everyone would agree with this assessment, preferring to emphasise the benefits of the new circumstances. While there is a debate between advocates of globalisation (see Scholte, 2005; Held, 2000), at the heart of the change taking place in international society is the threat posed to our sense of collective identity. Everyone needs a sense of who they are, a sense of belonging, and in modern society this has been primarily given to us by the nation-state. The strength of allegiance to the nation-state is highlighted by the large number of people who have been – and still are – willing to lay down their lives for their nation. Since the end of the eighteenth century the pre-eminence of the nation-state as the primary collective entity has remained unchallenged. It has offered 'a stronger sense of security, belonging, or affiliation and even personal identity, than does any alternative large group' (quoted in Horsman and Marshall, 1995: xi). In prosecuting war, negotiating peace, enacting laws, filling prisons, educating people, policing borders, collecting taxes and regulating daily life, the nation-state has appeared supreme. The word 'appear' is important here as nation-states have exerted considerable effort to propagandise their unity, inviolability and sovereignty. National identity is a constructed, imagined condition, often only held together by force or the threat of force and the imposition of values. The fragility of the nation-state has been exposed since the last great, global war of 1939–45 and is now challenged by forces of globalisation.

Enacting global change by promising to erode the imaginary boundaries which distinguish one group of people from another is a threat to the nation-state. Supranational organisations such as the European Union have established markets and industries, enacted laws and regulations and engineered electoral and political processes that have taken power away from the nation-state. They have superseded the old customs and ways of doing things, the old laws and politics. Multinational companies are wresting economic decision making away from national governments. Within nation-states, older and more ancient loyalties have re-emerged following changes in technology, the international economy and the Cold War. Basques, the Welsh, Catalans, Scots, Sorbs, Serbs, Croats, Slovenes, Chechens and Frisians are among a variety of sub-national identities that have attempted to assert what they see as a more authentic sense of belonging. Nation-states are being squeezed from above and below. The result is an increasing insecurity over identity, manifest in the United Kingdom, for example, in the debate over Britain's relationship with Europe (Anderson and Weymouth, 1999; Gavin, 2001). Minority cultures and global interests have used television and radio and other forms of mass media to promote a new sense of common purpose and shared rituals

(Sinclair et al., 1996; de Moragas Spa et al., 1999; Straubhaar, 2007). The predominance of American and western programmes on world screens and the portrayal of previously submerged cultures and languages in regional and local audio-visual systems has drawn attention to the importance of the issue of representation in a swiftly changing world.

Contesting foreign news

Many nations and peoples, particularly in the non-western world, complain about the way in which they have been represented by international news and foreign correspondents. Since de-colonisation in the 1950s and 1960s people in the so-called 'Third World'*, that is, the countries of Africa, Latin America and Asia, have protested about their portrayal and called for fundamental change in the operation, organisation and working practices of international journalism. Their grievances stemmed from the realisation that political independence did not lead to an increase of control and sovereignty over their economic, military and cultural affairs. Matters culminated in the publication of the MacBride report in 1980 by United Nations Educational, Scientific and Cultural Organisation (UNESCO), which supported calls for the establishment of a New World Information and Communication Order (NWICO). The report was highly critical of the western news agencies that dominated the gathering and processing of international news and helped to perpetuate an imbalance in international news flow in favour of the West. The western news media and international news agencies responded defensively. UNESCO was accused of seeking to control and censor the news, restricting the free flow of international information (Righter, 1978). Several leading international journalists highlighted some of the most blatant forms of repression perpetrated by the governments who were calling for a fairer and more balanced reporting of their societies (for example, Sussman, 1981; Meisler, 1978; O'Brien, 1980).

The complaints about international journalism made by UNESCO, the MacBride Report and the Third World rested on two basic criticisms. The first was that little coverage was devoted to what happened in Africa, Asia and Latin America, even though two-thirds of the world's population, land and natural resources were located in these parts of the world (Gerbner and Marvanyi, 1983). The limited and routine coverage of these countries was explained by the belief that not much happens in the Third World. As former journalist, UN official and politician Conor Cruise O'Brien stated: 'there are indeed

---

*The term 'Third World' is seen as problematic for some, who prefer 'Global South' to describe the countries of Asia, Africa and Latin America. However, it was a term regularly used during the NWICO debates in the 1970s and 1980s and appears in much of the literature at this time, including inside the Global South. For consistency the term is used throughout this book, whilst recognising its limitations.

many parts of the world in which not much is happening except that people in considerable numbers are suffering and dying' (O'Brien, 1980). The scarcity of material in the news about the Third World was added to by the negative ways in which what did appear was covered – the second criticism levelled at the world's media. What happened in Asia, Africa and Latin America was primarily reported through the prism of what was referred to as the 'coups, famines, earthquakes' syndrome. News about the Third World tended to be only 'bad news'. According to Paul Harrison and Robin Palmer (1986: 82), 'only the spectacular, the bizarre and the truly horrific reach our screens' from Africa. Without routine coverage the picture that appeared in the pages of newspapers and on television screens of the Third World was one of instability, violence and irrationality. With neither context to give to these events nor any countervailing picture of the day-to-day life in these parts of the world, viewers, listeners and readers were left with stereotypical images of developing societies. The intensity of feeling that many in the developing world felt about their misrepresentation led to calls for a new information order.

Attempts to bring about a new international order in the 1970s were ultimately unsuccessful. Alternative arrangements to gather international news were embarked on. National news agencies inside the Third World were brought together in regional groupings such as the Pan African News Agency (PANA) and Caribbean News Agency (CANA) as well as broader based efforts such as the Non-Aligned News Pool (NANAPOL). New independent, alternative news agencies such as the Inter Press Service (IPS) and Gemini emerged in the West and there were some changes in the mainstream western media with newspapers such as the *Guardian* in Britain beginning a 'Third World section' in 1978 (Giffard, 1998; Sosale, 2003: 386). More positive stories were reported and the development efforts of the Third World received more coverage. Regional exchange mechanisms and alternative news agencies and organisations improved the flow of news between the nations of the Third World as well as adding to what audiences in the West read, saw and heard about the Third World (see Boyd-Barrett and Thussu, 1992). However, the contribution of these arrangements to the international flow of news was limited; severe financial constraints, the indifference of many Third World governments and media outlets as well as the quality of the product and the restricted coverage of certain parts of the world meant these efforts did not do much to rectify the one-way flow of news and information from the West to the Third World.

It was the entry of new actors into the field of international news in the late 1980s, the rise of neo-liberal economic and media policies around the world and the advent of new technology that had a more profound impact than the political efforts to establish a new information order. CNN and other 24-hour news channels that followed not only increased the flow of international news and information but also began to provide alternative perspectives on the news, in some cases challenging western interpretations of what was happening in the world. The channel that has come to epitomise the 'new world' of international journalism is Al-Jazeera, which from its base in Qatar provides a service in English and Arabic, delivering a picture of the world that challenges many of the preconceptions audiences in the West have of international events (El-Nawaway and Iskandar, 2003: 155–7). Direct satellite broadcasting has changed the way foreign news is gathered, processed, disseminated and consumed. The internet has also had a significant impact on international journalism. It was seen to come of age as a news medium during the 2003 Iraq War. Stuart Allan (2004, 2006), in his study of the internet's coverage of the war in Iraq, documents the growth of traffic to online websites when George Bush announced that the conflict had started – *Yahoo* reported a 600 per cent increase in the volume of hits on its news section the following day (Allan, 2006: 103). Many Americans, according to Allan, turned to other international news sites as a result of their disillusionment with the war coverage provided by the US mainstream media. At a click of the mouse they could find alternative views and accounts.

Much of this alternative news and opinion, however, was provided by mainstream media sites such as those of quality British newspapers including the *Guardian* and aljazeera.net. Similarly, many of the 'warblogs' were part of the established media's effort to report the war; CNN correspondent Kevin Sites – until his employers stopped him – provided his own personal blog accounts alongside his reports for the channel. However, there were also bloggers who had no connection with established media, most famously the Baghdad Blogger, Salam Pax. They provided eyewitness accounts of the fighting and suffering often neglected in mainstream media. Other bloggers, often operating far away from the fighting itself, searched out and documented what they saw as political 'bias' in official accounts and mainstream media coverage of the war and its aftermath. Many sought answers to their questions online. The internet had become an important source of international news, opinion and information. Subsequent events such as the Asian tsunami and Hurricane Katrina have shown that the internet is a source to which people, especially younger people, will turn to for immediate news of breaking events. Correspondingly, eyewitness accounts are now not only showing up in mainstream media but are also disseminated on the net via email, blogs and other new media devices as citizens around the world make use of new technology, particularly the mobile phone, to practise their own personal form of 'citizen-journalism'.

New forms of international journalism

Political, technological, economic and cultural changes as well as the attempts to establish a new international order have led many to question the practices, performance and preconceptions of international journalism. International journalism is in a 'state of flux and subject to deep, multi-dimensional change' (Preston, 2008a: 1). In particular, western journalism – what is labelled variously as the Anglo-American, liberal or professional model – is under attack. It is seen as inimical to the fair and balanced reporting of the Third World. Not only are western foreign correspondents held responsible for the misreporting and misrepresentation of world events but also the values of western journalism are being transferred to the countries of Asia, Africa and Latin America, producing a profession that is discordant to the needs and requirements of these societies. Peter Golding (1977) has described the variety of ways in which values, practices and routines have been transferred from the West to the rest of the world. The incorporation of these values into the work of Third World journalists has been described as 'nothing more than their increasing integration into a community sharing values and standards developed by major western news media' (1977: 104). The professionalisation of Third World journalism into the western model is seen as a means to reinforce the dependency of Latin America, Africa and Asia on the rich industrialised countries of the West and their news media. Anglo-American journalism and news-making values and practices are becoming 'a universal standard for the remainder of the world' (Preston, 2008a: 1). This has coincided with increasing criticism of the model from within western societies, as many professionals call into question its usefulness in addressing the radical transformations that are taking place. These developments have produced new ways of thinking about how journalism should be practised.

In questioning the growing hegemony of the Anglo-American model of journalism, new forms and practices of journalism have been articulated. Practitioners in the Third World espoused the concept of 'development journalism'. Development journalists reject many of the basic tenets of western journalism, particularly the commitment to detachment and objectivity. The role of the neutral observer was regarded as problematic in newly independent societies that were seeking to build their nation and grow economically. They were at war: a war against poverty and under-development. Many of the early advocates of development journalism had their views of the role of journalism shaped by their experience of the struggle for decolonisation and national liberation. Kwame Nkrumah, the first President of Ghana, had used the press as an integral part of the political fight for independence. He saw the duty of the journalist being to 'help establish a progressive political and economic system', to work for the 'betterment of his fellows and the society of which he is a worthy member' and to educate and inspire them to 'work for equality and the universality of men's [sic] rights everywhere' (Nkrumah, 1965). Proponents of development journalism emphasised the importance of educating people about 'how serious the development problem is, to think about the problem, to open their eyes to possible solutions ...' (Chalkley, 1970: 2). Development journalists were 'soldiers of development' whose job was 'not only to give the facts of economic life and to interpret those facts, but to promote them and bring them home to [their] readers'. The active role in pressing for change was the characteristic that separated development journalism from western reporting with its emphasis on objectivity (Kariithi, 1994: 28). As Nkrumah said, 'we do not believe there are necessarily two sides to every question. We see right and wrong, just and unjust, progressive and reactionary, positive and negative, friend and foe. We are partisan' (quoted in Hatchen, 1971: 45).

The shifting nature of world events led many western correspondents to question their practices and performance. In the face of covering conflicts in the late twentieth and early twenty-first centuries, particularly in the Balkans, some foreign correspondents began to equate 'doing journalism' with 'doing good' (Seib, 2002: 119), arguing that journalism should be seen as a 'moral enterprise'. Former BBC foreign correspondent Martin Bell (1995, 1998) is one of many who have called for journalism to be more involved in the issues and events that are shaping the modern world. Bell, a veteran correspondent who covered conflicts for the BBC for over 30 years, found the journalism he had been practising all his life insufficient to address what he was confronted with in the Balkans. He is critical of the detachment and distance which characterises the tradition of what he labels 'bystander' journalism'. Faced with the suffering and 'evil' he found in the Balkans, Bell (1998: 16) was 'no longer sure of the notion of objectivity, which seems to me now to be something of an illusion and a shibboleth'. He argues for the replacement of the dispassionate approach which has been part of Anglo-American journalism for much of the twentieth century by the 'journalism of attachment'; 'a journalism that cares as well as knows; that is aware of its responsibilities; that will not stand neutrally between good and evil, right and wrong, the victim and the oppressor'. Bell's experience is replicated in different ways in the attitudes of other leading reporters such as CNN's Christine Amanpour and ITN's Michael Nicholson, highlighting how moral and humanitarian pressures have forced journalists to reassess the profession's guiding principle of objectivity and detachment.

Another concept of journalism that has emerged in recent decades in response to the growing instability of international society is 'peace journalism'. Postulated as a normative theory in the 1970s by Johan Galtung, this approach to reporting developed after the 1991 Gulf War. An international network of over 200 correspondents, 'Reporting the World' was established which is committed to privileging peace in their reporting. Two leading figures in the network produced a handbook for peace reporting which examined how journalists could become more socially responsible and part of the attempts to resolve conflict (Lynch and McGoldrick, 2005). The notion of the journalist as a neutral observer was again identified as a crucial barrier to journalism playing an effective role in society. Peace journalism is regarded as controversial within the profession. Practitioners in western media organisations have been hostile to an approach which they believe compromises the integrity of the profession and confuses their role as detached reporters (Loyn, 2003). However, within the war-torn societies of the Third World peace reporting has received much more support, with many journalists attempting to apply the concept to what they do.

It is not only those committed to the cause of peace that question the relevance of objectivity. One consequence of the aftermath of 9/11 was the growing adherence to 'cheerleader journalism' in the US. Manifest in the output of stations such as Fox TV, journalism took sides. During the 2003 Iraq war Fox News practised 'patriotic journalism'; a pin of the American flag appeared on reporters' lapels and the Stars and Stripes adorned the studio (Zelizer, 2005: 209). Patriotism and partiality became comfortable bedfellows and Fox's formula of 'opinionated news with an America-first flair' was popular with US audiences (2005: 202). Fox's owner, Rupert Murdoch, realised that in an increasingly competitive environment television news that confirmed people's prejudices could be successful in ratings terms. His commitment to 'openly biased news' is based on the conviction it is what people want – and with Fox surpassing CNN as America's favourite cable news channel this view appears to have been confirmed (Allan, 2005: 9). Fox's coverage led to considerable consternation within the journalism profession in the United States, spawning a debate about the appropriateness of such reporting. Failures within the mainstream media enhanced the search for new ways of practising the profession – the *New York Times* had to apologise for failures in its coverage of the decision to go to war with Iraq in 2003 and the fabrication of stories by one of its leading reporters, Jayson Blair. The success of satirical news programmes such as Comedy Central's *The Daily Show* not only attests to the entertainment driven environment in which television news operates but also to the growing public mistrust of mainstream journalism.

If journalism has had to become more reflective of its performance, the profession of journalism is an increasingly precarious practice. The retrenchment of foreign correspondents has been accompanied by the growth of freelance reporters and 'stringers' in the coverage of international events. The rise of the freelance reporter is a feature of the era of globalisation as news organisations around the world have slimmed down their staff to adjust to the increasingly competitive market in which they have to operate (Gynnild, 2005). The ability and capacity to operate as a freelance correspondent has been facilitated by technology as well as the expansion of media outlets to which freelancers can sell their product. The relationship between journalists and their news outlets has changed; for some it has enabled the reporter to free him- or herself from the editorial restrictions of single organisations. The Norwegian freelance war reporter Asne Seierstad, besides gaining international acclaim as the author of the bestselling novel, *The Bookseller of Kabul*, was able to sell her stories from Baghdad in 2003 to a variety of media outlets around the world, and these were translated into more than seven languages. She was also able to produce a documentary and book about her life as a war correspondent in Iraq that was sold to several countries (2005: 115). To achieve her success Seierstad, like other freelance correspondents, has taken 'extreme risks' to get the story. Economic insecurity and a lack of organisational ties encourage greater risk taking. For some there is a correlation between the increased number of freelance reporters and the rising death toll within the profession (Smith, 2009: 55). It also seen as changing the way in which the story is written. Many leading freelance reporters subscribe to a more literary style of journalism, eschewing the traditional news writing format to present a more vivid, narrative-driven and personal take on the news.

What all these calls for change have in common is a belief that the traditional ways of 'doing' international journalism are no longer viable in a world in which rapid and deep-seated transformation is occurring. They reject many of the fundamental tenets of the mainstream media, including what have been seen as the guiding lights of 'good journalism', namely fairness, objectivity and balance (Loyn, 2003: 1). Representatives of the mainstream media are reluctant to acknowledge these new ways of thinking. Martin Bell (1998: 18) describes how a middle ranking BBC executive perceived him as 'a heretic and backslider from long-established truths'. The BBC in the wake of its struggles with the British government over its reporting of claims about weapons of mass destruction in Iraq has attempted to reassert traditional values through more closely policing what its correspondents report and what appears on screen. Anything which may, in the view of BBC senior management, impair its commitment to objectivity, including a humanitarian appeal for the civilian population of Gaza, is not broadcast (see Llewellyn, 2009). In spite of the corporate effort to reassert the importance of objectivity, it is clear that many reporters believe that new forms of practice are required with which to engage, understand and explain the increasing complexity of the contemporary world – and for some there should be a moral and ethical dimension to what they do. For Jake Lynch, one of the leading advocates of peace journalism, journalists must confront their own role in international events as well as develop strategies to 'use the power of the pen to ethical ends' (Lynch, 2004: 261). This view accords with the position of many Third World journalists, who have long advocated the need for a more engaged form of reporting.

Information and power

Debates about the practice and performance of international journalism and the delivery of foreign news and information have relevance which extends beyond the remit of the profession. They are central to the conduct of international affairs. Politics and culture, economics and science, public health and education, technological and social progress, international relations and other spheres of human activities are 'interlocked by the information media' (Vidyarthi, 1988: 3). Control over the provision and packaging of international news and information is an essential ingredient to the exercise of global power. Power, commonly defined as 'the ability to exercise control' in order 'to get others to do what they might not otherwise do' has been central to relations between nation-states since the birth of the modern world system (Alleyne, 1995: 4). How international power is exercised has been a subject of study for diplomats, political leaders and scholars for a considerable time. There are differences of opinion over how best to exercise power, not least because power can take a number of forms, tangible and intangible (Mowlana, 1997). Coercion, the use of force, control over resources, economic wealth and advantage and the capability to shape opinion and knowledge are among the factors determining the exercise of power. Traditionally military and economic muscle – what is labelled as 'hard power' – has been emphasised. Threats and inducements, 'carrots' and 'sticks', are the means by which 'hard power' is applied (Nye, 2004: 5). However, there is another, less transparent, face of international power which gets people to do what you want by co-opting rather than coercing them. Soft power 'rests on the ability to shape the preferences of others' by 'attraction and seduction' (2004: 5). Susan Strange (1994: 24), in her influential book *States and Markets*, makes the distinction between relational and structural power. The former is the power of A to get B to do something they would not otherwise do; structural power is 'the power to shape and determine the structures of the global political economy within which other states, their political institutions, their economic enterprises, and (not least) their scientists and other professional people have to operate'. It is the ability to shape the rules, regulations and customs, as well as the ideals and dreams, by which international relations is conducted. Information, and how it is communicated and interpreted, are central to the exercise of structural power.

The Canadian scholar Harold Innis (1950) has shown how information, communication and literacy have played a key role in the establishment, expansion and maintenance of empires and power blocs since pre-Roman times. In recent years, with the advent of new information technologies that can process information more quickly, more widely and in greater quantities than ever before, the notion that information is power has never been truer. Information obtained from satellite communication is able to provide economic advantage. The capacity to better exploit the world's resources is enhanced; for example, international fishing companies by their use of this technology are able to compete with local fishermen in locating shoals of fish. But as globalisation changes our sense of time and space, some scholars have drawn attention to the expansion of the ability and capacity to shape people's understanding, knowledge and analysis of what is happening, in other words, the extension of structural power. Whether it is a small number of transnational corporations that promote 'global dreams' or a global elite that peddles consumerism or America Inc that puts forward the 'American world view', structural power is seen as exercised in a more assertive way by a decreasing number of global actors (Schiller, 1969; Barnett and Cavanagh, 1994; Sklair, 2001). Contrary to the view that new technology liberates individuals to tell their own stories, it is possible to argue that it is furthering the capacity of powerful interests to set the international news agenda. New forms of control and surveillance are a feature of contemporary global society. Propaganda, as Philip Taylor (1995) reminds us, has always been a characteristic of the interaction between states. The relentless rise of the public relations industry in the twentieth century, however, has extended the global reach of spin and news management (Sriramesh and Vercic, 2007; Miller and Dinan, 2008).

Governments, corporations and many other international actors have increasingly deployed public relations (PR) to sell wars, policies and their image abroad. The most famous example of this was the PR campaign waged by US agency Hill and Knowlton in 1991 on behalf of the Kuwaiti government to gain public support for US military action against Iraq. In 2003 several PR firms and advertising agencies were at the heart of efforts to convince domestic and international audiences of the rightness of the cause. The centrality of the information war to the 2003 invasion of Iraq is illustrated by the US incorporating 'total information dominance' as a central component of its military strategy and foreign policy (Miller, 2004). But it is not only western governments and organisations that have become skilled in the practices of PR. Many governments in the Global South have abandoned resorting to the use of force, denial of access and intimidation to control foreign media. Unhelpful and obstructionist Ministries of Information have been replaced by western PR companies, hired to cajole, persuade, sell and package the policies, actions and images of the most repressive regimes. The ability to improve visibility and decrease negative images of foreign nations in the US media by hiring PR firms has been documented (Zaharna and Villalobos, 2000; Kiousis and Wu, 2008). Non-governmental organisations have also developed their packaging skills. Protest groups from the Zapatistas in Mexico to the anti-globalisation movement have made considerable use of new technologies such as the internet to organise their campaigns of civil disobedience. The 1999 'Carnival Against Capitalism', which brought hundreds of thousands of demonstrators on to the streets of cities all over the world, is an example of the power of the web to mobilise protest (Chadwick, 2006: 127). Terrorist organisations such as Al-Qaeda have also developed their propaganda skills, using the internet to communicate effectively with the outside world. However, it is the world's leading powers that have had the resources to deploy 'structural propaganda', utilising overt and covert forms of manipulation to ensure that the 'global village' is 'still dominated by elite conversations, ideas and prejudices' (Alleyne, 1997: 43).

In the face of the growing sophistication of international image and information management, which has helped to extend the exercise of structural power, the capacity and ability of foreign correspondents to interrogate accounts of world events has declined. The demands of a 24-hour news culture appear to preference filling airtime and pages over checking facts and providing interpretation. Foreign correspondents in the global era are regarded as more susceptible to spin because they are 'ill-equipped to read foreign texts' and often over-dependent on national or domestic sources (Louw, 2005: 260). Foreign correspondents usually see international events and issues through a domestic lens, taking on their own government's perception and interpretation of events, especially at times of crisis. However, it is the decrease in resources associated with economic retrenchment and the shrinkage of time and space brought about by technological innovation that are seen as undermining the work of the foreign reporter.

Structure of the book

This book examines the impact of technological, cultural, social, economic and political change on foreign correspondence. It does this within the context of growing sophistication of sources, particularly official agencies, to manage the media and manipulate information in the exercise of international power. Foreign correspondents would appear to be crucial actors in the production of global consciousness. However, this assumption seems to be contradicted by many in the profession who believe that foreign correspondence is a 'dying occupation' (Hannerz, 2007: 309). They believe that the correspondent has been superseded by other forms and ways of gathering international news. There are two basic questions:

1   Is foreign correspondence changing and to what extent is it becoming more global in its outlook and practices?
2   Does the way in which international journalism reports and represents the world differ in the digital age?

In answering these questions we examine both the occupational culture and organisational structures within which foreign correspondents work

(Chapters 3 and 4) and the 'standard techniques' by which the raw data, facts and information that foreign correspondents collect is manipulated by sources of information (Chapter 5). The content of international news and the output of international journalism in a digital age is investigated (Chapter 6). The book begins with a section that locates foreign correspondence within a historical context, without which we would be unable to understand the contemporary conditions under which foreign reporters work and the parameters within which they can exercise initiative and enterprise (Chapter 2). The opening chapter provides a theoretical overview within which we can make an assessment about the impact of globalisation on foreign correspondence and as a consequence on our understanding of the world.

1

GLOBALISATION AND INTERNATIONAL JOURNALISM

Globalisation and the internet have created a space for news and political discourse that overrides geography and increases opportunities for non-mainstream, citizen based news sources ... the deterritorialised and globalised online zones for news and political discussion have led to important new questions about the future of traditional news media and the shape of political discourse. (Reese et al., 2007)

This chapter examines the different approaches to understanding the impact of global change on the nature of international journalism. To assess the impact we must be clear about what we are discussing. Both 'globalisation' and 'international journalism' are simple but elusive concepts. Traditionally, international journalism is equated with foreign correspondence. Many assumptions are made about the nature of 'foreign correspondence' which ignore the porous borders that have always existed between domestic *and* foreign news. Foreign news comes in different shapes and forms and the gathering, reporting and dissemination of international news has been undertaken by a variety of actors in a range of organisational contexts serving numerous objectives and interests. Understanding what is meant by 'globalisation' is not easy (McGillivray, 2006). There is 'no single coherent theory of globalisation' and the empirical data generated to assess the impact of global change is limited and contradictory (Held et al., 1999: 436). The media are full of references to 'globalisation', with newspapers, magazines, television news and other media forms carrying stories, comment and analysis of how globalisation is responsible for a plethora of events and occurrences. It seems that, every day, politicians around the world call forth 'globalisation' to justify support for this policy or to extol us to take that form of action. Everything from the problems of the collapse of the banking system to the decline of English football is attributed to what former British Prime Minster Tony Blair described as the 'inevitable and irresistible' process of globalisation. Despite having 'invaded our consciousness' (Tae Kim and Weaver, 2003) uncertainties cloud the meaning of the concept of globalisation.

As well as defining the terms that are central to our discussion of the way in which the world is reported, the chapter outlines three different approaches to understanding international journalism in an 'age of globalisation'. The first approach is to focus on the *homogenisation* of foreign news and reporting brought about by the standardisation of journalism around the world. According to Mark Deuze (2005: 444) 'the twentieth century history of ... journalism can be typified by the consolidation of a consensual occupational ideology among journalists in different parts of the world'. Globalisation is seen as encouraging the development of a universal set of values around the practice and output of the contemporary international journalism. The way in which international journalism has been universalised is a matter of debate. It is most commonly argued that the Anglo-American model has become the universal yardstick by which the profession should be practised. However, the export of Anglo-American journalism is not uniformly regarded as a positive development.

The second approach postulates the emergence of a radically new form of journalism described as *global journalism*. It is seen as a response to the new realities of a globalised international society that is more 'transnational' or 'cosmopolitan' in composition. Globalisation has 'weakened the connection between journalism and its traditional nation-state base ...' (Reese, 2008: 240). For Peter Berglez (2008: 847) 'global journalism is endowed with particular epistemology, defined as the global outlook', which produces interpretations of the world that are different from the national outlooks within which journalism has traditionally framed social reality. Globalisation and technology are also seen as undermining the professional and industrial foundations that have traditionally supported international reporting, removing the need for specialised foreign correspondents. The rise of 'do-it-yourself' foreign reporting facilitated by the internet has, some would argue, increased the number of 'foreign correspondents' who, 'equipped with camcorders and computers will send out and receive more foreign dispatches' (Utley, 1997: 9). The third approach asserts, or perhaps we should say reasserts, the role of the nation-state in determining the theory and practice of journalism in the global era (see de Burgh, 2005). It seeks to emphasise that foreign correspondence remains *heterogeneous* in its practices, performance and values. National cultures, polities and societies shape the practice and performance of foreign reporting throughout the world. This can be seen in a number of different ways: the 'domestication' of foreign news, the desire of news audiences around the world for local interpretations and analysis of events, the rise of new regional and local news actors, and the advent of new media organisations that are non-western in outlook.

Foreign correspondence

Foreign correspondence – or international journalism[1] – usually describes news media coverage of what is happening outside the home state and the processes by which it is obtained. What constitutes 'foreign' news is delineated from 'domestic' news with the presumption that there are clear differences between the peoples of different nations. It is what happens to 'them', and the implication is that what happens to 'them' has nothing to do with 'us' (Vargas and Paulin, 2007: 20). The word 'foreign' implies that what is reported is alien, strange and unfamiliar. This clear delineation of 'domestic' and 'foreign' news is the product of the development of nation-states and national media systems. Print and broadcast journalism has grown within the framework of the nation-state: newspapers, radio and television have been organised on a national basis serving the informational needs of the state, commerce and civil society.

The close connection between modern national identities and the media is emphasised by Benedict Anderson (1983) who theorises that individuals were able to imagine themselves as members of the modern nation through their consumption of the newspaper and print media. The growth of print culture enabled people who never met one another to feel, for the first time, that they were part of the same 'imagined community' – the nation. Broadcasting in most parts of the world has been committed to 'serving the nation'; the motto of the British Broadcasting Corporation (BBC) that 'nation should speak truth unto nation' illustrates the national remit of public service broadcasting. Most countries in the late nineteenth and early twentieth centuries established national news agencies to communicate national news to the world. These agencies played a crucial role in the consolidation of the modern nation-state, participating in the national rivalries that characterised international relations in this era.

The centrality of national interests, needs and considerations to the emergence of the media ensured that international news would be defined as news about and between nations. National news agencies were closely associated with government, usually financed and funded by them and highly dependent on official sources of information. Many had started as commercial ventures to provide foreign news to their national and provincial newspapers, but most of them came under the aegis of state control and/or patronage. While legally and politically committed to independence from political influence, national news agencies closely identified with the nation-state perspective of events and issues.

> The agencies were vital components in the armoury of the nation state: then as now, the agencies were among the range of institutions which new nation states came to feel they had to establish in order to be seen as credible as nations and in order to project or control the dissemination of the 'national image' on global markets. (Boyd-Barrett and Rantanen, 1998: 5)

This close identification not only shaped the practices of the national agencies and national media but also influenced the values used to select foreign news.

The notion that foreign news is about events that happen outside national borders is deemed inadequate by many scholars and practitioners in capturing what appears – and has appeared – in print and on screen. International news comes in different packages: foreign news abroad, home news abroad and foreign news at home (Hahn and Lonnendonker, 2009: 6). What we take as the customary form of international news is that which covers stories about countries and peoples abroad which have no impact, effect or relevance to home audiences. However, most news media focus more on the latter two categories; according to Kai Hafez (2007: 39) 'most of the time, international reporting in media systems around the world is produced for domestic audiences, not for the regions in question themselves'. Adapting international stories to domestic concerns and interests is a means of ensuring that foreign news relates to the viewers, readers and listeners at home (Golding and Elliott, 1979: 156). *Home news abroad* concentrates on events which are directly linked or of direct interest to domestic audiences. What happens to fellow citizens abroad or the foreign travels of domestic leaders or celebrities are examples of such stories. *Foreign news at home* is the other side of this coin; such stories include visits by foreign heads of state or dignitaries, international conferences on home soil or domestic reactions to major international issues. Foreign correspondence often involves making a 'link between foreign news coverage and domestic coverage' and 'transporting domestic references or concerns to foreign news abroad' (Hahn and Lonnendonker, 2009: 6).

This has implications for understanding what foreign correspondents do and what foreign correspondence is. Definitions of the 'foreign correspondent' are few and far between. Scholars have bombarded foreign correspondents – mainly those working for western organisations or in major news centres such as Washington and London – with mailed questionnaires since the mid 1950s (for example, Lambert, 1956; Mowlana, 1975; Ghorpade, 1984; Morrison and Tumber, 1985; Hess, 1996; Wilnat and Weaver, 2003; Wu and Hamilton, 2004). While generating considerable information about their background and working practices, no-one has provided a detailed definition of foreign correspondence and foreign reporting. One standard way of defining a foreign correspondent is 'a journalist who works in a state different from one in which his [sic] information-medium is located' (Hahn and Lonnendonker, 2009: 3). Traditionally, the largest employers of foreign correspondents have been the international news agencies – a select number of national news agencies that morphed in the nineteenth century into international news providers (see Chapter 2). Their allegiance to the 'nation' has been a matter of conjecture as a result of their commercial objective of providing news for outlets in a variety of countries. Many national news organisations have for most of their history maintained their own correspondents in key locations abroad.

Most of those we characterise as 'great foreign correspondents' worked for distinguished national titles. These are usually believed to be nationals of the country in which the news organisation is located – history indicates that this assumption is problematic. The gatherers of foreign news have traditionally come in many shapes and sizes, and from numerous national backgrounds. Long stay correspondents, the men and women assigned to cover a country, region or beat – the bureau correspondents – are seen as typifying the foreign news reporter. But from the very early days the roving reporter sent to cover 'hot spots' or major news stories in remote parts of the world – what we label parachute journalism today – have figured prominently in the foreign news gathering business. Long before air transportation enhanced the ability of reporters to drop into breaking news stories across the world, reporters jumped off trains, boats, horses and carriages or whatever form of transport was available to cover stories (Erickson and Hamilton, 2007). The distinction between the long stay reporter and the parachute journalist has been a feature of foreign correspondence since its earliest days. The struggles between the two types of reporters and their different *modi vivendi* have always had a bearing on the nature of international news.

Much foreign news is not gathered in the field but by other kinds of correspondents based in the home country. Tensions between the 'field' and 'home office' figure prominently in the history of international news gathering. This is not only a product of the way in which those in the home office edit copy, crop pictures and splice film to fit their understanding of the story but also the result of the flow of information from diplomatic, political and other home-based correspondents. The reporting of one of the 'big stories' of the twentieth century – the Vietnam War – is often characterised as a battle between two press corps, the Washington-based reporters and the Saigon correspondents, which fed the media two different and mutually exclusive pictures of events. Several Saigon-based reporters spoke of their editors ignoring what they were telling them in favour of the Washington version (Knightley, 1975: 376). Struggles inside media organisations are a feature of all kinds of news reporting but are keenly felt in the case of foreign news stories: a large newspaper such as Japan's *Yomiuri Shimbun* would have – on an average news day – two pages of foreign news, which means its large network of 60 foreign correspondents based in around 30 countries faces acute competition for space (Hannerz, 2004: 67).

Another important distinction in the world of foreign correspondence is between full time and freelance reporters. Mark Pedelty (1995), in his examination of the press corps covering the bitter civil war in the El Salvador in the early 1980s, differentiates between A Team and B Team correspondents. The A Team are usually staff correspondents who work for major news outlets, have regular access to official sources of information, a regular salary, reside in the best hotels and usually appear when the story enters its crisis phase. The B Team are part timers who are hired for their local knowledge. They can be local nationals or foreign nationals who are resident in the country. 'Stringers' and 'fixers' are often local journalists who supplement what is in many parts of the world a meagre income to supply news for larger and usually foreign news organisations. The 'staff' and 'stringers' distinction is a feature of the reporting of many major foreign news stories. Pedelty (1995) describes the tensions and interdependency of the two groups, drawing attention to the different type of foreign news reporting produced by each. The staff reporter is perceived as trapped within 'disciplinary apparatuses' (1995: 5) that favour particular forms of knowledge and privilege certain discourses. He or she is subject to the 'editorial discipline' of the news organisation (1995: 76). While stringers are not 'under the editor's constant eye' they are subject to the commercial pressure to sell their expertise and stories to different media outlets. They are also perceived as less detached from local conditions – stringers are seeking to sell their familiarity which, in the words of one staff correspondent who covered the war in El Salvador, 'can lead to pretty strong emotions towards the story' (1995: 75). Hannerz (2004: 74) makes a distinction between 'freelancers' and 'stringers'; the latter have 'a bit longer term relationship with media organisations'. Many stringers seek to advance to a staff position. Freelancers on the other hand struggle to maintain their independence from editorial control. Writing for a variety of publications is part of this struggle but the commercial need to 'sell' stories means they are enthralled to the news organisations as much if not more than staff reporters.

The 'team' aspect of foreign news reporting must be emphasised – while the audience is accustomed to seeing star reporters on their screens (such as CNN's Christine Amanpour and BBC's John Simpson) or reading them in print (such as John Pilger), most foreign news gatherers work relatively anonymously and as part of a team. Covering a story for television has for most of the post-war period involved a sizable entourage, including a sound recordist and camera worker. Many print reporters are accompanied on their travels by photographers. The relationship between reporter and support staff has often been characterised as difficult, with camera workers and photographers portrayed as taking greater risks to get the story (Behr, 1978; Marinovich and Silva, 2001). Getting the pictures, particularly in relation to television, is as important as the words and the outcome of an often uneasy collaboration. The notion of the lone correspondent perpetuated by news organisations and practised by a few mavericks such as Ryszard Kapuściński (see Chapter 4) belies the fact that for most of the post-war period foreign reporting in the field has been done by a team of media workers. This is changing with the advent of new technology but traditionally foreign correspondents are involved in a process of conflict and collaboration which determines the kind of news we receive.

Supply-side explanations of foreign correspondence must also focus on the role of home editors in determining what foreign news is. News organisations are hierarchical and editors exercise considerable control over the news agenda. The contours of the foreign news coverage, it is argued, reflect the ways in which editors deploy their correspondents. Some parts of the world 'generate more foreign news because they have more foreign journalists' (Van Ginnekin, 1998: 143). Economic and organisational factors are crucial in determining what is reported. Surveys have also shown that home editors perceive their audiences are relatively uninterested in foreign news. This perception shapes their coverage of events overseas. It leads us to ask what readers, listeners and viewers actually want. The audiences for foreign news have not figured prominently in the discussion of foreign news reporting (Berger, 2009). The limited attention paid to what people want produces a range of contradictory data: more people appear to be interested in foreign news than editors believe and they appear to want different kinds of stories than they often receive. It is also possible to say that audiences in certain parts of the world have historically been more open to news from abroad.

There are two final points about the nature of foreign correspondence. The first relates to the variety of forms of knowledge by which correspondents and their organisations serve up accounts of what is happening in the world. Scholarly literature tends to focus on the 'news' – this is the primary way by which what foreign reporters see, hear and are told reaches the majority of the public. The restrictions that news as a form of knowledge places on what is reported have been thoroughly dissected. However, there are other outlets that foreign correspondents – as with other specialist reporters – use to tell us what is happening. Backgrounders, features and more analytical pieces, columns and special documentaries – recently joined by blogs – are some of the means by which foreign reporters escape the straight jacket imposed by news on what they can communicate. The BBC's John Simpson used a column in the *Sunday Telegraph* to express his opinions about world and other events – something his employers eventually believed impaired the commitment to objectivity they demanded. Over the years reporters have resorted to books to convey their truth of the events they have witnessed. In fact, reporters such as Kapuściński, who spent most of his working life as a reporter for the Polish National News Agency (PAP), have acquired their reputation as foreign correspondents based on their 'literary' not their news output.

The second point is intrinsic to the word 'foreign': foreign correspondents continually have to make the unfamiliar familiar to their audiences. Crossing cultural barriers and interpreting cultural difference is central to activity of foreign correspondence. A critical aspect of this is the process of 'translation'. Bielsa and Bassett (2009: 2) relate how international journalism conceives of translation as more than an inter-lingual activity; it is a process by which information is 'reshaped, edited, synthesized and transformed for the consumption of a new set of readers'. INAs produce news texts for the different markets they serve; linguistic and cultural knowledge combine to produce information that conforms to the journalistic norms of the regions and satisfies the demands of their audiences. The dominance of languages such as English – one in three internet users is an English speaker and more than 50 per cent of the content of the medium is English – means many stories are 'translated' into English before being re-translated into other languages. The translation of global news therefore has implications for how readers, viewers and listeners around the world understand what is happening and the meaning of events. There are 'serious questions about the extent to which we can ever know what was and what was not said in another cultural context' (2009: 132).

What is globalisation?

We can all accept that the world is undergoing considerable change. More problematic is how we make sense of the change and its impact on our lives. Globalisation is a catch-all concept used to explain the effects of the growing interaction of the international economy, the rise of supranational entities that limit or bind the actions of nation-states, the increasing intermingling of cultures across the world and the rising awareness peoples in all parts of the world have of what is happening elsewhere. Robertson (1992: 8) describes globalisation as 'the compression of the world', emphasising the increased interactions and interconnectedness between peoples, groups and organisations across national borders and boundaries. Interaction and interconnectedness is enabling the emergence of a transnational or global culture or society. While travel, tourism and migration fuel connectivity, there can be 'no globalisation without media and communications' (Rantanen, 2002: 1). The growth of the global media and cultural industries is perhaps the most significant of all the transformations that are supposedly bringing us all closer together. These industries have increased the speed and volume of information, images and entertainment that the individual receives on a daily, hourly or minute by minute basis. They are making people more aware of the commonality of the problems the world faces as well as enhancing consciousness of other places, other peoples and other lifestyles. New media technologies are singled out as central to the weaving of a web of interconnectivity between people, cultures and countries, breaking down the limitations of geography and nation, of time and place.

The globalisation debate is characterised by a 'wide array of claims and counterclaims' (Scholte, 2005: 2). Sceptics believe globalisation is neither inevitable nor widespread and some dismiss the concept as a 'myth' (Hafez, 2007; Ferguson, 1992). For Hafez (2007: 159), increased cross border exchange is not necessarily leading to greater connectivity, or changing the political, social and cultural systems of the nations involved or acting as the midwife to the emergence of a global public sphere or civil society or culture. He argues that globalisation is developing to 'a far more modest degree and at a far slower pace than is generally assumed'. For sceptics nation-states, which are supposedly withering away in the face of greater global interconnectedness, retain their hold over political, economic and cultural life and activity. They see globalisation as a 'flawed conceptual tool' which has significant limitations in helping us to understand contemporary international relations (Hirst and Thompson, 1996; Sparks, 1998, 2008). It is important to emphasise that 'globalisation' is a contested term; it is also the case that there are different kinds of proponents of globalisation.

Among those who embrace the view that globalisation is 'real and tangible', there is a distinction between *positive* and *pessimistic globalisers*. The former focus on the capacity of globalisation 'to improve the quality of life, raise living standards and bring people together, which, in turn, promotes the sharing of cultures and understanding among nations around the world' (Held, 2000: 22). The transfer of values, resources, goods, aid, technology, ideas and media and communication systems across the world is beneficial; it helps these nations to grow economically, develop politically and socially and ultimately contributes to the eradication of poverty and backwardness. *Pessimistic globalisers* believe that the world is becoming 'less diverse and more homogeneous' with the dominant world powers able to 'impose their own agenda on the world' with 'a diminution of national identities and sovereignty' (Held et al., 1999: 22). They deem the interaction to be harmful, imposing alien values which undermine the cultural identities of most of the peoples of the world and removing their cultural autonomy. Both concur that greater interconnectivity is breaking down national boundaries, diminishing differences between nations and peoples and promoting the development of new global structures (Held, 2000: chapter 2). Globalisation assumes some degree of homogeneity resulting from the exchange of goods, values, ideas and beliefs. It is the consequences theorists disagree over. Simon Cottle (2009: 28) draws a distinction between these two approaches on the basis of power, pitting the 'global public sphere' against the 'global dominance' paradigm. Positive globalisers embrace the notion that people are coming together to create a 'world cosmopolitan citizenship' (2009: 28). People are described as having a disposition that not only takes them beyond the concerns of their immediate locality but also makes them more open to inter-cultural knowledge (Hannerz, 1992, 1996; Holton, 2009). They have a sense of global belonging and an international outlook – they are 'citizens of the world' (Norris, 1999). Globalisation is seen as a process of 'hybridisation', which focuses on different cultures travelling across borders to influence one another and create out of their interaction a new culture that respects and embraces difference. Pessimistic globalisers, on the other hand, stress the inequality of global interaction, focusing on the extension of capitalism, corporate power and American or western influence. Interconnectedness is determined by the few rather than the many – and in particular by the US which, in spite of the vast changes that are taking place, is 'still in charge' (Schiller, 1998: 17).

The global village

Positive globalisation is often associated with the Canadian philosopher Marshall McLuhan, who coined the notion of the 'global village' in the 1960s. McLuhan emphasised the role of new media technology in shaping international relations. He believed in an equality of exchange between those involved in interactions across national borders and asserted that increased international interaction results in better understanding between peoples, cultures and countries. He concluded that the expansion of television and satellite technology would bring about a world in which we could all live alongside one another as neighbours in a global village. He wrote that 'after more than a century of electronic technology we have extended our central nervous system in a global embrace, abolishing both time and space as far as our planet is concerned' (McLuhan, 1964: 3). Suffused with an overly romantic view of village life, McLuhan was positive about the impact of technology on social relations. McLuhan's small world was characterised by greater understanding, better cooperation and a more fully developed sense of community. Peace and harmony, watchwords of the 1960s when his work was published, were the outcome of greater understanding and cooperation. The universalising of values such as democracy and greater access to ideas, values and even material goods were the foundations of life in the global village. For McLuhan the explosion of communication, information and interconnectivity was a liberating force.

McLuhan's conceptualisation of globalisation as a positive, unifying force was not new. Usage of the term 'globalisation' may be relatively recent but the developments it refers to have long antecedents. Attention has been drawn to the 'ahistorical manner' in which contemporary discussion of globalisation often takes place (Morley, 2006). Armand Mattelart (1996) has traced the discourse of 'globalisation' and its attendant hype back to the end of the eighteenth century. He reminds us that every technological innovation in media communication that has speeded up international interaction has been accompanied by the propagation of 'the grand narratives of general concord and social reconciliation' (1996: 19). The remarks of the novelist and journalist Victor Hugo, in his opening address at the International Congress of Peace, 1849, remind us that the connection between the shrinkage of time-space by the extension of international communication networks *and* the expansion of peace and understanding between nations and peoples is a recurrent theme in the history of new media forms (Hugo, quoted in Mattelart, 1996: 20).

How peoples touch each other! How distances are growing shorter! And growing closer is the beginning of fraternity ... in a short time man will be able to travel the Earth just as the gods of Homer travelled the sky, in three steps. Just a few more years and the electric wire of concord will embrace the whole world.

Philip Taylor (1997: 7–9) highlights how Hugo's sentiments have echoed down the years. There is the belief that new means of communicating between peoples help to 'transcend ... race, creed, culture, class and country'. Every media technology has been seen as the internet is today, as a means of promoting international understanding.

Putting aside the crude assumption that the more we know about and interact with one another, the better we get along, the concept of the 'global village' was problematic in the eyes of many, particularly those who lived in villages in the developing world. Not all villagers had access to the benefits of the new media technologies. A variety of critics have drawn attention to the disparities between the nations, peoples and individuals in this world of ever expanding media hardware and software. Cees Hamelink (1983) challenges the basic assumptions on which McLuhan's concept of the 'global village' is constructed. For him the world is not a place where everyone talks to everyone else, where people know a great deal about each other and where everyone has social and cultural experiences in common. On the contrary it is a community in which only a few voices are heard, opinions expressed and images viewed (Traber and Nordenstreng, 1992). Distinction is made between the *information rich* and *information poor* in the global village. Many parts of the world are deprived of access to the benefits of the global information and communication revolution. Considerable disparities exist between developed and developing countries. Nation is not speaking unto nation in a world dominated by an unequal distribution of information and information technology.

Emphasising such disparities is regarded by some commentators as out of date, associated with old technologies whose usefulness to the world of international communication is fading away. Today's new digital technology is bridging the information imbalance, turning a monologue into a conversation between many. The internet, mobile phones and other forms of digital technology offer new opportunities, enabling those previously lacking access to information the chance to join in the global chatter. Mobile phone usage has increased considerably everywhere, even in Sub-Saharan Africa, one of the world's most information poor regions (James and Versteeg, 2007; Tenhunen, 2008). The rate of acceptance of the internet in Africa is described as 'the most remarkable in the world' (Sonaike, 2004: 46). However, the facts and figures show that Africa, like the rest of the Third World, is on the wrong side of the digital divide. With one user per 190 people, Africa compares unfavourably with the world average of one user for every 15 people.

Many people do not have access to the new media technology, in the same way as they were deprived of the old media. Similar complaints are levelled at the new technologies; the language of the internet is primarily English and the costs of accessing mobile telephony and the internet are prohibitive for most of the people who live in Asia, Africa and Latin America. Golding (1998: 79) points out that the 'arrival of new communication and information technologies has offered the promise of a more egalitarian, participatory and progressive structure', but 'in practice, the reality has been of their rapid incorporation into familiar structures of inequity and commercial exploitation'. He prefers to describe international interaction as 'cultural pillage', placing his analysis firmly in the camp of pessimistic globalisers.

The global village is also imbalanced in terms of values, ideas and lifestyles. What villagers are talking about, the products they are buying and things they are doing are seen as overwhelmingly shaped by 'western values'. The huge global audiences attracted by television programmes such as *Dallas*, *Bonanza* and *Hawaii 5-0* in the 1970s and 1980s are cited as evidence of the dissemination of western values and lifestyle around the world. The success of western products such as Levi jeans, Ford cars and Nike shoes is seen as an example of the disproportionate emphasis attached to western lifestyles. The growing similarity of downtown city centres on all continents with their Holiday Inns, McDonalds and shopping malls attest to the increasing replication of western urban structures. The emergence of English as a global lingua franca reinforces the notion that western ways of doing things are more valued. These are all examples of how local, authentic cultures around the world are, in Jeremy Tunstall's graphic description, being 'battered out of existence' by the flow of images, ideas and products from the West or, more specifically, from the United States (Tunstall, 1977). The predominance of western products, lifestyle and values around the world is evidence that undermines McLuhan's view of an exchange of equals. Technological change and the global marketplace of ideas and experience might bring the world closer together, drawing in even the most remote areas of the world. But for McLuhan's critics this is happening on the terms of the few; the global village is steeped in western values, beliefs and lifestyles.

Local and/or global

One major assumption of positive and pessimistic globalisers is that expanding interconnectedness threatens the ability of nation-states to exercise control over their territories and citizens, making state governance increasingly unviable. Globalisation is leading to the 'withering away' of the nation-state. Nation-states in the form of territorial, bureaucratic and centralised entities which govern virtually every aspect of social relations within their borders have 'reigned supreme over the vest majority of humanity' for the last 350 or more years (Scholte, 2005: 188). National sovereignty – that is – the exclusive right of the state to exercise power within its own territory, was established by the Treaty of Westphalia in 1648. The quantity and speed of contemporary global information flows impedes the efforts of the state to exercise surveillance over its borders. Citizens are every day making more and more connections with one another outside the control of the nation-state, and in the process forming new identities and weakening their allegiance to the nation. In addition, supranational bodies of one form or another reduce the legal, economic and political powers of the nation-state.

Supranational actors come in a variety of forms – positive globalisers tend to emphasise the rise of non-governmental organisations (NGOs), people power and global political actors such as the EU, while pessimists concentrate more on multinational or transnational corporations (TNCs). Positive globalisers focus on transborder links between organisations ranging from sporting bodies such FIFA to NGOs like Greenpeace and Amnesty International, from the proliferation of regional, multilateral agreements and organisations to the expansion of international political bodies such as OPEC, NATO and the OECD. They tend to foresee this expansion of global political activity as leading to the emergence of global governance, usually based on the extension of democracy and human rights. The most optimistic globalisers believe technology offers the possibility of global democracy by liberating individuals everywhere to communicate their views and opinions. Pessimistic globalisers stress the negative impact of global economic interaction, especially the rise of the global firm. Global media firms such as Rupert Murdoch's News Corporation have become key players in determining the nature of global communication and act as the main gatekeepers of the flow of information around the world. They have been described as the 'lords of the global village' and the 'new rulers of the world' (Pilger, 2002). They are represented as 'operating unchecked in national, regional and global settings, creating their own rules, acting at will, constantly expanding and having limitless power to grow larger than ever' (Picard, 1996: 24). This may exaggerate the power of TNCs which are subject to vagaries of competition (see Compaine, 2002). It is also challenged by free marketers who ascribe to the benefits of the extension of capitalism. But the growing concentration of economic and cultural power in the hands of a smaller number of international corporations is seen as a threat to democracy, cultural diversity and the capacity and ability of governments to make economic, cultural and political decisions. TNCs are seen as the 'missionaries' of capitalism and consumerist values (Herman and McChesney, 1997).

The media are undergoing a fundamental transformation in the era of globalisation. Previously bound within the parameters of the nation-state, national in their scope and output, the media have played a key role in helping to forge national identities (Anderson, 1983; Gellner, 1983;

Billig, 1995). By contrast, the global media are producing material that is 'increasingly detached from the specific tastes of national audiences'. Now the media facilitate the emergence of a transnational culture, drawing on symbols, products and images that come from anywhere in the world. The relationship between the 'local' and the 'global' is posited in theoretical terms primarily as either/or, as mutually exclusive categories, and the rise of the global is portrayed as happening at the expense of the local or national. This binary approach is problematic. The interaction between the local and global is characterised by a variety of forms: the emergence of cultures which combine global and local elements, the adoption of the values of another, alien culture and the revitalisation of traditional sub-national local cultures. Hafez (2007: 5) draws attention to the 'complex processes of indigenization and local adaptation which play a role both in the import of media and the construction of world views within international reporting'. The complexity is acknowledged in the term 'glocalisation' (Robertson, 1994).

Globalisation is not simply a clash between the 'global' and the 'national', a collision of opposing trends juxtaposing homogenisation *and* heterogenisation or assimilation *and* resistance. The presentation of the global and national as antagonistic ignores the fact that as a result of the new media technology we can be in two places at once; the global and local are part of the same process. Global change may be transforming national culture, media and identity but the nature of this transformation is unclear, often exaggerated and it is something that has been taking place for much longer than many proponents of globalisation believe. Things national are not disappearing, they are merely adapting as they have always done. Interconnectivity has its roots deep in history; whether you identify different stages or phases of globalisation or whether you describe globalisation prior to present times as 'incipient', making international connections in a sustained and organised way started way back in history. The growth of 'empire', which saw European societies make connections with all parts of the known world, is associated with the rise of the nation-state and modern society from the late fifteenth century onwards (see Darwin, 2007; Brook, 2008).

The theoretical differences between positive and pessimistic globalisers resonate in the debates within UNESCO in the late 1970s and early 1980s over calls to restructure the international information order. In this debate positive globalisers were associated with 'modernisation theory' while pessimists with the concept of 'cultural imperialism'. These different theoretical outlooks laid down much of the thinking that has shaped the contrary interpretations of globalisation discussed above. If modernisation looked forward to the possible benefits and opportunities posed by technological progress and commercial change, cultural imperialism looked back to the political certainties of colonialism, which had been the primary defining experience for most peoples, nations, communities and individuals in encountering each other at the global level. This theoretical disagreement has shaped not only our understanding of globalisation but also the nature of foreign correspondence.

Both theoretical approaches accept that there is a transfer of resources, values and practices from the West to the rest. Modernisation theory believed that the transfer was an integral part of the efforts to promote development in Africa, Asia and Latin America during the 1950s and 1960s. As part of the efforts to bring about social and economic change, attempts were made to create a 'professional class of communicator'. Golding (1977) describes how western forms, practices and norms were imitated by professionals in the Third World. Most of the models for selecting, gathering and processing news inside the Third World are based on US, British or European newsroom structures and norms. American structures were often – and still are – trans-ferred as part of 'tied aid' packages with finance made available to replicate US practices and news values. Training and education programmes supported by the UN and western government and non-government programmes incul-cated western skills, values and attitudes. Journalism schools were set up with funds from the United States across many parts of the Third World (Schiller, 1976: 11). Based on programmes patterned on those in the United States and Western Europe, trainees absorbed Anglo-American notions of journal-ism and the role of journalism in society. The commitment to objectivity, the basis for selecting news and the autonomy of the professional, as well as the verbal and visual techniques required to present the news, were implanted into the emerging professional in the Third World. Media scholarship was also dominated by Anglo-American thinking and provided a readily acces-sible theoretical model – the 'Four Theories of the Press' – which pushed aside other ways of conceptualising journalism and media systems (1976: 257).

Ignoring the question of whether these values actually capture how the media perform in western societies, the Anglo-American model of journalism was seen by the cultural imperialism thesis as not appropriate to conditions in Africa, Asia and Latin America. The failure of UN efforts to bring about development in the Third World meant that the gap between rich and poor actually widened as the take-off predicted by modernisation theory failed to materialise. This led to a reassessment of the impact of western products, val-ues and ways of doing things on Third World societies. Westernisation came to be seen as detrimental to development. Western countries, and in particu-lar the world's dominant power, the United States – according to cultural imperialism theorists – exploited the countries of the Third World to serve their own economic and political interests. Scholars such as Dallas Smythe (1981), Armand Mattelart (1979), Cees Hamelink (1983) and, above all, Herb Schiller (1969, 1976), described how the importation of western prod-ucts and values maintained the 'structural under-development' of the Third

World. Michael Traber (1985) was one of many who called for the development of a form of journalism more conducive to Third World societies. He called for alternative news values which emphasised non-prominent people, 'good' news, a new way of writing about events and an emphasis on stories which stressed social processes rather than events. Traber's questioning of the appropriateness of the western model of journalism was part of a broader re-evaluation of the impact of western values and practices. This re-evaluation became highly politicised in the 1970s as pressures for change grew.

MacBride and a new order

The battle of ideas between 'modernisation' and 'cultural imperialism' was not simply a dispute between academics. Waged with some intensity during the 1970s, it often spilled over into real war as the struggle for national economic liberation inside the South was subsumed into the rivalry of the Cold War. More often it was fought out within the UN system with calls for a NWICO as a necessary step toward the restructuring of the world's economic system. Many Third World governments and their supporters in the West were critical of the way in which calls for economic reform and justice were either ignored or misinterpreted by the international media. The MacBride Report,[2] published after nearly four years of discussion, debate and disagreement (Alstchull, 1995: chapter 17) defined communication as a human right and criticised the international coverage of the western media, blaming misrepresentation of the Third World on the market and commercial considerations which dictated the work of the news agencies and international broadcasters. To rectify the imbalance in the international communication flows and structures MacBride made a number of recommendations. As with all UN Reports they were expressed in broad and sometimes vague terms in order to attain as much agreement as possible. Besides calling for more resources and technical aid, MacBride put forward a number of recommendations to make media systems around the world more responsive to their own particular needs as well as redress the imbalances and distortions seen as endemic to international news. Encouraging national news agencies, preferencing public service media, promoting radio over television, limiting the concentration of media ownership and providing a right of reply to misreporting were among the proposals made.

The report said a lot about journalistic standards and the news values that underpinned the reporting of international news. Standards could be improved by more appropriate training for journalists in the Third World, the introduction of a code of ethics and the improvement of accountability to the public through the establishment of press or media councils. However, it was the means to improve international reporting that took up much of the discussion of journalism standards. All countries were urged to make greater efforts to admit foreign correspondents and facilitate their reporting. Better education in the languages, politics and cultures of the nations to which correspondent were assigned was advocated. The report recommended that editors in developed countries – the international news 'gatekeepers' – become 'more familiar with the cultures and conditions in developing countries'. More protection for journalists to do their job everywhere was proposed. The Commission also wanted a thorough reassessment of conventional news values, which it believed were at the heart of the poor reporting of the Third World.

> Conventional standards of news selection and reporting, and many accepted news values, need to be re-assessed if readers and listeners around the world are to receive a more faithful and comprehensive account of events, movements and trends in both developing and developed worlds. The inescapable need to interpret unfamiliar situations in terms that will be understood by a distant audience should not blind reporters or editors to the hazards of narrow ethnocentric thinking … (quoted in Richstad and Anderson, 1981: 391)

This call was made in the context of a critique of the negative influence of market pressures in shaping the nature of national and international news and the dominance of global corporations over international communication and media structures.

The failure of the MacBride Commission to criticise government involvement in the media and the restrictions placed by some Third World governments on the flow of information at the same time they condemned the market was the basis of its rejection by many western organisations and journalists. MacBride was charged with seeking to impose state control over the media. The system he proposed would, according to one Fleet Street editor, 'impose a State version of truth: a monotonous official lie' (O'Brien, 1980: 7). Western editors found support from some of their colleagues in the Third World who saw UNESCO as strengthening the power of governments at the expense of an 'independent press'. As one East African editor put it: 'People forget that government held all the power before independence. It still holds all of the power. My fight for intellectual freedom is more important to me than the fight against Americanisation' (quoted in Smith, 1980: 40). While the debate about a new information order was conducted in the corridors of the UN by national governments, journalists all over the Third World struggled to establish independent centres of opinion against the increasingly authoritarian stance their governments took to media freedom. UNESCO's efforts to implement a NWICO were ultimately stymied by Britain and America's withdrawal from the organisation in the mid 1980s (see Atwood and Murphy, 1982; Roach, 1987, 1997). They were eventually swept away with the fall of Communism and the vast and rapid technological changes that spread through the international media and communication industries. The ideological struggle around a NWICO prevented a full and informed discussion of the nature and the impact of western values, attitudes and practices on developing societies.

Westernisation or what?

The debate over McLuhan's concept of the 'global village' highlights two different and diametrically opposed views of interaction between the 'West' and the rest of the world. Whether detrimental or beneficial, the impact of the West and western values is central to the debate about global change and international journalism. Identifying what is meant by 'western values' is problematic, as is any assessment of the impact of these values on other societies. Many scholars have questioned the notion of westernisation (Latouche, 1996). Jonathan Hardy (2008: 1) notes the term 'western' has 'various dimensions and patterns of inclusion and exclusion' that are 'complex, deeply contested, dynamic and changing'. Several scholars have described how the concept came to be constructed historically and used to classify societies into different categories to serve ideological and political purposes, emphasising the qualities of some societies – the West – in contrast to the failings of other societies – the rest (see Said, 1978). Unpacking the components of what constitutes 'the West', it is apparent that each of these is a contested area within western history, society and culture. Some scholars have fallen back on a narrower definition of cultural transfer by emphasising the notion of 'Americanisation' or the transfer of the 'American way of life'. It was not just the peoples of the Third World that expressed concern about the 'Americanisation' of their ways of life. Europeans have a long tradition of complaint about the influence of the relentless flow of US popular culture into their continent during the twentieth century.

A variety of terms including McDonaldization, Coca-colarization, Disneyfication, CNNization and even the 'Levi's generation' – have been used to describe the process by which American values are disseminated (Campbell et al., 2004). Putting aside the problem of identifying what values constitute the 'American way of life', it is not clearly articulated how media products such as Hollywood films, American TV drama serials and international news reports represent and convey American values. The problem of defining a 'culture' is not confined to trying to identify the values of the dominant culture. There is some confusion over what constitutes the local, authentic cultures of the Third World that are being eradicated by western values and media. In one of the most rigorous interrogations of the concept, John Tomlinson (1991: 17) draws attention to the emphasis on 'national cultures' in the discourse of 'cultural imperialism'. Differences within the countries of the Third World – either in economic or cultural terms – are rarely acknowledged. Tomlinson (1991) sees this as a product of the deployment of the theory within the UN system, which is dominated by nation-states and national governments. Equating cultural identity with national cultures reflected the pressing concern of many Third World nations to ensure the political stability of the highly fragmented and fragile entities they inherited following decolonisation. The disposition of national governments and political elites towards traditional cultures inside their own countries was never that favourable; they often shared the view of proponents of modernisation that rural and minority language cultures were inimical to national development. The state-centric bias of the discussion led to a re-evaluation of the nature and process of the impact of western media and products on the Third World.

Seeing international information as a struggle between nation-states or national governments *or* the First and Third Worlds *or* the West and the Global South *or* America and the rest neglects the information imbalances within regions and societies. The growth of media strength in the non-western world has led to charges of 'little cultural/media imperialism' (Sonwalkar, 2001: 505). Within southern Asia, for example, concern has been expressed among India's neighbours about the impact of Indian satellite television on their cultures (2001: 507). Gross inequalities in access to information and communication hardware and software also exist within nations. Global change cannot simply be seen in terms of the transfer of western values from one nation to another, in which the culture of one nation is made subservient to another. Leslie Sklair (1991, 2001) attempts to understand global society and international relations in non-'state centric' terms, applying the Marxist notion of dominant–subordinate classes to international society. Rather than divide the world between states, he distinguishes the emergence of a class of people throughout the nations of the world who benefit from the economic, cultural, technological and political changes that are associated with globalisation. These elite people are found in Asia, Africa and Latin America as well as the nations of the West. They enjoy the benefits of global citizenship: travelling the world, consuming the world's media and purchasing the products that can be obtained in the downtown shopping centres that are replicated throughout the planet. Sklair's global elite – or what he prefers to call the 'transnational capitalist class' – is based on the expansion of the global reach of multinational corporations. Global citizens tend to work for these corporations or for the businesses and service industries that supply them or the state enterprises that support them. They reproduce a culture of capitalism throughout the world, promoting consumerism, advocating liberalisation of trade and emphasising the profit motive. According to Sklair they are responsible for the widening gap between rich and poor, between the transnational elite and the masses, as well as the ecological crisis which is the by-product of the workings of the present international economy.

Sklair's class analysis is criticised for presenting a negative interpretation of global interaction. A more positive analysis is found in the notion of 'cosmopolitanism' – the emergence of what is essentially a group of 'citizens of the world' who have a broad internationalist perspective and outlook (see Holton, 2009). This perspective is critical of Sklair's analysis in two respects: it extends 'global citizenship' beyond the confines of business and economic elites *and* perceives it as something which emerges from below rather than driven by the needs of multinational capitalism. Ulf Hannerz (1996: 105) describes cosmopolitans as those who seek 'to immerse themselves in other cultures'. These are not 'global tourists' who travel the world as a 'spectator sport' but the community of diplomats, bureaucrats, educationalists, aid workers, military personnel and businessmen and women and their sons, daughters, families and friends who have eschewed their local and national attachments to become 'world citizens'. Academic guru Ulrich Beck (2006: 3), in more prosaic prose, describes the cosmopolitan outlook as comprising 'global sense, a sense of boundarylessness ... awareness of ambivalence in a milieu of blurring differentiations and cultural contradictions ... the possibility of shaping one's life under conditions of cultural mixture'. There are people who have been able to throw off their national shackles to be able to imagine belonging to a worldwide community. The 'intellectual and aesthetic stance of "openness" to peoples, places and experiences from different cultures' is deemed a crucial characteristic of these people (Holton, 2009: 19). What they imagine appears similar to the vision McLuhan had of his global villagers. These elites make a contribution to the cultivation of an enhanced sense of 'global civic responsibility'. Cosmopolitanism is a positive development as it favours more 'inclusive arrangements of compassion, human rights, risk management, solidarity and peacefulness' (Hannerz, 2007: 301).

Foreign correspondents can be identified as part of the 'world making cultural apparatus' by the role they play in the 'management of meaning across spatial and cultural distances' (Hannerz, 1996: 113). While foreign correspondents may be accustomed to crossing borders, comfortably living and working in different places, they are not necessarily cosmopolitan in their outlook. Hallin and Mancini (2004: 258–9) note that international journalists are heavy consumers of Anglo-American media. Journalists in many parts of the world regularly tune into the BBC and CNN as well as read global business publications such as *The Economist*, *Wall Street Journal* and *Financial Times* and news magazines such as *Time* and *Newsweek*. A study of Greek international news gatekeepers identified the influence of US news magazines as well as CNN International in shaping their organisations' concept of newsworthiness (Roberts and Bantimaroudis, 1997). While the study found that 'European influences are not negligible', with *Le Monde* and the French TV channel TV5 figuring prominently, American media played a central role in shaping professional judgements on foreign news. Most international news gatherers are employed by international news agencies, which can be seen as primarily US and UK companies. They serve as vehicles to bring Anglo-American news values and news practices into newsrooms around the world (Tunstall, 1977: 45–6). They are also part of a highly competitive business that with the arrival of the internet and 24-hour news channels, has become even more cut-throat, thereby militating against the 'electronic empathy' that Hannerz (1996: 121) describes the international media as being able to promote.

Globalisation and international journalism

It is commonly held that globalisation has changed the ways in which foreign correspondents work and the nature of international news. With globalisation generating greater interconnectedness between peoples and nations it is often assumed that there should be a growth in the demand for foreign news. Similarly, international news should promote a growing awareness of what is happening elsewhere in the world. Outside these commonsense assertions the exact nature of the changes is a matter of debate. There are adherents of modernisation, cultural imperialism and globalisation who in their different ways believe that journalism is becoming increasingly standardised in its practice and values and that international news in the world's media systems is more and more similar. Both positive and pessimistic globalisers argue that standardisation is based on the expansion of the Anglo-American model of journalism. British and American news organisations, news agencies and newspapers dominate the flow of news around the world (Tunstall and Machin, 1999: chapter 8) and journalists as insatiable consumers of global news increasingly look to these organisations and publications to provide them with the model of how they should understand their role in society and how they should do their job. The INAs are conceived as playing a crucial role in having 'successfully spread worldwide the narrative forms and values of western journalism' (Bielsa, 2008: 364). The hegemony of the Anglo-American model – also described as the 'professional' or 'liberal' model – is sustained by the role of English as a world language, the concentration of academic and textbook publishing in Britain and America and the long tradition of journalism training and research in the US (Joesphi, 2005). What constitutes international journalism is determined by Anglo-American news values and practices.

The liberalisation and deregulation of media systems around the world in the 1990s is seen by some scholars as increasingly leading to the global media system becoming consolidated as a single commercial entity dominated by western TNCs. This development is resulting in a further homogenisation of international news which ever more reflects the agenda of western nations and governments and the negative imagery associated with this agenda. Several studies since the 1970s have indicated that there is considerable similarity in what is reported as foreign news in media systems throughout the world (see Chapter 6). The consolidation of the power of 'communication cartels' such as Murdoch's News Corporation and Disney has reinforced the hold of the West – and in particular America's dominance – over people's understanding of international relations (Thussu, 2006).

The commercialisation of national media systems and the deployment of 'soft power' by successive US administrations are crucial factors in this respect. Reference is made to the 'Murdochisation' of journalism and the media in non-western countries due to the dramatic rise in entertainment-oriented news, sensational style journalism and the commodification of news (Sonwalkar, 2002; Rao, 2009). The shift in the balance between public service and commercial media and journalism highlights a contradiction at the heart of what is understood as the western or Anglo-American approach. Daya Thussu (2002) emphasises the extension of commercial media in the context of the increasing importance attached to the exercise of 'soft power' in the post-Cold War era. The US government and the Pentagon in particular have become more skilful in using the international media and information system to persuade the world of American views of events and issues. He notes that the extension of US military power in the form of interventions in many of the world's hot spots since the 1990s have 'dominated the foreign reporting agenda' and they have been 'invariably presented in the context of how they fitted into the American view of the world, with most reports based on information … provided by US sources' (Thussu, 2002: 206).

Veteran television and newspaper correspondent Philip Seib articulates the notion of the 'global journalist', arguing that global change requires of the correspondent that 'much new information must be mastered, which involves learning the substance of new issues and acquiring new sources'. Global reporting 'seeks to understand and explain how economic, political, social and ecological practices, processes and problems in different parts of the world affect each other, and are interlocked, or share commonalities' (Seib, 2002: 25). It is not grounded in Anglo-American or other national assumptions of how the world should be reported. Going online or producing a global news service is seen as changing the relationship between the news media and their audiences. The 'death of distance' means that national media can become 'global' in their reach and with readers, viewers and listeners across the world their product will be adapted to respond to the needs of a global audience. The instant interconnectedness of the online world in particular is changing the national orientation of news journalists around the world and undermining reporters who cover foreign news from one nation. There are a growing number of news workers who supply content to global corporations, produce news for a global audience and adopt a global outlook on world events. The huge packs of reporters – the same reporters – turning up time and again at the major news events can be seen as a physical manifestation of this phenomenon. The INAs in this scenario are increasingly decoupled from their

Anglo-American and European roots in order to embrace this global perspective. The emergence of a new form of journalism that is distinctly 'global' in practice, values, nature and dimension is underpinned by a positive approach to understanding the process of globalisation. It associates 'global journalism' with democracy and the potential of the internet to advance a 'more engaged and active citizenship' (Reese et al., 2007: 237).

There are, however, differences in understanding the way in which foreign correspondence is becoming more 'global'. Some commentators, such as Philip Seib (2002), locate the changes within the confines of the profession. They tend to see it as an extension or evolution of journalism: the net and other technological advances, the expansion of global agencies and organisations and the growth of an audience that has escaped from national frames of reference are identified as factors that transform the mediating role of the foreign correspondent. For other scholars the new environment is undermining the need for specialist foreign news gatherers. Global news can be produced from anywhere and by anyone. The internet means that a foreign news-gatherer does not need to travel to another country to report on events. Home based reporters can trawl the web for information and news about foreign locations. A 'news species of unintentional foreign correspondents' is emerging (Berger, 2009: 366). With foreign news media accessible online local reporters around the world have become sources of international news. Official and non-government websites also act as a source of foreign news for residents of other countries who can become 'do-it-yourself' journalists. Such transformations are also weakening the hold of INAs as the primary provider of foreign news; many of the traditional clients of Reuters, AP and AFP can now turn elsewhere for foreign news. The new landscape is threatening to make the foreign correspondent as a specialist news gatherer redundant.

Scholars such as James Curran and Myung-Jin Park (2000) highlight what they see as the limits of 'Anglo-Americanisation'. They are critical of the 'self absorption and parochialism' of much of the contemporary study of the mass media and journalism and the 'routine' way in which 'universalistic observations about the media' are 'advanced in English-language books on the basis of evidence from a tiny handful of countries'. John Downing (1996) talks of the conceptual impoverishment of extrapolating theoretically from such unrepresentative nations as Britain and the United States. By prescribing the Anglo-American model as the only valid way of practising the profession other journalism traditions have been ignored or neglected. Hugo de Burgh (2005: 2) asserts that the notion that 'all journalisms were at different stages on the route to an ideal model, probably Anglophone, is *passé*'. He and his fellow authors in *Making Journalists* describe different forms of journalism. They draw attention to the range of conventions, practice and values that differentiate between journalism in different cultures. They emphasise that 'how journalism operates ... is a product of culture' and that while globalisation has shared more widely techniques, formats and professional attitudes, it has also 'brought about an intensified awareness of the power of culture' (2005: 17). Some of the basic tenets of Anglo-American journalism are simply not workable in different cultures and political systems. While that most precious of principles, 'objectivity', might be operationalised within a two-party political system, it is 'almost impossible within an intricate and fragmented panorama in which a greater number of political forces act and in which even the slightest shades of meaning in a story risk stepping on the positions of one of the forces in the political field' (2005: 9). The MacBride Report (1980) drew attention to the problems of performing objective journalism in a highly politicised society. It also emphasised that the wide dissemination of the US model made it difficult for any journalist to advocate practices that violate principles of autonomy and private ownership.

Notes

1 The terms 'foreign', 'international', 'global', 'transnational' and 'cross-cultural' are often used in the literature on international news and communication. There are differences in the way in which they are used but sometimes they are used interchangeably to refer to the gathering, production and dissemination of news about international issues and events. Berger (2009) provides an interesting discussion of the geo-spatial conceptualisation of news produced outside the boundaries of the nation and the challenges posed by technological change. In this book foreign correspondence and international journalism are used to mean the same thing, as the notion of 'foreign' has traditionally been central to our conceptualisation of international news gathering.

2 The MacBride report was produced by the International Commission for the Study of Communication Problems chaired by former Irish Foreign Minister, Sean MacBride, and was composed of 15 members representing all parts of the world.

2

'THE COLONIAL LEGACY': THE HISTORY OF INTERNATIONAL JOURNALISM

Foreign correspondence has a natural history. Like a living creature, it has adapted over time to a changing environment in order to survive. (Cole and Hamilton, 2008: 798)

The first exposure to Africa for North American and European readers has come through the words of the slave owners. I mention this because the legacy of 300 years of slavery and colonialism runs deep in your culture. Your history books influence your analysis. A journalist from a developed country is not isolated from this legacy. (Mandaza, 1986: 133)

The roots of contemporary international reporting are deeply embedded in the expansion of the communication system in the nineteenth century. Many of the organisations devoted to the gathering of international news emerged out of the commercialisation of the press in the 1850s. The routines and practices we associate with the occupational culture of foreign correspondents developed with the 'great foreign reporters' of the late Victorian period who voyaged to the far flung corners of the world to report of wars and uprisings. Where foreign stories are from and what they focus on are a product of this history. However, foreign news appeared in the very first newspapers that were established in the early seventeenth century. Europe's first newspapers were full of stories or hearsay about events across the length and breadth of the continent and beyond. This was a response to the demand for news of the cataclysmic occurrences associated with the wars of religion that impacted on the lives of everyone in European society. It also reflected the first tentative steps Europeans had taken into the unknown worlds of Asia, Africa and the Americas. Reporting foreign news was less risky than covering domestic affairs. Monarchs and the dynastic order that ruled Europe rigorously prevented news and information about their affairs reaching the public unless they were specifically sanctioned accounts of their rule. Printers had their ears and nose cut off for breaking the law and some were put to death. Foreign news became easier to gather with the expansion of postal services and transport systems. To satisfy the public thirst for news and to exploit the emerging communication infrastructure the early newspapers established foreign news as a staple feature of their output.

This chapter traces the history of international news reporting and the emergence of the foreign correspondent as a specialist news gatherer. It begins by examining how international news figured in the daily press as it developed in the eighteenth century and the close connection between the expansion of foreign trade and foreign news. It was the rise of colonialism which ensured that the gathering of international news and information was organised and put on a regular footing. The imperial ventures of the European nations produced an invisible cash crop – information – which international news agencies sought to harvest for profit. The psychological insecurities of imperialism shaped the kind of foreign news that was reported, including the stereotyping of 'native' peoples. The advent of new technology in the form of cable, telegraph and telex enhanced the reach of the international newsgathering system and laid down the structure within which international journalism was to operate. The present international information order was established between 1870 and the 1914–18 War. It was effectively dominated by a small number of international news agencies closely linked to the imperial powers. Colonialism not only moulded how international news is gathered, processed and disseminated today but also had a profound impact on audience expectations of what international news should be.

The early foreign news gatherers

Anthony Smith (1980: 19–28) locates the antecedents of the foreign correspondent in the world of exploration. Foreign reporting 'is exploration carried on by other means' (1980: 24). The early explorers were not necessarily motivated by the pursuit of information for its own sake – although curiosity did play its part for some individuals. According to Smith, 'each unit of information filled in the uncertainty about the nature of the world' (1980: 21) that existed outside of Europe. More significantly, the acquisition of information could ultimately lead to power and wealth, and information gathering was an element in the economic and industrial exploitation of the world by Europeans. Fashioned out of words and pictures, information is the basic product of journalism and it is sometimes forgotten that the journalist has always been a trader. News is a commodity bought and sold around the world, and the emergence of international journalism and reporting should be seen as part of the expansion of international trade. The link between international news and international trade is as strong today as ever: 'trade between nations has been found to be one of the most conducive factors in augmenting press coverage in foreign countries' (Pietilainen, 2006: 217). The pattern of trade between countries has taken on different forms, and the evolution of foreign correspondence as a result has, over the last 350 years or more, gone through several stages, including exploration, slavery and colonialism.

The link between trade, adventure and news was apparent in Europe's first newspapers. The *corantos* that emerged in the 1620s were almost exclusively devoted to foreign news (Stephens, 1997: 153). This is highlighted by their titles – what is regarded by some as the first *coranto* published in England was entitled *Corante, or Weekley Newes from Italy, Germany, Hungary, Poland, Bohemia, France and the Low Countreys*. Domestic news was absent. When Count Mansfeld visited England in 1624 the *corantos* covered his trip over and his trip back but reported nothing about his stay (1997: 153). The dependence on foreign news is usually attributed to the rigorous system of licensing and censorship which prevented any publication of domestic news. Early English and French *corantos* were published in Amsterdam, where enterprising printers such as Peter de Keere and Caspar Van Hilten translated and reprinted their Dutch publications – cutting out news of the countries they were supplying (1997: 145). Amsterdam was a cosmopolitan city, one of the main trading and shipping ports of Europe, and its *coranto* publishers acquired their news from merchants, traders and seafarers who brought stories not only from around Europe but also from America, Africa and Asia. They were responding to strong public demand for information about events in Europe, which was engulfed in the Thirty Years War (Brownlees, 2005). According to one news writer of the period 'the subject of Newes most enquired for, is for the most part of *Wars*, *Commotions* and *Troubles*, or the *Composing* of them' (Arblaster, 2005). The pressure of filling pages on a regular basis was assisted by the availability of material that could be translated from foreign journals and publications – and it is no surprise to know that the world of news at this time was dominated by the plagiarism of stories, as printers reprinted material from rival publications. The gradual weakening of licensing and censorship led to the growth of domestic news but foreign stories remained the main feature of the newspapers in most parts of Western Europe well into the eighteenth century and beyond.[1]

Much of the early foreign news was phantasmagoria. Fear of the unknown, of lands unexplored and peoples undiscovered led to tales of monsters, make believe and mystery (Smith, 1980: 19–21). Accounts of the extraordinary proliferated. Typical was a report in a French news sheet of 1576 of a 'monstrous and frightful serpent' found in Cuba, illustrated with a woodcut of a two headed, winged serpent (Stephens, 1997: 123). Sensational, hyperbolic language was used to describe the creatures, peoples and places found in the unexplored world – terms such as 'frightful', 'horrible' and 'marvellous' tended to prefix the monsters mentioned while the men who sallied forth into the unknown were 'gallant' and 'mightie' (1997: 123). Because much of this material was gathered from seafarers who regaled the customers of taverns and alehouses in Europe's ports it was unreliable. Foreign news was the product of gossip, tall tales and rumour, gathered in an unsystematic and unverified manner. It is noteworthy that such stories featured in the early attempts to organise the collection of news from abroad. Those involved in business and commerce required reliable news from afar. They could not rely on printed material which was 'too crude' or on spoken news that was 'too unreliable' and sought to establish their own collection system of written news (Smith, 1980: 66–68). They set up private postal networks whereby local agents acted as correspondents, sending news in handwritten letter form to their employers.

The most advanced networks were those established by financiers, the Fuggers of Augsburg and the Rothchilds of London, in the second half of the sixteenth century. News was essential to financial dealings – the Fuggers, for example, lent money to a great many of Europe's leading families and as a result of the high rate of bankruptcies among these households early intelligence was required (Smith, 1979: 19). In addition to information about exchange rates, insolvencies and prices, these newsletters contained reports of battles, disasters, plots, miracles, royal births, deaths and marriages as well as executions and 'weird happenings' (Smith: 1979: 67). Intelligence was not confined to financial and business information: it was also about more general events and rumours that traders, financiers and bankers had to keep abreast of. This system of news gathering was a form of private news; it was not at this time sold to customers, although it is suggested that the Fuggers sometimes passed on their service to clients (Hohenberg, 1993: 6).

Private networks of correspondents had existed since the late Middle Ages, sending military, diplomatic and ecclesiastical information across Europe (Smith, 1979: 18). Well trodden paths were developed to ensure that the Church and monarchs obtained the information they required to pursue their affairs. Diplomacy was established as an essential part of how the European monarchies conducted international relations. Rules and regulations were quickly developed in order that governments could 'talk' to each other: embassies and ambassadors became sources of information about what was happening in their part of the world. It is not surprising that much of the news that travelled throughout Europe concerned political, religious and financial matters and events. This is the kind of news that Kings, prelates and bankers demanded and they were the only actors in the medieval and early modern period that had the resources, money and manpower to gather and transport news on a regular basis across the dangerous and difficult roads and routes of those times.

Newssheets and newspapers of Restoration Britain relied heavily on overseas newspapers for their foreign news. They concealed their sources by using phrases such as 'They write from Vienna', or 'We have advice from Turin', or 'It is reported from Frankfurt' (Sutherland, 2004: 126). It was with the emergence of daily newspapers that the sources of foreign news began to be made transparent to readers. Britain's first daily newspaper, *The Daily Courant*, told its readers on the 22 October 1702 that foreign news:

> will be found by Foreign Prints, which, as Occasion shall offer, will be mention'd in this *Courant*, that the Author had taken care to be duly furish'd with all that come from Abroad. And for an Assurance he will not impose any *Feign'd Additions*, he will always quote the *Papers* from whence he makes his extracts, and represent *Foreign Affairs* just as he finds them in the Foreign Prints ... (2004: 126)

Foreign stories in the British press that were not taken from continental newspapers originated from official sources, diplomatic communiqués, war news from officers and commanders in the field or the official government newspaper, the *London Gazette*. These accounts were often either bland or highly dubious in their veracity. To supplement such accounts news was also taken from the letters of private correspondents (Clarke, 2004: 201). They were often published well after the occurrences they were relating had taken place. Reliance on foreign papers and private correspondence from abroad meant that foreign news gathering was an uncertain business. Disruptions in the mail service caused by bad weather could result in empty pages, stories printed in a larger type face or extraneous accounts of this or that (Sutherland, 2004: 126–128). Newspapers tried to avoid reproducing empty pages or printing irrelevant material; apologies were common and a few of the more conscientious news writers would fill up space by providing general accounts of the situation in this or that country.

During most of the eighteenth century foreign news was collected in a casual and haphazard way. This began to change in the early nineteenth century, particularly in the US and Britain, when the press demanded a more professional approach to foreign news gathering. Faced with the cataclysmic events in revolutionary France, the London newspapers showed some initiative in covering them. The *Morning Post* actually sent out a man in early summer, 1789 only for him to miss the fall of the Bastille – the opening salvo of the revolution – by a 'lamentable error of judgement' (Hohenberg, 1993: 3). It was left to *The Times* to employ reliable correspondents and organise them into a network of reporters, covering the major capitals of Europe. The newspaper's owner, John Walter I, deployed staff including translators and messengers to get dispatches back to London and in the process established the first independent foreign news gathering service for a newspaper. With the Napoleonic wars severing Britain's links with the European continent, *The Times* appointed Henry Crabb Robinson as the first correspondent sent abroad with the purpose of covering the news (Hohenberg, 1993: 4). It was Robinson who persuaded *The Times* to set up a network of regular foreign correspondents, which helped to establish the latter part of the nineteenth century as 'the era of great reportage'.

Birth of the foreign correspondent

Henry Crabb Robinson was appointed as foreign correspondent to Germany in 1807, served as special correspondent during the Peninsular War in Spain in 1808–9 and became foreign editor of *The Times* after that tour (Boston, 1990: 75). He was instrumental in the newspaper locating regular correspondents in Paris, Vienna, Berlin and St Petersburg with the task of providing regular weekly round ups of the news (Mansfield, 1936: 191). From this initiative the newspaper built up a formidable network of international reporters. *The Times* dominated the British press in the first half of the nineteenth century, and the scale and scope of its foreign intelligence outstripped the country's other newspapers (Tunstall and Palmer, 1991: 49). Much of the prestige of *The Times* derived from the fact that it had 'more correspondents, reporting more frequently and fully from more European capitals than its rivals' (Brown, 1977: 43). This network led the newspaper to reject offers from the newly formed news agencies to provide it with foreign news: 'they generally found they could do their own business better than anyone else' (Griffiths, 2006: 122). While the rest of the press signed up, *The Times* resisted for several years. However, by the 1860s it found it impossible to compete with the speed of the agency service, which had become indispensable.

The first major private news agency was established by Frenchman, Charles Havas, in 1832.[2] Created before the days of the telegraph, *L'Agence Havas* depended on carrier pigeon and semaphore to disseminate news. Much of this news was financial information, particularly stock market quotations, which Havas sold to the newspapers and other clients. Taking over its main rival, *Correspondence Garnier*, in 1835, Havas established itself as a supplier of national and international news with its headquarters in Paris employing a growing number of translators, writers, messengers and clerks to serve its clients. With French newspapers unable to afford their own correspondents, Havas gained a virtual monopoly of foreign news in France, with offices in London, Brussels, Vienna and the major cities of Germany. With the invention of the electric telegraph, Havas consolidated its service across Europe. Unlike in other countries, the telegraph in France became a state monopoly, and Havas's close connections with the government guaranteed the agency preferential access. This arrangement helped Havas to cement its position as 'the first disseminator of cheap, mass produced news that was reasonably fast and reliable …' (Hohenberg, 1993: 7).

It was not long before rival international news services started up – most of them founded by former employees of Havas. In 1849 Bernard Wolff, with the support of the Prussian government and banking interests, set up *Telgraphisches Bureau* (WTB) in Berlin. Wolff's compatriot, Paul Julius Reuter, started to provide stock exchange prices for London merchants and brokers in 1851. Reuter saw the opportunity of exploiting the new cable laid between London and the continent. It was not long before the three agencies began to cooperate, signing an agreement in 1856 to exchange stock prices between the three financial centres, which was later extended to political news (Smith, 1980: 77). Unlike other agencies that continued to operate within a national framework, Reuters, Havas and WTB became international news agencies within the first few years of their establishment. Britain, France and Germany were the countries with the most developed telegraph networks. They, in Reuter's words, started to 'follow the cable' and, as undersea cables linked Europe and America, and then extended to Africa and India in the 1860s, and China, South America and Japan in the 1870s, these agencies opened offices around the world (Rantanen, 1997: 612).

For Reuter and his rivals, their main clients initially were financial bodies, particular those associated with the emerging stock exchanges. It took more time to sign up the press, as many newspapers used their own correspondents. Reuter spent several years attempting to convince *The Times* to subscribe to his service. It was only in the late 1850s when the repeal of press taxation in Britain encouraged the emergence of new, more commercially inclined newspapers that Reuter was able to acquire sufficient subscribers to make his service profitable. The lack of subscribers meant that Reuter was not able to cover the Crimea War (1854–6) and it was left to *The Times* correspondent, William Howard Russell, the 'first war correspondent', to report in graphic pen pictures the setbacks and vicissitudes faced by the British army and their French allies (Read, 1992: 29). Russell's dispatches were sent by sea – not telegraph – and took nearly three weeks to get back to London. His reports brought down the government but, more significantly for the history of foreign correspondence, he participated in the first organised effort to report a foreign war. Reuter's efforts to convince the press to take up his service were initially stymied by the poor quality of the early telegraph line, and the way in which news was lost in translation as it passed through the hands of operators who failed to fully and correctly copy down the story.

In the process of attracting custom from the press, the international news agencies (INAs) developed a style and form of foreign news which was to characterise 'agency copy'. With established newspapers of the 1850s such as *The Times* using their own correspondents, Reuter placed their emphasis on their being first with the news, providing short accounts of action in plain language. He also ensured that his correspondents covered events from more than one side or perspective, guaranteeing full coverage and gaining a reputation for objectivity (Read, 1992: 31). The speedy provision of accurate, statistical data to keep the stock markets informed was transferred to the political domain. 'Brief bulletins' were provided without comment and 'without a tinge of sensational prose' (Read, 1992: 94). It was left to the newspaper correspondents to file detailed accounts. The business manager of *The Times* summed up matters thus:

> Reuter's agent has one business, to pick up the facts, not to bother his head about anything but the bare facts, and to wire them at the earliest moment he can acquire them. A *Times* correspondent has a great deal more to do [his] duty being to comment on the news rather than give it .... (Palmer, 1978: 209)

Short, succinct hard news accounts became the provenance of the INAs. The competition was to ensure that your agency was the first with the news. Hard facts also made business sense. Factual accounts of what had happened enabled the INAs to sell their stories to newspapers of different political persuasions. And it reduced costs: using the telegraph during its early years was expensive. With the price of sending a telegram between London and India in the 1860s as much as £1 per word, a short message could save considerable money (Read, 1992: 92). This meant that 'telegrams are for facts; appreciation and political comment can come by post' (Palmer, 1978: 208). The advent of 'telegraphic journalism' drew a distinction between 'fact' and 'comment', which became a feature of journalism in the twentieth century. But gathering early intelligence and hard facts was not easy. Many of the telegraph services around the world were controlled in one way or another by governments,[3] many of whom were unsympathetic to a free press. The INAs entered into agreement with national governments and national news agencies to extend their newsgathering effort, reproducing communiqués and information from official sources. The earliest Reuter's agents simply collected official pronouncements and reproduced stories from local newspapers (Read, 1992: 29). Close ties with government were also established through subscriptions or 'subsidies' for telegraph services to certain parts of the world (Read, 1992: 63).

The breakthrough for the INAs came in the 1860s with the rapid expansion of the commercial press. This was more pronounced in Britain than in either France or Germany, thereby benefitting Reuter more than his competitors. From the 1860s onwards there was an increase in demand for foreign news. Provincial newspapers in Britain which had few or no foreign reporting staff came to depend on Reuters' telegrams. A systematic communication of information from the Continent to Britain, the Reuters service included regular telegrams offering summaries of news that was in the public domain in the country it reported from: appointments and resignations, new legislation, weather reports, crop and harvest information, and disasters and accidents

(Brown, 1977: 27). While this service was not a substitute for a correspondent on the spot it did enable the rest of the British press to compete with the sophisticated network of correspondents that had been developed by *The Times*.

The importance of foreign news to the London press is attributable to the dominant position of *The Times*. The supremacy of the Thunderer's foreign news service was one of the primary features of its role as market leader. A leading *Times*' foreign correspondent was Paris-based Henri Stefan Opper de Blowitz, who specialised in obtaining exclusive interviews with the leading European statesmen of the day. His greatest scoop was at the Congress of Berlin in 1878 when, in addition to a rare interview with Reich Chancellor Bismarck, he secured a copy of the Treaty which *The Times* was able to publish as it was being signed (Griffiths, 2006: 112). *The Times*'s rivals struggled to compete with such coverage but compete they had to. Not only did readers expect foreign news coverage but it was soon apparent that foreign news stories could generate a large boost in circulation. De Blowitz and his colleagues produced a long letter, outlining in detail the events that they were describing and providing their interpretation of what had happened. Sent by mail their reports usually took up a prominent place in the newspaper when they were published. It was also the tradition not to edit the letters in *The Times*; it was not until 1891 with the setting up of the Foreign Department that editorial control was imposed over the newspaper's correspondents (Brown, 1985: 240).

The main challenge was the speed of getting the news home. *The Times* from the 1830s sought to develop the fastest possible routes to receive reports from its men in the field. No matter what route and method were discovered a time lag occurred. The electric telegraph changed this, making news available within hours rather than weeks. Expectations that foreign news would be available for the next morning's edition rose and it was the Franco-Prussian war (1870–71) that brought home to British newspapers the increasingly competitive nature of foreign news coverage; this war was the 'beginning of the rush to get news first and to be ahead of the other newspapers' (Hampton, 2004: 78).

Responding to the huge demand for news of the war, the practice of making a distinction between the letter and the telegram unravelled. It failed to produce either the latest news or a coherent account of events. The long letters appeared 'stale' and the telegrams 'inadequate' to cover events that were unfolding quickly. The *Daily News* directed its correspondents to telegraph their long account directly. Other newspapers followed suit and correspondents in the field were soon developing arrangements to ensure their copy was back in the home office within 24 hours. This was to have a profound impact on the perception of the time frame within which the 'newsworthiness' of events should be assessed. The then editor of *The Times*, John Delane, believed that the requirement for immediate reports marked the end of the foreign correspondent. Echoing debates about the internet today, he held that the telegraph removed any necessity to maintain permanent correspondents abroad. Correspondents had to change their style: 'they would have to be more reflective than narrative, with a wider scope and greater breathe of views' (Palmer, 1978: 208).

Hard news could now be clearly distinguished from features and comment, and correspondents were required to file shorter news pieces more quickly to satisfy the changing news culture. The necessity for a regular and rapid supply of news was exploited by those in power. For example, the Prussians allowed unprecedented access to the battlefield as German Chancellor Bismarck recognised the propaganda value of press coverage: 'Nothing will be more favourable for our political standing in England and America than the appearance in the two most influential newspapers of these countries ... of very detailed accounts of our army in the field' (quoted in Knightley, 2003: 47). The war did not bring about the end of the foreign correspondent as Delane predicted but it did finish the career of those who failed to adapt to the more concise, factual writing style of the telegraph era and the demands of ensuring that copy reached home promptly.

Establishing a reputation for speed, usefulness and trustworthiness, Reuters became a limited company in 1865. Business grew as the newspaper industry flourished and the cable network expanded in the late nineteenth century. Increased demand brought more competition – Central News was established in 1863 and started employing foreign correspondents in 1871. It was joined the following year by Exchange Telegraph, which deployed reporters in major news centres (Boyd-Barrett, 1978: 196). These agencies forced Reuters to pay more attention to what the press wanted; the emerging 'penny newspapers' had a different conception of foreign news from their more serious counterparts of earlier years. Demand for more 'exciting news' brought a response from the agencies. Reuters informed its agents and correspondents in 1883 that:

> In consequence of the increased attention paid by the press to disaster &c., of all kinds, agents and correspondents are requested to be good enough, in future, to notice all occurrences of the sort. The following are among the events that should be comprised on the service: – fires, explosions, floods, inundations, railway accidents, destructive storms, earthquakes, shipwrecks attended with loss of life, accidents to war vessels and to mail steamers, street riots of a grave character, disturbances arising from strikes, duels between, and suicides of persons of note, social or political and murders of a sensational or atrocious character. (Cited in Read, 1992: 100)

The search for more sensational stories led one of Reuters' rivals – the New York based Dalziel's News Agency – to overreach itself, providing inaccurate stories which compromised its standing with clients (Palmer, 1978: 215). Reuters in the face of competition established a close relationship with the Press Association (PA), which was set up in 1868 to represent the leading provincial newspapers in Britain (Read, 1992: 45). In exchange for domestic news from PA, the agency supplied international news to the provincial press. As a result Reuters was able to establish a 'secure domestic market ... without having to involve itself greatly in the activities of domestic news-gathering' (Boyd-Barrett, 1978: 194). If the PA agreement helped to stave off competition inside Britain, it was the agreement that Reuter signed with Wolff and Havas in 1870 that 'was destined to form the basis of the international news order until the 1930s' (Read, 1992, 55).

Institutions of empire

Fear of renewed competition led to the Agency Alliance Treaty, which divided the world into 'spheres of influence' for international news gathering and dissemination. Given the close relationship each of the agencies had with their national governments, these spheres corresponded with the political and economic influence of their respective governments (Smith, 1980: 78). Reuters served the British Empire and the Far East; Havas was furnished with Italy, Spain, and the French and Portuguese empires; and Wolff acquired Austria and her satellite territories, and Scandinavia and Russia. Reuters and Havas shared Latin America but it was eventually handed over to the French agency. Reuters was the most important member of this cartel; its sphere of influence was the most extensive and it had more bureaux and correspondents than its rivals. The agreement allowed the free exchange of news between the agencies and provided each with a virtual monopoly of news in their territories. Other agencies had to fit into this cartel and much resentment was caused, particularly among the American agencies, which were not treated as equals. Associated Press (AP) and United Press (UP) were marginalised, although the former became linked to the cartel when it was sub-contracted by Reuters to gather news in the Americas in 1893. From the 1870s onwards the cartel members proceeded to 'wire the world' by becoming involved in the companies that developed much of the world's cable system, expanding offices in the major cities reached by the rapidly expanding cable system, entering into agreements with or taking control of national news agencies in different parts of the world and building close ties with the imperial ventures of the nations with which they were associated (see Winseck and Pike, 2007).

The cartel exercised hegemony over international news between 1870 and 1917, although it was not formally dissolved until 1937. The internationalisation of news and journalism accompanied the expansion of commerce and the development of empire in the late nineteenth century. International communication was an integral component of sustaining imperialism and capitalism. The communication networks developed between 1870 and the

First World War served the political, military and commercial interests of the colonial powers. The transport infrastructure inside the colonies connected the economically profitable parts of the country to the coastal ports. All routes led to the sea in order to facilitate the trading interests of the European countries. Similarly, the international network of news and information that developed served the colonial powers: they connected the metropolitan centre of the empire to their administrative centres in the colonies (Harris, 1981: 11). The colonies were never connected to one another, which meant even after decolonisation the countries of Africa, Asia and Latin America had more difficulty communicating with their neighbours and one another than they did with Europe's capital cities. The international information order was monopolised by the interests of European traders, businessmen and colonial administrators and the nature of the news and information transmitted reflected this bias. The cartel extended its influence as the telegraph and more significantly the undersea cable stretched further around the world.

The spread of the INAs was accomplished by a series of arrangements made with national agencies, most of which were government owned. The expansion of the telegraph from the 1850s was designated a matter of national security by most governments, and multilateral agreements were made to facilitate telegraphic connections across continents. The International Telegraph Union (ITU) was founded in 1865 with the aim of regulating the network in order to prevent the transmission of private telegrams 'that threaten state security, or violate the laws of a country, public order or morals' (Mattelart, 1994: 9). Only one of the ITU's 22 founding members was not European. Telegraphic communication increased rapidly, rising from 29 million transmissions in 1868 to 329 million by the end of the century (1994: 11). With the increase in international information flows many governments merged the administration of their postal and telegraph services, and codified their power in an ITU convention held in St Petersburg in 1875 (Hills, 2002). The cable system was developed primarily under private finance although the colonial governments were involved in providing subsidies and facilitating mapping and navigation (Thussu, 2006: 8). Companies had to gain licences from government to bring cables ashore, which could sometimes lead to tensions in some part of the world (see Winseck and Pike: 2007). The potentially ruinous cost involved in laying cables and the political difficulties that could arise led these companies to cooperate with one another, across national borders, in what has been described as 'a complex series of monopolies and cartel arrangements' (Pike and Winseck, 2004: 645). Close connections with national governments meant imperial rivalries sometimes manifested themselves in the expansion of cables but it was the degree of cooperation between the colonial powers in the development of this international information structure that is noteworthy. British companies came to dominate the manufacture and laying down of cables and by 1900 they owned almost two-thirds of the world's cables (2004: 646). This enabled Britain to exert considerable control over the transmission of information at this time.

The expansion of the cable was in the hands of private companies but dictated by the needs of government. Less financially viable lines were laid in order to satisfy the political and imperial ambitions of the colonial governments. The telegraph and cable enabled governments to communicate directly with their colonies: 'for the first time in history, colonial metropoles acquired the means to communicate almost instantly with their remotest colonies ...' (Headrick, 1981: 129). This facilitated the rapid execution of colonial policy as well as ensured that local administrators were placed more fully under the direct control of the imperial power. The amount of international news also increased. INAs became 'assiduous users' of the cable network from very early on (Mattelart, 1994: 15). As the cable reached further into India, Australia, South Africa and the Far East, the agencies opened offices along the route, usually establishing firm ties with the local colonial administrators. Chandrika Kaul (1997: 67) describes the 'close links' that Reuters formed with 'successive viceroys and the political elite' in India. By 1870 Reuters had six offices in India, in the major conurbations, establishing Britain's major colony as a central component of the Reuters international news network (Read, 1992: 60). The agency dominated the news going in and out of India as well as supplying commercial information and private telegrams. Much of this news focused on keeping settler communities aware of events in their home countries as well as ensuring that the home countries were in touch with the men and women who left their shores to serve in the colonies.

Settler press

The large migration of Europeans to settle in all corners of the world had major implications for the ways in which those societies developed. The social and cultural institutions of the home country were replicated inside the colonies, with more or less rigour depending on the colonial power (Rodney, 1988). The settlers' established their own newspapers, which served the interests of the European community as well as the native elites who were co-opted into European culture in order to run the colony under the metropolis and the colonial administration. They not only were clients for the INAs but also provided many of the correspondents employed by the European press and news agencies to gather information from their part of the world. Most of the early newspapers were started by missionaries or the colonial authorities. They were produced in the language of the colonial power, and indigenous language newspapers were either discouraged or subjected to tight control. The French colonies in Africa up to the 1930s forbade anyone but a French citizen from starting a newspaper and the British used the law to prevent the publication of material that would 'inflame an excitable and ignorant populace' (Mytton, 1983: 52). The uneven development of the colonial press left a 'discontinuity in communication' between the elite and masses in many parts of the world which remains today (Mytton, 1983: 41).

The indigenous elites and the European settlers shared an international news system that provided them with more information of what was happening in Europe than in their own countries. Many correspondents of metropolitan newspapers and the INAs worked for the settler press – Kaul notes that, 'frequently correspondents from among conservative sections of the Anglo-India press establishment' were recruited by *The Times* (Kaul, 1997: 74). Much of the news of India, Africa and other colonial outposts was gathered in the European capitals from which they were governed. Official sources of information dominated. In 1909, the foreign department of *The Times* consisted of four men in London, 'one or other of these four is continually in direct relations with the Foreign Office, India Office and Colonial Office' (Kaul, 1997: 72). Special correspondents would travel to imperial outposts to familiarise themselves with the situation or to cover breaking news events. Long stay bureaux were located in the more important colonies – in the case of Reuters this was India, South Africa, Australia and the Far East, especially Hong Kong and Singapore. Other colonies were peripheral in news terms, including most of colonial Africa, which remained the domain of stringers from local newspapers.

The maintenance of contact between the settler communities and the 'mother country' was a major determinant of international news. Settler-oriented news was crucial in order that 'he [the migrant] is in touch with what is happening at home and, more importantly, in his own home locality, he feels less isolated …' (Harris, 1981: 13). Integrating the settlers into the empire was seen as a crucial function of international journalism:

> There can be no essential unity of corporate life in the Empire unless every part is supplied with news of common Empire interest … British news, that is, news interesting or important to British subjects, should be widely disseminated to the farthest frontiers and recesses of the Empire. (1981: 13)

It was the telegraph and the news that bound the British Empire together. The strategic importance of the press was recognised with the establishment of the Empire Press Union (EPU) in 1909 (Kaul, 2006). Founded at the inaugural Imperial Press Conference held in London that year, the EPU had as one of its major aims the expansion of the news service to settler communities, and to this end it successfully pressed for reduction in the cost of telegrams to India (Harris, 1981: 13; Kaul, 1997: 63). Bringing together Fleet Street and provincial newspapers of all political persuasions and their colleagues in the colonies, the conference sought to shape and guide public opinion throughout the empire. The representatives of the settler press to the conference were mostly expatriates; the Indian representatives, for example, were primarily drawn from pro-government, Anglo-India newspapers such as the *Civil and Military Gazette*, the *Madras Mail*, the *Englishman* and the *Pioneer*, which stated that 'an Anglo-Indian journalist is an English man first and a journalist second' (cited in Kaul, 2006: 131). The representation of the Indian press by British journalists was to change as the number of Indian newspapers with offices in London grew from eight in 1901 to 47 in 1914 and 63 by 1921 (2006: 132). The EPU as a result became more critical of the imperial venture.

But the dominant theme of the early years was a better news service for expatriates. The extent of the hold that empire exerted over Fleet Street is manifest not only in the launch of a Sunday newspaper, *The Empire News*, but also in the vast number of the leading lights of the industry who were outspoken and enthusiastic supporters of empire. Leading editors such as Garvin (*Observer*), Spender (*Westminster Gazette*), Strachey (*Spectator*) and Dawson (*The Times*) were 'journalists for Empire', helping to make the Empire 'one of the commanding subjects of the time' (Startt, 1997: 65). The mass circulation popular newspapers that emerged in the late 1890s extended news of the British Empire to a wider readership. Britain's first million-selling daily newspaper, the *Daily Mail*, was 'the embodiment and mouthpiece of the imperial idea' (Kaul, 2000: 49). Its owner, Lord Northcliffe, attempted to infuse 'living patriotism' into his newspapers and to this end he expanded the number of travelling correspondents, encouraging them to make liberal use of cable and wire services, to the extent that the *Daily Mail* became the largest international news operation in Britain behind *The Times* and Reuters. More human interest stories were produced as the *Mail's* correspondents dug out stories from the overseas Dominions; colonial warfare was a particular interest of the *Daily Mail* and other popular newspapers. Increased circulation attests to the way in which these newspapers captured the 'imperial' mood of the country.

Development of agency journalism

The imperial parameters within which the INAs operated appeared to contradict the independence and impartiality they claimed for their newsgathering operation. However, there were other problems that confronted the operation – not least the quality of their journalism. The first employees of the INAs were not trained journalists. They were agents whose job it was to simply collect and convey official pronouncements and stock market prices and information. In addition they would copy stories out of the local press in the country and region in which they were based; 'the idea of original reporting or of obtaining stories at the same time or before local newspapers was the exception' (Lawrenson and Barber, 1986: 39). The number of paid, full time correspondents remained relatively small until the 1930s. Considerable debate took place over the adequacy of Reuters news service in the 1920s: the agency's chief editor admitted in 1922 that few of their correspondents 'have had actual experience of newspaper work or have been trained to look at matters from the sub-editor's desk in a newspaper office' (Read, 1992: 196). Concerns were raised about the lack of Reuters' correspondents to fully cover the world – between 1920 and 1930 the number of 'stringers' trebled (1992: 195). The employment of too few of their own reporters led critics to accuse the agency of recycling propaganda from foreign agencies it had contracts with.

As the demand from newspapers for more general news increased, the agency men and women became more professional in their news gathering and processing. The focus on hard news and the essential facts emphasised the importance of speed, immediacy and succinct prose, which required a more professional approach to the reporting. The Reuters' news employees were described as:

> ... Bohemian types, a cosmopolitan bunch who took pride in being able to compress as much information as possible into the minimum number of words, whether the language was French, German or English. (Read, 1992: 195)

The compressed style reflected the increase in cost that would result from extra words. Reuters refined a telegram code system that helped to put more information in fewer words. It was also a response to growing public demand for the latest accurate, up-to-date information of world events. However, the agency's news service maintained an uneasy relationship with the commercial operations conducted by the company. Money-making activities such as the Reuters Bank, and its advertising operations and remittances business, were seen as potentially damaging the quality, reliability and objectivity of the agency's news operation.

Reuters' reputation for objectivity was vital to the success of its news business. The furnishing of facts and the latest information, however, was a continuous struggle. The late 1920s and early 1930s have been described as 'a nadir in the fortunes of Reuters' (Boyd-Barrett and Rantanen, 2001: 133). Reuters' journalism was accused of appointing employees with the 'right background' rather than the appropriate professional skills. Criticism of Reuters' performance centred on the agency's often being late with news, producing copy which suffered from too much wordage and being happy to act as 'mere purveyors of Foreign Office and Embassy statements' (2001: 133). A British official wrote in 1917: 'At Reuters the work done is that of an independent news agency of an objective character, with propaganda secretly infused' (quoted in Thussu, 2006: 11). Ten years later the agency's proclivity for writing news from a British perspective was no longer – if it ever had been – a secret. Cloaked by the anonymity of its correspondents,

Reuters was a British news agency, presenting British news and closely associated with the British government. The setting of the sun on Britain's colonial enterprise since the end of the Second World War has enabled the agency to gradually distance itself from the British State. However, it could not hide that for much of its history it has been a British operation, based in Britain, employing primarily British nationals and serving the interests of the British Empire.

Demise of the cartel

The operation of the cartel was never smooth or always financially successful. On several occasions one or other of the members, often under pressure from their governments, attempted to take over their rivals. The escalating cost of gathering international news pushed the INAs close to financial insolvency. It was, however, a series of changes in international politics that ultimately led to the break up of the cartel. Phil Harris (1981: 20) identifies three factors that propelled the collapse. First, there was the frustration felt by many national news agencies about the power of the INAs. The dissatisfaction of the national news agencies was led by the American agencies, AP and UPA (later re-named UPI). Kent Cooper, AP's boss, articulated their dissatisfaction when he said that Reuters was 'the leader of a monopoly of government influenced agencies, deliberately obstructing the free flow of international news, and misrepresenting America to the world' (Cooper, 1942: 12). He later explained what he meant by this misrepresentation: 'So Reuters decided what news was to be sent from America. It told the world of Indians on the warpath in the West, lynching in the South and bizarre crimes in the North. The charge for decades was that nothing creditable to America was ever sent' (Cooper, quoted in Smith, 1980: 98). Similar criticisms were levelled at Havas by agencies and newspapers in Latin America which condemned the French agency for reporting the region as 'conquered lands'. Second, the wartime blockade of news from Europe in 1914 provided the American agencies with the opportunity of supplying news to Latin America. The outcome of the war also led to the demise of Wolff as an international agency, leading to its withdrawal from the cartel. The third factor was the rise of America as a world power, and in particular the growth of its political and economic interests in the Far East, which provided the foundation for the expansion of US news agencies into that part of the world.

The growing damage to the reputation of Reuters cannot be discounted as undermining the cartel. The independence of the company was gradually compromised by its close ties with the British government. This was manifest in the person who was to be Reuters managing director in the years of its pre-eminence. Roderick Jones started working for Reuters in South Africa where he served in an editorial capacity for settler newspapers such as *The*

Press and Cape Times (Harris, 1981: 17). He was a close confident of the leading politicians who were his main sources of information; they shared a 'common settler ethos'. Jones defined impartiality within the context of serving the British Empire. While his company asserted its independence and impartiality, this was undermined by its actions and the activities of those who worked for the agency. The limit to Reuters' objectivity was seen in its reporting of Britain's colonial wars; defeats were reported as well as victories but the British cause was 'always assumed (even if tacitly) to be "right" and the British troops "ours"' (Read, 1992: 65). The copy also reflected the attitude of the settlers to native populations: guidelines issued in 1906 to correspondents in the Far East stressed that the murder of Europeans, however obscure, should be reported while 'the murder of one Chinaman by another under the most atrocious circumstances is invested with little or no interest in European eyes and can therefore be ignored' unless 'the outrage is of a political nature' (Read, 1992: 104). The pro-British bias of the agency was confirmed for its critics by Jones's appointment in 1918 to the post of Director of Propaganda for the British Ministry of Information.

The cartel was also undermined by the arrival of the wireless. Cable and telegraph were supplemented and then superseded by radio broadcasting, which began immediately before the 1914–18 war. The evolution of wireless communication followed the same pattern of international development as the cable and telegraph – only it was more rapid and spread more widely (Winseck and Pike, 2009). Initially, the cable companies sought to cast doubts on Marconi's transmissions, refusing to retransmit his messages, which they labelled a 'fairy tale of science' (Winseck and Pike, 2009: 36). Wireless provided greater competition for the cable companies and the initial impact of regular wireless services was to reduce the cost of transmitting messages. Price differences soon disappeared as the control of the new media passed into the hands of a small number of companies. These companies sought to manage relations between cable and wireless interests, establishing an international wireless cartel that indicated its preference for cooperation and collusion rather than competition. This was to lead to the merger of cable and wireless interests, notably in the company Cable & Wireless, which formed in 1927. Technological, political and financial challenges led to the demise of the cartel in 1934. The European hegemony of the international news market was effectively over; national news agencies were free to make arrangements with whoever they wanted and the increased competition placed Havas and Reuters in an increasingly precarious financial position (Boyd-Barrett, 2004: 14). They turned to their government for support, and with the outbreak of the Second World War were incorporated into the State.

Colonialism played a considerable role in shaping the institutions that underpinned international journalism. The roots of colonial interaction are to be found with the explorers who first left Europe in the late fifteenth century.

Their adventures were the beginning of a process of economic, cultural and political subjugation. The colonial experience was not uniform or homogeneous, and it is difficult to generalise as some parts of the world were better able to resist the efforts of the colonial powers to impose control over the lands they penetrated. For most people in the Third World, their first interaction with Europeans was steeped in an experience that devalued their societies and culture. This was institutionalised in the nineteenth century with the laying down of administrative structures by the European colonial powers. The system of foreign news gathering that developed, especially the INAs, reflected the values, attitudes and priorities of colonialism.

Colonial imagery

Colonialism not only shaped the structures and processes that underpin international news gathering. It also shaped how audiences in the West – and elsewhere in the world – came to perceive and understand the events, peoples and places that existed outside their borders. It is important to stress the factors that shaped European intervention into the rest of the world. Early European expansion into Asia, African and Latin America was motivated by the stifling conformity of European society in which the Church dominated not only what men and women believed but also what they thought, what they thought about and how they behaved. Papal control over the institutions of mental production was nearly complete and by managing the means of mass communication of the day, the pulpit, altar and religious rituals and imagery, the Papacy was able 'to transmit not merely its claims of church leadership but an ideological perspective of the world that legitimated its domination of Christendom' (Curran, 1982: 209). To escape the social claustrophobia many set sail for the new World. They were never able to totally escape the Church. Priests accompanied the early expeditions and the Church saw exploration as a 'means to the higher end of saving the soul of the unbaptised from perdition' (Worsley, 1984: 8). The spiritual mission to bring the Christian faith to the poor, benighted natives of Asia, Africa and Latin America initially fell on barren ground. It was only when the force of arms accompanied the propagation of the gospel that converts were made. Conversion was brought by conquest not conversation. Christianity, for example, did not catch on in Africa until the armies of missionaries were replaced by real armies. It was under colonialism that the systematic restructuring of non-Western societies took place, but propaganda was, from the very earliest days, part of the efforts of the European invaders to subjugate peoples in other parts of the world.

The urgency to 'civilise' the people they subjugated can only be partly explained by the need to propagate the gospel. It was also driven by the irrational fears that Europeans had of the unknown world they were violating. Fear of the unknown conjured up the most disturbing images of these lands and the people who inhabited them. Exploration brought knowledge and enlightenment and as contact with the worlds outside Europe increased so the myths and monsters dissipated. As Anthony Smith (1980: 21) notes, 'exploration was a pursuit of information and each added unit of information filled in a troubling uncertainty about the nature of the world'. However, the phantasmagorical imagination left a legacy: a residual fear and loathing of the indigenous peoples of the New World. Bringing civilisation to conquered peoples was not straightforward. Some parts of the world were more receptive – particularly those without a highly developed social and economic infrastructure. It was less easy to apply the 'civilising mission' to the Orient, parts of which were never fully colonised and had civilisations which could be distinguished by the colonial powers from the 'tribal' societies that characterised Africa. Edward Said (1981: 25) argues in relation to the study of the Orient in the nineteenth century that:

> Familiarity, accessibility, representability: these were what Orientalists demonstrated about the Orient. [It] could be seen, it could be studied, it could be managed. It need not remain a distant, marvellous, incomprehensible and yet very rich place. It could be brought home – or more simply Europe could make itself at home there, and subsequently it did.

Said draws attention to the psychological insecurity that underlay expansion from the known cultural world to the unknown. This led the colonial powers to try and cast the unfamiliar in terms of the familiar – which became the basis of many of the stereotypes and misrepresentations that have culturally imprisoned the peoples of Asia, Africa and Latin America today. To 'manage' the colonised peoples for their economic and political benefit, the colonial powers sought to propagate the perception of their cultural inferiority.

> Since a civilised society was defined as one that had a strong and centralised state, a firm sense of national identity, a competitive capitalist economy and a high level of technology and a civilised man as one who had drive and ambition, who was competitive, individualistic, calculative and ruthless in pursuit of his interests, non-European societies and their members were by definition uncivilised. (Parekh, 1988: 116)

The notion of delivering civilisation hid the economic and political interests – as well as the use of force, violence and sometimes wholesale genocide – that drove colonial conquest. The economic motive was closely tied to the work of the Christian missionaries, for whom Christianity and capitalism went hand in hand. Journalist H.M. Stanley, who was sponsored by the *New York Herald* to search for the lost missionary David Livingstone in Africa in 1869, returned to Britain to tell the Manchester Chamber of Commerce of the potential market opportunity that existed in the new world:

> There are 50 millions of people beyond the gateway to the Congo and the cotton spinners of Manchester are waiting to clothe them. Birmingham foundries are glowing with the red metals that presently will be made into ironwork for them and the trinkets that shall adorn those dusky bosoms, and the ministers of Christ are zealous to bring them, the poor benighted heathens, in to the Christian fold. (Stanley, quoted in Smith, 1980: 25)

Stanley was a news reporter but the information he collected and disseminated was undertaken within a conceptual framework which celebrated 'the pursuit of loot, markets and Christian faith' (1980: 25).

The representation of colonial peoples must also be located within the changes in European societies that made empire more appealing to the domestic audiences. Europe at the outset of the nineteenth century was in a state of turmoil. The French Revolution cast a long shadow over the political and social development of the continent; the voice of the previously disenfranchised under-classes was beginning to be heard in a struggle for political reform. Radical politics accompanied the socio-economic upheavals created by the Industrial Revolution. The breakdown of traditional society created dislocation and tension as the emerging working class found its voice. Fear was aroused among the established order, the ruling gentry and bourgeoisie, about the threat posed to their power and influence. The response of those in positions of political and economic power was twofold: the *suppression* of all forms of agitation for change and the *substitution* of radical ideas by values that upheld the status quo, most clearly promoted through the development of state run education. Different European societies combined suppression and substitution in different ways but all sought to use imperial ventures to unite the nation around a set of consensual values. The European nation-states started to proselytise imperial values. Selling the empire was part of a process by which political order and stability was established at home. John MacKenzie (1986) has documented how the imperial idea was sold to the British people through propaganda, education and the use of the mass media and popular entertainment, including the emerging popular press and music halls, popular songs and verse in the nineteenth century, and film and radio in the early twentieth century. He shows that:

> through the colonial connection domestic 'under classes' could become imperial 'over classes'. They could feel part of a national enterprise on which the majority had been able to agree ... it was an enterprise tinged with a sense of moral crusade, aided by

periodic war, led by charismatic figures, both alive and dead. In its ancestor worship, its emphasis on authority, it linked tribal atavism with cultural self satisfaction and technical advance. (MacKenzie, 1984: 254–55)

Studies of British popular culture in the late nineteenth and early twentieth centuries show that colonialism was presented for public consumption as a civilising mission and the peoples of Asia, Africa and the New World were the beneficiaries of the process (see, for example, MacKenzie, 1984, 1986; Kiernan, 1995). This view remained deep-seated within British society; for example, as late as 1956 a school textbook could state:

... the significant fact remains that the Europeans have brought civilisation to the peoples of tropical Africa, whose standard of living has, in most cases, been raised as a result of their contact with white peoples. (MacKenzie, 1984: 193)

The colonised and their societies were represented as culturally inferior. Their peoples were variously depicted as stupid, savage, childlike and backward as a means of delineating the 'superiority' of the colonists. Africans, for example, were a source of fascination and fear in popular theatre in nineteenth century Britain where they were shown as 'light fingered, prone to irrational violence and rampant sexual desire'. Indians were depicted as, in the words of a popular song of the 1870s, the 'dusky sons of Hindoostan', willing serfs of the British Empire, standing by the mother country against her imperial competitors (MacKenzie, 1984: 50). Their societies were deemed primitive as they did not conform to what Europeans identified as a civilised society. Mentally and materially the world was seen by the imperial powers 'in terms of the West's need for it' (Smith, 1980: 24). Jan Nederveen Pieterse (1995) highlights the extent to which western identity is constructed on negative and stereotypical images and representations of other cultures.

These images were propagated and promoted by the imperial authorities. In the 1920s the efforts of the British state to promote 'empire' as the core ideology of 'Britishness' were formalised in official bodies such as the Empire Marketing Board (EMB), which was established by the Baldwin government as part of the conviction that imperialism offered a solution to the political and economic problems that beset Britain. It promoted trade with the Empire, and imperial values were seen as a means to counter the expansion of socialism. The EMB sought to persuade people to 'buy British', using all means of mass communication to induce people to change their purchasing habits, which the EMB believed could only happen by 'bringing the Empire alive' (Constantine, 1986). The campaign had limited success in the face of the economic realities of the depression years but, according to one scholar, it had greater success in reinforcing in the public mind the ideological message of the virtue and validity of Empire (1986: 224).

The legacy of empire

The collapse of the western empires did not sweep away the values, perceptions and understanding that accompanied the colonial era. International news and international news gathering is steeped in the residue of colonialism. Martin Woollacott, a former foreign correspondent for the *Guardian* newspaper in London, argues that:

> The western press ... has since decolonisation acted as a sort of international monitoring agency, whose inspectors – foreign correspondents – tour the Third World to measure how far away from proper standards Asian and African societies have fallen ... and right-wing, liberal and left-wing reporters and news organisations share at least one attribute – the notion that it is their role to judge and apportion praise (if any) and blame. (Woollacott, 1976: 14)

Ill-informed, lacking background knowledge, unable to speak local languages and spending only a short period of time in any locality, many correspondents from western countries feel able to comment on and criticise societies and cultures of which they have little understanding. Some attribute this to arrogance but it is perhaps more appropriate to see it as part of the experiences of empire which differentiated between peoples and nations. It reflects 'the West's deep disillusion with nearly all post-colonial societies as well as our assumption that we are still the ultimate arbiter of the rest of the world' (Woollacott, 1976: 14). International reporting – and the people, organisations and values that shape it – represents the world through the prism of colonialism. For a majority of people in the Third World, colonialism not only is responsible for many of the political, economic and social problems they struggle with on a daily basis, but it also shapes how people understand them and their ability and capacity to put their own interpretation, analysis and outlook forward. As Govind Vidyarthi (1988: 13) emphasises: 'relying on its powerful propaganda apparatus, the West seeks ideological domination of the developing world, presenting its spiritual values and world outlook as the only rational and indisputable ones'. Foreign correspondence is part of 'the legacy of several hundred years of western expansion and hegemony, manifested in racism and exoticism' and 'which continues to be recycled in western cultures in the form of stereotypical images of non-western cultures' (Pieterse, 1995: 9). Many of those who serve the large western news organisations that dominate international news provision have to satisfy the needs and requirements of western audiences and western clients – or what they perceive as the needs and requirements – and in doing so cannot escape the legacy of colonialism.

Notes

1 Research indicates that by the 1730s nearly half of the news items in British newspapers were domestic and by the early twentieth century domestic stories made up nearly four-fifths of the news coverage in the *Daily Telegraph*. It took longer for the shift to take place in German and French newspapers. Newspaper such as the *Hamburgischer Correspondent* carried more foreign stories than home news until 1906. See Wilke (1987).
2 The discussion of Havas is based on Hohenberg, 1993: 6–8; Boyd-Barrett, 1980: 122–26; Stephens, 1997: 250.
3 The British government, after a campaign from the press and agencies, national-ised the telegraph system in 1870.

3

THE BIG THREE: THE ORGANISATIONAL
STRUCTURE OF INTERNATIONAL JOURNALISM

Knowledge of foreign affairs actually comes to us from a system of news gathering deeply flawed by the subtle interplay of ideology, ethnocentrism, dubious professional practice and economic forces. (Dorman, 1985: 419)

Keep in mind that our news gathering system is no public service ... Forget the rhetoric: the news business sells a product that is blended and packaged, and the competition is cutthroat. When the product doesn't sell, its marketers tinker with the mix. (Mort Rosenblum, former Associated Press correspondent, 1993: 8)

The contemporary international information order within which foreign correspondents work has until recently been dominated by the international news agencies. They have played a 'pivotal role' in the spread of international interconnectedness since their advent more than 150 years ago (Bielsa, 2008). Exploiting various innovations in technology, from the telegraph, telex and telegram to the fibre optic cable, satellite and the internet, they have over the decades disseminated news and information more quickly and over greater distances. They have ensured that events in far off places have intruded into everyday consciousness ever more regularly. As the primary gatekeepers for the supply of foreign news to the world's media, the agencies have had a key role in defining what is foreign news and influencing the way in which it is gathered, processed and distributed. They are the basic organisational foundations on which the international news system operates. National news organisations such as the US networks and newspapers such as *The New York Times*, *Le Monde* and *The Times* of London operate their own foreign news services. They are joined by national news agencies, alternative news agencies as well as 24-hour rolling news stations and websites and bloggers in ensuring a flow of news and information in international society.

This chapter examines the development of the organisational structure of international journalism since the end of the Second World War, documenting the considerable changes that have taken place, particularly in the activities of the INAs. The monopoly they established over international news has gradually been eroded by competition, technology and increased costs. They have had to diversify their operations, branching out into activities that are less to do with news and journalism and more focused on other forms of information and commercial transactions. This shift is mirrored elsewhere in the production of international news. It is the commercialisation of their operations that is the most significant factor in the agencies' development. The widescale deregulation of media markets has placed profit making and commercial considerations at the forefront of the industry. Rising costs and increased competition in the international news market have led to the disappearance of significant players. It has also contributed to the emergence of new forms of competition with the proliferation of news channels and internet news sites. The most significant innovation is the rise of 24-hour news channels such as CNN and BBC World, which provide a stream of international news on a continuous basis. Among the new sources of international news and information is the appearance of alternative agencies, many of which are non-western players. The growth in the number of organisations able to gather and disseminate international news and the changing nature of their operation are features of the contemporary international news system. The erosion of the distinction between wholesale news producers and retailers as a result of economic and technological change poses a threat to the continued influence of the agencies in the international news market. Some scholars see the increasing uncertainty surrounding news agencies and what they do as constituting a 'crisis' (Boyd-Barrett and Rantanen, 2004b: 35), and the notion that the INAs will continue to be the key providers of international news appears anachronistic.

The growth of a post-war international news system

The changes to the international news system that had begun in the 1930s were completed by the Second World War, which swept away the remaining vestiges of influence the established agencies exercised. Indeed Reuters was the only 'imperial' agency to survive the war. Wolff was closed down with the rise of Nazism in Germany. Havas disappeared when France was occupied; it was turned into the French Information Office during the war (Alleyne, 1997: 8). It was revived in 1945 as Agence France-Presse (AFP), which was granted independence and financial autonomy by government in 1957. The links established with government during the war and the immediate post-war years reinforced the perception that the agency is closely aligned with the French State – the provision of government subsidies and official support accentuated this view. AFP has throughout the post-war period retained a strong presence in parts of the world where French political influence continued to be exercised. Reuters survived but it emerged from the war with its reputation and finances in a precarious state. Understandably, it had become closely associated with British government policy between 1939 and 1945 and it was bailed out financially when the British press took a 50 per cent stake in the company. It remained financially insecure throughout the 1950s and 1960s and it was only following a reorganisation in 1974 that it returned to profitability.

The greatest beneficiaries of the upheavals of the war were the American news agencies, AP and UPI. UPI – formerly UPA – was formed in 1907 with the intention of challenging AP's dominance of domestic news in the Unites States. Both agencies benefited from the growing demand for news from American subscribers in the 1930s – emerging from isolationism American audiences were interested in the events that were unfolding in Europe. Jonathan Fenby (1986) shows how AP and UPI developed their international newsgathering operations prior to the war, developing a 'fast breaking' style of news coverage which was well suited to reporting the dramatic events of the Second World War. AP built up its photographic service which produced vivid pictures of the fighting, and UPI's focus on human interest stories enabled the agency to convey what was happening to audiences in the US and, ultimately, around the world. The rise of the American agencies coincided with a change in the nature of news. The French and British focus on commercial and diplomatic affairs was broadened out to include more features, sports and human interest stories (Tunstall, 1977: 30). The extension of American power facilitated the expansion of their national agencies in Europe and other lucrative news markets. The US occupation of Germany and Japan helped AP and UPI to attain an advantage over their rivals in these countries. Their aggressive selling of their services sometimes went to ludicrous extremes if one UPI executive is to be believed:

> After 1945, some of the UP correspondents went into the newly liberated countries with contracts in their pockets. In Belgium, one UP man couldn't find any newspapers to sell the service to, so he signed up a butcher after convincing him that he would do better business if he was in touch with what was going on in the world. (Fenby, 1986: 57)

The extension of American media influence throughout the world, of which the agencies were a part, was seen by some as a continuation of the imperial agenda of the European nations; it is described by many in the Third World as neo-colonialism (Vidyarthi, 1988).

The history of the INAs up until the 1980s was characterised by the diversification of output. The 'Big Four' (Reuters, AP, AFP and UPI) experienced financial difficulties in the immediate post war years. Printed news was ceasing to be profitable and the agencies began to incorporate other kinds of information provision, including news photographs, radio and television pictures and faxes. Television services became an important part of their activities. In the 1970s the international television market was controlled by Visnews, which was owned by Reuters, the BBC and the US network NBC and UPITN, a partnership between UPI and the UK broadcaster, ITN (Boyd-Barrett, 1997: 135). Between them they exercised a duopoly over the provision of international television news pictures, controlling an estimated 90 per cent of the trade. It was the diversification into the provision of business information and financial data that proved most significant. The rapid expansion of international trade, business and finance initiated by the post-war reconstruction of Europe increased the involvement of the agencies in the supply of information and data related to these activities. Reuters was at the forefront of the shift into economic services. In the 1960s such services provided between 30 and 50 per cent of the agency's revenues; by 1980 this had increased to 80 per cent, attaining a level of 95 per cent by 1997 (Boyd-Barrett, 1997: 139; Palmer et al., 1998: 63).

Oliver Boyd-Barrett (1997: 139) describes the growth of bureaux and personnel employed by Reuters to gather news, as well as the 'massive investment' in new technology in the 1980s. However, it was a period of some turbulence within the organisation; 'much public success' was accompanied by 'some private tension' (Read, 1992: 283). For the first 120 years the agency had become at least for its employees synonymous with one thing – general news from abroad (Bartram, 2003: 389). This is a slight misnomer as economic and financial information has always been part of the news agency business (see Chapter 2). Reuters, Havas and Wolff concluded their first agreement over the exchange of stock market prices (Tunstall and Palmer, 1991: 53). Nevertheless it was the growth of the press and its demand for copy that drove the development of the international agencies. Yet at times of financial trouble Reuters returned to its commercial roots and 'rediscovered' the provision of financial and business information. At the end of the First World War it set up Reuters Trade and Reuters Economic Services, which were heavily invested in at the end of the 1960s as a means of responding to dwindling revenue (1991: 54). The changes in the 1980s represented a shift in the balance of power within Reuters from the general news towards the economic services. Formerly two divisions within the agency, general news and economic services were merged with an impact on news priorities and writing styles.

The INAs are the largest employers of foreign correspondents. Retrenchment among national news organisations has seen a decline in their capacity to gather their own news from abroad (see Chapter 4). The withdrawal from the more 'peripheral' parts of the world is a feature of the retrenchment. The outcome could sometimes produce bizarre situations; for example, it was revealed in 1978 that BBCs correspondent Ian Mills covered news in Zimbabwe under a variety of names for several international outlets including the *Guardian, Daily Mail, Daily Telegraph, Newsweek,* Reuters, UPI and

AFP (Carver, 1982: 55). Often it was only through a sole representative of the INAs that a country was covered.

The western based INAs were joined during the Cold War by the Telegraph Agency of the Soviet Union (TASS), which had formally been created in 1926. TASS – as well as China's Xinhua at this time – was not considered as an INA. According to Boyd-Barrett (1998: 20) there was no clear dividing line between what it did as a news agency and as a department of government, and it did not operate commercially, providing its news services free of charge. TASS served as a 'mouthpiece' of the Soviet government and the Communist Party, controlling the supply of foreign news into and out of the country and the countries of the Eastern Bloc, mostly providing a positive picture of events. TASS's limited contribution to the international flow of news clearly distinguished the service from that provided by the western agencies. However, the role of TASS and Xinhua during the Cold War was important; they sometimes were the only source of information in the closed societies of the Communist Bloc and their services were subscribed to by many Third World countries as an antidote to what they regarded as the partiality of western news. TASS's influence was tied to the power and influence of the USSR and as that waned so did its international reach. The collapse of the USSR brought to an end the role of TASS as an international news player. Xinhua continues to play an important role in international newsgathering with the growth of China as a major player in the international economy. Set up in 1931, has the agency acted as a voice for the Communist Party for most of its history. Its employees still enjoy diplomatic immunity when working abroad and the agency receives subsidies from government. Since the decision of China in 1978 to develop a free market economy Xinhua has increased its output and provided more credible and reliable news (Horvit, 2006: 431).[1]

INAs in the satellite age

The 1990s marked another stage in the evolution of international news gathering with de-regulation, technological change, political revolution and the influence of the NWICO debate bringing about the 'dissolution' of the Big Four (Boyd-Barrett and Rantanen, 2004a: 42). Two factors were particularly important: the increasingly competitive market for international news and the growth of satellite broadcasting. Just as cable meant the international news agencies could cover the world in the nineteenth century, satellite links have enabled television to embrace the globe today. From the early 1960s, communication satellites such as Telstar and Earlybird beamed pictures and sound around the world irrespective of land, sea and in most cases terrain (Thussu, 2007b: 45). With the liberalisation of the global satellite infrastructure in the 1990s many countries – including from the Third World – launched communication satellites. The growth of satellite broadcasting brought a new dimension to international news and was epitomised by CNN.

Global TV, pictures and sound first became important in the collection and dissemination of international news in the late 1980s. CNN started as a cable TV station in Atlanta and grew into one of the world's major news providers in the 1990s. The advent of new technology and the deregulation of the broadcasting industry propelled it to prominence (Kung-Shankelman, 2000). It took advantage of satellite technology to 'blanket the world' through a mixture of satellite networks (Thussu, 2006: 135). The Gulf War in 1991 affirmed its position as a major supplier of international news, in particular of on-the-spot coverage of breaking news events. CNN pioneered the use of new media technology such as portable satellite newsgathering equipment, cellular phones and miniature cameras to bring instant and immediate coverage of breaking events such as the Tiananmen Square massacre, the collapse of the Berlin Wall and the Gulf War. It established itself as a primary source of news for other news organisations and policy makers. As a 24-hour rolling news service, by 1992 CNN had built a global audience of over 53 million viewers in 138 countries (Friedland, 1992: 11). By 2007 it operated 36 international bureaus, employing 150 correspondents serving a global audience estimated at around 260 million households (Thussu, 2007b: 66). CNN's success placed considerable pressure on established broadcasters to adapt their coverage as well as encouraging the entry of other players into the global news game. BBC World Service Television appeared on the scene in 1994, serving a similar sized audience in 200 countries and territories (2007b: 66). These two news channels have been joined by several other television broadcasters over the years. It is estimated that more than 100 international news stations have been established since CNN's arrival on the scene (Painter, 2008: 9). Many of these are described as 'counter hegemonic' in that they claim to offer 'a different vision of news content to the main western media ...' (2008: 14). Stations such as France 24, Euronews, Iran's Press TV, China's CCTV and Russia Today broadcast in English or partly in English, seeking to have some impact on an international audience.

The growth of these stations was triggered by increasing dissatisfaction with CNN's American perspective (Paterson and Sreberny, 2004: 10). While foreign journalists regularly appeared on screen for CNN in the 1990s, this did nothing to ameliorate the view, particularly from the Middle East, that CNN presents the news from an American perspective. CNN founder Ted Turner threatened to fine or sack any staff member who used the term 'foreign', as he believed no CNN viewer should ever be made to feel that he or she lived in a foreign country (Hannerz, 2004: 85). The arrival of more stations contributed to the broadening of international reporting. The most significant station to emerge was Al-Jazeera. It is one of several stations that was set up to provide an Arab perspective on world events. Based in Qatar, Al-Jazeera employed reporters who had worked on the BBC Arab Service before its closure. Broadcasting in English and Arab, it was able to challenge the western news agencies and international broadcasters as a source of news and information following 9/11. During the wars in Iraq in 2003 and Afghanistan in 2001, Al-Jazeera attracted a global audience, many of whom had been frustrated by the coverage provided by western organisations. The welcome given to the station by western commentators and governments soon turned to hostility when Al-Jazeera started to broadcast images and opinions that challenged western interpretations and understanding of the situation in the Arab and Muslim world (Zayani, 2005). Hostility turned to outright hatred in some quarters when the channel broadcast tapes from Osama bin Laden. Charges of being the mouthpiece of Al-Qaeda were levelled and Al-Jazeera was accused by, among others, Tony Blair's spin doctor Alastair Campbell of broadcasting lies (Zayani, 2005: 21). However, its growing importance in international news was emphasised by the increasing number of western leaders, politicians, officials and spokespersons who appeared on the channel (El-Nawawy and Iskandar, 2003: 155–7). Al-Jazeera's capacity to 'envision' the emerging world order differently, challenging dominant western interpretations of world affairs and the hegemony of the western media, has been a significant development in the international news environment. Together with other non-western international news stations it has changed the structural context within which international journalism operates.

Changes in broadcasting technology had an impact on the international television agencies. Visnews and UPITN went through considerable adjustment. Reuters bought out its partner in Visnews to establish Reuters TV in 1992 while UPITN turned into WTN, which came under the control of Disney in 1996, only to be taken over by APTV which had been set up in 1994 by AP. Reuters TV and APTN supply most of the international news footage to broadcasters around the world, including BBC and CNN, which operate the world's leading 24-hour news channels (Thussu, 2006: 133–4). In addition to Reuters TV and APTN, the European Broadcasting Union (EBU) and CNN provide international news: the EBU operates a satellite news exchange distributing material from Europe's public service broadcasters but allows commercial broadcasters associate membership, and CNN sells its output to national broadcasters (Baker, 2004: 71). Changes in the news footage market were accompanied by the increasing burden of adapting to the rapidly emerging new media technologies. Upgrading computing systems, introducing digital services and developing online news provision is a costly business which eventually had a profound impact on the operation of one of the INAs – UPI. The 'world's largest privately owned news service' faced mounting losses, estimated at $7million during the 1980s (Hamelink, 1995: 54). Declared bankrupt in 1992 it was bought by Saudi Arabian interests. This did not arrest its misfortunes, and ownership passed into the hands of News World Communications, whose most significant media outlet is the conservative *Washington Times*. These changes of ownership and continuing financial problems undermined the agency's credibility. Today the 'Big Three' of Reuters, AP and AFP dominate international news.

The 'Big Three' operate in a world in which the provision of news and information has become less stable and more competitive. At a global level there is more competition. Business news and financial information have witnessed a proliferation of global players, including financial news TV channels such as CNBC, operated by NBC and the European Business Network, AP-DJ economic news service and Bloomberg, a worldwide financial information network set up in 1981 that has expanded into a news service for newspapers, radio and TV stations around the world (Thussu, 2006: 133). Changes are also taking place at the national level, with national news agencies experiencing considerable problems. The post-war years witnessed a huge growth in national news agencies. These agencies struggled to survive, including those larger regional exchanges set up in the 1970s as part of UNESCO's efforts to establish a NWICO (see below). Many national agencies closed or became moribund in the 1990s (Boyd-Barrett and Rantanen, 2004a: 46). Cutbacks have taken place in the agencies of the newly free countries of Eastern and Central Europe. With few exceptions national agencies are encountering considerable difficulties in the highly competitive environment which has emerged in media markets across the world in the last decade or so (Boyd-Barrett, 2003). Some agencies such as Germany's Deutsche Press-Agentur (DPA), Spain's EFE and Japan's Kyodo are establishing a significant international presence. However, most are in decline, buffeted by the increasing costs of operating news services and the growing competition from new media outlets. The growing weakness of national news agencies, the increasing concentration of international news agencies and more competition within the news and information business created a very unstable environment for international journalism as it entered the twenty-first century.

Market for international news

International agencies in the contemporary world are increasingly commercial entities. They exist to make a profit to either satisfy shareholders or plough back into the running of the company. Government subsidies have dwindled – although AFP still depends on government for more than 40 per cent of its revenues (Boyd-Barrett, 2000: 9) – and competition has intensified in a deregulated world. This has led to the 'bottom line' playing an ever important part in their operation. The failure to take account of the market can have dire consequences, as the demise of UPI and the reduction of the number of national news agencies illustrates. A seasoned observer of INAs talks of the 'current crisis' facing the agencies, which is reflected in growing uncertainty as to what the proper role of such organisations *is* in the contemporary world (Boyd-Barrett, 2000, 2001). Much of this uncertainty is a consequence of the changing market for international news and, in particular, the primary characteristics that shape how the major newsgathering organisations operate: concentration of ownership, rising costs, increased competition and the commodification of international news.

Traditionally the INAs have dominated the wholesale market for international news. Between them the 'Big Three' are calculated to have a virtual monopoly over the flow of international news reports and photographs. They also exercise a similar hold over television news; Reuters TV and APTN dominate the market. Reuters claimed in the early 1990s that more than 1.5 billion people saw their pictures every day (Baker, 2004: 63). The increased competition for political news from television operators such as CNN, Sky and MSNBC and the challenge from Bloomberg in the supply of financial news have undermined the hold of these companies over the market – something accentuated more recently by the advent of new technology (see below). The world's news media perhaps depend less today on the international agencies – although in certain parts of the world they are still relied on as much as they ever were (Wu, 2003: 21). They are still major players in the international news market – AP employs 3,700 staff in 242 bureaus in 121 countries and services more than 8,500 subscribers. Reuters has 2,400 editorial staff members in 196 bureaus in 131 countries, while there are around 2,000 AFP employees based in 110 bureaus operating in 165 countries (Horvit, 2006: 429; Schlesinger, 2009: 22–3). The substantial reach of these organisations is complemented by their annual turnovers.

News is increasingly a business and the fact that the international market for news has traditionally been dominated by western media organisations has a number of important consequences for how news is defined, traded and produced. Primarily, international news agencies seek to make money. As we have seen this has not been a straightforward activity – reliance on government subsidies has always been part of the history of these agencies. There are differences between the 'Big Three' in the way in which they are constituted which places different pressures on them in their attempt to earn revenue. Reuters became a public limited company in 1984 when it was floated on the New York and London Stock Exchanges (Tunstall and Palmer, 1991: 68). This tied the organisation closely to the market, integrating it more firmly into the world of business and commerce. The economic downturn in 1987 saw the company lose 50 per cent of its share value but the growing demand for information and trading services in a volatile financial market ensured that it quickly recovered.

If Reuters' fate became increasingly tied up with Mammon (Tunstall and Palmer, 1991), AP remained a 'news co-operative' owned by more than 1,500 newspapers (Owen and Purdey, 2009, 22). The growing crisis within the US newspaper industry is putting pressure on this arrangement (McPhail, 2006: 183). AP has extended its news services, for example joining with Trans World International (TWI) in 1996 to launch a sports video news agency (McPhail, 2006: 181). AFP has considerable state involvement in its operation, with government a major client of its services, its representatives sitting on the board of the organisation. Unlike the other agencies it has not 'substantially diversified' into the non-media market – this has not been for want of trying but obstacles emanating from its close ties with the French domestic market and the involvement of the government have impeded this development (Bielsa and Bassett, 2009: 47; Tunstall and Palmer, 1991: 73–82). AFP has introduced new services and new media provision, specialising in a sports service with the objective of developing it as the equivalent to Reuters' economic service and establishing a renowned international photographic service (Bielsa and Bassett, 2009: 47).

The reasons for making money may differ but each agency acts as a commercial operator in a highly competitive market. The agencies have always striven to be the 'first with the news'. Nigel Baker, former head of APTN, describes how in the TV agency business 'the difference between success and failure … is measured in minutes' (2004: 65). Being first and being fast determine coverage and with the wire services the clients' judgement of the product is based on the ability 'to react swiftly and cover the story immediately' (2004: 65). As Baker says, 'in a time sensitive business' the TV networks 'prefer part of the story by their main deadline, rather than the whole story five minutes after it'. Deadlines dominate the work of news agencies and wire services and provide the basic organisational context within which foreign correspondents operate.

The business of international newsgathering emphasises that 'news' is a tradable commodity; it is bought and sold in the marketplace and what is reported and what is filmed is determined by the demands of those who are the main purchasers of international news. Rather than a set of news values determining the nature of international news, the value of news should be seen in terms of what clients and subscribers are willing to pay for. Giving customers what they want is crucial. The customers who dominate the market for international news are western media organisations and western conglomerates and companies. They spend the most on international news and their priorities determine what is covered. The INAs have to produce a product which satisfies their main customers, subscribers and purchasers of news. The smaller news organisations of Africa, Latin America and Asia, for example, have to take what they are given. What they are given is news geared to the demands of western interests. In the 1970s Reuters, for example, gained more than three-quarters of its total revenue from Europe and North America (Boyd-Barrett, 1980: 39), and in 2000 67 per cent of APTN's subscription revenue came from these areas of the world (Baker, 2004: 72). Giving these clients what they want is a vital component of their business. The consequence of this is that stories about issues and parts of the world that clients in Africa and other Third World regions might want to report do not get regularly covered. These clients do not exert as much influence over the way in which the agencies cover the world. As the Managing Editor of Visnews in the mid-1980s stated:

> We didn't just go after the coups, war and disaster stories. We reported the development projects but when the demand for these stories dropped to such a low level, that only a few organisations in Africa were interested, we stopped reporting them. (*Consuming Hunger*, 1988)

Commercial considerations push the agencies into a constant search for ways to produce news at minimal cost. This means events that are costly to cover may not be reported. It is only with 'big stories' in far off places that professional notions of what is newsworthy appear to outweigh economic considerations. But even then the tensions between the two criteria play their part in shaping coverage. Costs influence the foreign newsgathering activities of all news organisations. Two of the 'big stories' of the post-war era – Tiananmen Square and the fall of the Berlin Wall – came at the end of the financial year for most news organisations in the UK, which limited the number of correspondents they deployed as well as the duration of their stay. A study of US network news coverage in the early 1980s found that many conflicts around the world received minimal or no coverage: 'there's little correlation between the amount of carnage and the amount of coverage' (Townley, 1984). Limited news budgets and increasing costs were identified as important determinants of this coverage. Thus, the market pressure is to produce coverage at low cost and serve up a standardised product that is acceptable to western organisations.

The nature of international news has also been influenced in recent years by a shift away from the traditional client base of news and media organisations. The transmission of financial and investment data is becoming more important (Thussu, 2006: 131). Reuters claims to be the 'largest financial information provider in the world'. Today it is estimated that virtually all of Reuters' revenue is derived from financial news for non-media clients, primarily stockbrokers, banks, money markets and commodity traders (Boyd-Barrett and Rantanen, 2004b: 38). The overwhelming importance of the company's economic services has 'ousted news as the agency's *raison d'être*' (Tunstall and Palmer, 1991: 58). Fuelled by the deregulation of markets pursued with such conviction by Reagan and Thatcher in the 1980s, Reuters' economic service has thrived. New ventures were launched such as Reuters Trader, a real time price data and news service for traders, and Reuters Knowledge, corporate information for investment bankers (Thussu, 2006: 131). Some believe the company can no longer be defined as a news agency, seeing it as 'a multinational corporation that sold news as just one dimension of its business' (Alleyne, 1997: 9). The implications of the shift away from news provision are a matter of debate. For some it had an impact on the supply of news, changing the kind of news provided and topics regularly covered. 'News' has been redefined to include 'everything from the murder of John Lennon to the movement of pork-belly futures' (Fenby, 1986: 78). There was a move away from human interest news, detailed coverage of regions which could not provide a lucrative market of subscribers, and items of 'secondary interest'. Many old Reuters' hands were unhappy at what they believed had become a focus on 'major stories' only and the provision of services for economic clients at the expense of other considerations. The collection of economic data was seen as distorting news priorities. Several senior members of Reuters news operation left the company in the mid-1980s, some to launch the new British daily newspaper, *The Independent*, 'in disgust' at the 'increasing subordination of Reuters news operations to financial services' (Alleyne, 1995: 82).

The shift to economic news is less apparent with AP and AFP. The former touts itself as the 'essential global news network', claiming that 'more than a billion people everyday read, hear or see AP news' (Thussu, 2006: 130). Its news service has increasingly faced competition in the provision of international news to the US market from syndicated newspaper services of national organisations such as the *New York Times* and the *Los Angeles Times* (Boyd-Barrett and Rantanen, 2004b: 38–9) as well as the mushrooming of US news websites. As a non-profit cooperative, its financial situation appears to have become increasingly fragile. In the 1990s it teamed up with Dow-Jones to set up the AP-DJ economic news service (Thussu, 2006: 132). AFP entered into a similar arrangement with the *Financial Times* in London to provide an economic service with a European focus (Thussu, 2006: 131). AFP's efforts to develop its economic services have been less successful than Reuters and AP. The 'longest strike in the agency's history' in 1986 illustrates the high degree of resistance encountered by the attempts to restructure the agency (Tunstall and Palmer, 1991: 80). While downturns in the international economy have their impact on these financial news operations, and the recessions in 2000 and 2008 bit hard into their revenue, the success of the economic news services is illustrated by the arrival of new competitors on the scene.

Bloomberg was founded by a former investment banker in 1981 and by 1990 it was, as a result of its success, able to launch a news service and expand its operation to include some 1,100 reporters and editors in 80 bureaus based in 50 countries (Bartram, 2003: 391). By 2006 it was providing financial information to users in 126 countries in five languages. Bloomberg News is syndicated in 250 newspapers across the world and its radio service has 840 affiliates, and a television service claims to reach 200 million homes (Thussu, 2006: 133). Bloomberg's activities – as well as those of other financial agencies – provided a direct challenge to Reuters, which in 2007 – after more than 150 years as a separate company – combined with Thomson to become the world's largest purveyor of financial information and data. Thomson Reuters is primarily a financial information news service whose services to the media are a small component of its activities. The diversification of the Big Three into other areas of news and information, and the arrival of financial information and data agencies which have added news services to their operations, indicate the increasing economic value of international news. The extent to which economic, business and finance news, information and data have become central to the activities of the international agencies represents a shift in the international news system. This is highlighted by Jonathan Fenby, a former top executive at Reuters.

> The ... agencies exist to serve markets ... their prime concern is with the rich media markets of the United States, Western Europe, and Japan, and increasingly with the business community, which requires fast information services that can be used to make money ... the result of this application of the commercial market approach to news is that an agency may well have more staff reporters in a single major European country than in the whole of Africa. (Fenby, 1986: 4)

The internet and international news gathering

Struggling in an ever increasing competitive market, INAs have been confronted by the proliferation of new sources of international news. Advances in new media technology have driven down the economic barriers to entry into the international news market, bringing about increased competition. The development of satellite broadcasting forced the agencies to re-adjust, as did the advent of radio and television. The internet presents a more fundamental challenge owing to the speed and broad-based nature of the news service the medium offers, as well as the capacity for users to access information directly. INAs have always presented a service 'on the wires' that serves up news which can be immediately pasted onto a page or dropped into a bulletin. Downloading from the internet is more instant than taking information off the wires. Anybody – group, organisation or individual – is now able to post news, information and comment on websites for others to select and shape if they are inclined. A proliferation of online news sites has occurred. Some of these are the web versions of already established broadcasters, newspapers or agencies. Others are exclusively internet institutions with no 'historical responsibility to prioritise the needs' of the traditional retail clients of international news (Boyd-Barrett, 2003: 376). The virtually unlimited space offers the opportunity to publish news of countries rarely covered in the traditional media; the sheer speed of information transmission and the gamut of the tools that enable users to access copy and audio and video clips from all over the world, as well as follow links to a range and diversity of other information sources, promise a product the traditional media cannot provide. The ability and capacity of users to write, publish and edit articles on the net allows the web to be a medium that can 'tackle the unmatched mission of receiving and disseminating international news ... narrowing the gigantic discrepancy between the news world and the real world' (Wu, 2007).

The new media by which international news and information can be accessed comes in a variety of forms. Google is the 'largest and fastest growing internet search engine' with, it is estimated, more than 100 million searches made every day covering 8 billion web pages (Thussu, 2006: 215). Google News was launched in 2002 and aggregates more than 4,500 English language news sources for users to access (Allan, 2006: 176). Updated every fifteen minutes, news on Google is grouped into a variety of categories such as world, sport, entertainment, business and science/technology, and in 2006 it could be personalised on the basis of news from 22 different regions and in ten languages (2006: 177). Google's news service has had several problems in developing its operation, most notably in China where access to its Chinese language site has been blocked. Under pressure from the Chinese government Google removed controversial and critical stories. Internet portals such as Google, Yahoo and MSN are becoming the most favoured source of news for an increasing number of people. Their speed and instantaneous quality attract younger consumers in particular.

Large news providers have been joined in cyberspace by smaller, independent news sites such as Indymedia (www.indymedia.org) and OhmyNews (http://english.ohmynews.com). They are seen as pioneers of 'citizen journalism'. Indymedia has its roots in the anti-globalisation protests and demonstrations in the late 1990s, culminating in what some have described as the 'siege of Seattle' in 1999 (Allan, 2006: 125). A number of activist organisations joined together to provide their own news of these demonstrations, criticising mainstream coverage for its focus on violence and confrontation. With the slogan 'don't hate the media, be the media' hundreds of volunteers armed with the latest recording technology provided their own view from the streets. Posting stories on their own website, there were around 1.5 million hits in the first week. A network of 150 independent media centres (IMCs) in 45 countries grew up, operated by volunteers who post stories anonymously on topics of their choice. Editorial guidelines focusing on honesty, accuracy and thoroughness determine the broad parameters within which news stories are posted. This has not prevented considerable controversy surrounding the output; the authorities in several countries including the UK have commandeered several servers and Google threatened to remove IMCs from their search engines.

Ohmy news emerged from a similar set of circumstances, as an antidote to conservative mainstream journalism but in South Korea, the 'most wired society' in the world. Launched in 2000, like Indynews it encourages ordinary citizens to participate in the production of news. Its English language version, OhmyNews International came on-stream in 2004. Funded by donations and advertising the site is financially profitable and has gained an international reputation for investigative reporting. Its hybrid operation combining commercial practices and progressive politics has led to some questioning of the venture (Kim and Hamilton, 2006).

The most significant change is often seen as the rise of individual websites and blogs and other forms of user-generated content (UGC). The mobile phone, email and text messages have communicated a considerable amount of international material to news organisations and agencies. So-called citizen journalists – often simply ordinary men and women who are caught up in events – have been the source of images and video on many major stories such as the 2004 Tsunami, the 2005 London Underground terrorist attacks and the 2007 execution of Saddam Hussein. Television news organisations emphasise the importance of this new source of international news. According to a BBC producer it means that:

> ... essentially we've got stringers in every corner of the world. It's a difference between getting the picture of the explosion as it happens and getting the picture of the firemen turning up afterwards and hosing it down ... we get the news as it happens. (Bivens, 2008: 117)

In some parts of the world bloggers and mobile phones play a vital role in informing the world of what is happening, compensating for the restrictions placed on the mainstream news media. The recent ban placed on the western media from entering Zimbabwe by President Mugabe meant that bloggers and mobile phoners became a crucial source of information for the world's news organisations (Bivens, 2008; Moyo, 2009). Mobile telephony and lightweight equipment also meant that many TV crews were able to enter the country clandestinely. Blogging and mobile telephony not only provide personal insights into political events and crises but also satisfy the need for breaking news and 'event oriented news', which drives the 24-hour global news media (McGregor, 1997).

With the replacement of tele-printers by the electronic delivery of news, agencies and news organisations have had to adapt to new delivery formats. The news agencies 'no longer have a choke-hold on the flow of information' (Bivens, 2008: 116). Reuters, AP and AFP, in soliciting UGC, are changing their relationship with the public. The business is no longer only about 'clients'. Individuals matter as they act as sources of breaking news. Newsrooms and news agencies increasingly use blogs and websites as sources to respond to the immediacy demanded in the global news market. The growth of 24-hour news stations, the growing availability of UGC and the convergence of media forms enhance the importance of immediacy and being first with the news (Bivens, 2008: 123). The constant pressure to be first and to be 'live' is, as Rena Kim Bivens documents, shifting resources away from investigation and severely reducing the time for reflection (see Chapter 4). Using the internet as a source of information is a challenge. Care has to be taken over the credibility and reliability of what is posted. In 2006 pictures used by Reuters during its coverage of the Israeli incursion into Lebanon were found to have been digitally manipulated. The episode threatened to compromise the trust clients place in the agency, a vital component of its competitiveness. The photographer involved was dismissed. The agency also distances itself from material from external sources; the notice posted beneath a list of links to blog posts on the agency's portal africa.reuters.com states that 'Reuters is not responsible for any content provided by external sources'.

Other forms of new media are slowly being populated by international news providers. Reuters opened a bureau in *Second Life* in 2007 (Beckett, 2008: 38) while YouTube has allowed a variety of individuals and organisations to post video clips; nearly as many people watch videos on YouTube as watch they do on the US TV networks' websites (2008: 23). Wikinews is an offshoot of Wikipedia, the highly successful online communal encyclopaedia launched in 2001 (Allan, 2006: 135). Wikinews allows individuals access to the net to post and edit news content on its site without prior authorisation or registration (Thorsen, 2008). Launched in 2004 it produces news which is of local, national and global interest by a process of collaboration. Users are able to edit, change and amend articles up to a certain time and within guidelines set down by Wikinews. The commitment to open content produced in what is described as an ideologically neutral way is deemed a 'fresh approach to journalism' (Thorsen, 2008: 937). Unlike the political agenda of Indymedia and subjectivity of OhmyNews contributors, Wikinews believes 'everyone can make a useful contribution to painting the big picture of what is happening the world around us' (Allan, 2005: 136). The promise of a 'non-hierarchical, collaborative news production cycle' is seen as 'an improvement to the traditional sense of journalistic objectivity'; instead of a 'single unbiased "objective" point of view' the site claims that its contributors collectively produce a fair representation of all viewpoints (Thorsen, 2008: 937, 939). Critics point out that not everyone can contribute to painting the big picture. A large number of people in the developing world, those living on the other side of the digital divide (see below) cannot access the internet and therefore cannot contribute to the editorial process on Wikinews. Wikinews is charged with reflecting news from an 'Anglo-American-centric point of view', an evaluation accepted by the site.

One aspect of the new media technology that has major implications for international news gathering is the customisation of content. The internet allows for the capacity to 'personalise the type of international news by region' (Berger, 2009: 365). Internet users can be much more precise about the international news that they want to consume. MSNBC's site allows consumers to personalise the type of international news by region while the *New York Times'* news tracker lets people create a subject or keyword-based filter alerting them when an article is published with those words (Hamilton and Jenner, 2002: 9). Yahoo added local news for logged-in users of the front page in 2007 and Google News features articles on its site selected by a robotic editorial program that 'trolls the web, picking out the most frequently repeated stories and angles – the concerns that already monopolise our attention' (Viviano, 2007). Users can surf for news stories within a designated proximity. The potential of this technology, with the possibility of linking mobile internet use with geographical positioning systems (GPSs), offers more radical localisation of international news (Berger, 2009: 365).

Impact of the internet

The impact of new technology on the structure of international news gathering and distribution is still a matter of conjecture – rapid technological change makes it difficult to assess clearly what is happening. Many scholars and commentators, as well as those working in the industry, hold 'high hopes' that the new technology is having a beneficial impact on international news gathering (Berger, 2009). At one level they may 'offer one of the best solutions to the dwindling foreign reporting by traditional media' (Hamilton and Jenner, 2002: 21). The arrival of new kinds of foreign correspondent – the man or woman who reports local news for local media but who can be accessed over the internet by users in other countries, the reporter who covers foreign affairs without leaving his or her own country and the blogger cruising the information super highway – promises to offset the decline in the professional foreign correspondent. The new technology means an infinite news hole, allowing the possibility of more international news and coverage of those parts of the world traditionally neglected by the mainstream media. New content producers such as bloggers can eschew the negative news values that pervade the coverage of international news and provide different forms of representation. The online world no longer requires that national perspectives dominate.

While much speculation revolves around the internet, other aspects of the technical changes that have occurred in the gathering, processing and distribution of international news have been less well discussed. Michael Palmer (2008) draws attention to ways in which the changing practices of international news agencies have had an impact on the notion of what news is. Palmer describes how attempts to make news formats compatible in the age of the internet and hypertext mark-up languages has led to a significant reclassification of news (2008: 815). Classifying material to ensure that news-purveyors and end users, as well as news agencies, can readily exchange material has been a feature of international news since the 1880s. Ensuring that computer-to-computer data transfer can be exchanged has led to systems such as the News Industry Text Format (NIFT), which divides up news, information and data streams into specific categories. The increase in the news outlets by which clients, professionals and individuals can access news and information, including podcasts, websites and SMS, leads to the further customising or tailoring of news to individual consumers. The increasing importance of non-media clients has resulted in a demand for shorter news packages. Traders, hedge fund managers and other members of the financial community require basic information; they do not have time to read news stories, preferring headlines that let them make decisions about whether to buy or sell. 'Moving market news' should be headlined in no more that 40 or 50 characters (Palmer, 2008: 816). What is categorised as news and how it is packaged is beginning to change in the digital world (see Chapter 6).

The change has to be kept in perspective; the internet has not led to the reduction of the inequalities in the international news system identified by the MacBride report. Much of the internet is 'primarily in English and has a US-centric bias' (McPhail, 2006: 302). In 2004 it was estimated that 50 per cent of the global internet usage was accounted for by the US with Europe taking up a further 25 per cent (2006: 304). Despite the increase in the presence of the new technology in many parts of the Third World – China, South Korea and Brazil are among the top ten countries with the highest internet use – a noticeable digital divide exists. In many parts of Africa, Asia and Latin America there are millions of people who do not have access to the old media, let alone the new media. The new media have been 'commandeered by the forces of global inequality which have carved the communications architecture of the past century' (Golding, 1998: 81). Consumption of the internet is confined to elites, elite people and elite nations. There are a host of restrictions placed on using the net: 'the points of access to the internet are still very much local, subject to the influences of a host of external factors that are rooted in the interplay between the state, the market and the media' (Chang et al., 2009: 154).

Where users are able to go into cyberspace, what they are allowed to see is subject to national political constraints as well as organisational considerations. Commercial and financial factors determine the links that news websites offer; media organisations are driven by the logic of the market to keep users of their news sites in the same domain. Encouraging users to go to foreign news sites, to jump from country to country, domain to domain, is a potential threat to their business. Most news websites are 'disinclined to make overseas websites available and accessible in their reporting of foreign news stories' and unless users actively search out related online stories they are 'denied the opportunities to learn more about the countries involved or read different perspectives of the same story' (Chang et al., 2009: 155). Research indicates that core countries such as the US and UK dominate the links made to foreign websites; news sites in countries on the margins of international society are often dismissed as 'propaganda or ideologically loaded' (2009: 155–56). Ben Scott (2005: 95) notes how the INAs 'very quickly' became major players in the internet news market, 'supplying ideally suited digital content ... to the portal aggregators, start-up news websites and traditional news vendors looking to strengthen their online presence'. The structural dependency of the web on the established newsgathering system means that the potential offered by the internet is not necessarily easily realisable in practice. The revolutionary transformation in journalism promised by many proponents appears to have a 'long way to go' (Robinson, 2006). One major obstacle is that access is often determined by political and corporate interests.

Global media ownership

International news organisations have become part of large media conglomerates which are extending their reach, power and influence over media markets across the world. CNN, for example, was incorporated into the Time-Warner conglomerate in 1995. Time Warner is typical of the large global firms that dominate international communication. It has interests in films, magazines, music, cable and satellite TV and now the internet. In 2000 it merged with America Online (AOL) to become the world's largest media firm – this lasted until 2009 when the entity broke up. Other large global media conglomerates include Sony, Viacom, Disney, NBC-Universal, Bertelsmann and the News Corporation. They have been joined recently by the new media giants who have benefited from the expansion of new technology – such as Google, Yahoo and Microsoft.

Most of the world's leading sources of news and information are part of corporate fiefdoms. General Electric owns NBC, Disney owns ABC, Viacom owns CBS, NewsCorp owns Fox and Time Warner owns CNN. Journalists are increasing employed by a smaller and smaller number of ever larger organisations. Most of the world's multimedia corporations are American owned, integrating new and old media in their portfolios. In 2006 News Corporation purchased MySpace, indicating the ever-increasing hold these companies have over the new media. The need to expand is essential to remain competitive in a deregulated, free market, which means that the growth of these companies is often at the expense of local or indigenous media – although 'merger mania' between the large players was a feature of the early years of the twenty-first century. Their relentless search for new markets and new consumers to attain an acceptable rate of return on their increasingly large investments in new media is the impetus that drives them on. The convergence of media forms and services brought about by digital technology also fuels the growth of larger corporations as they seek to gain the best advantage in the new multimedia world and consolidate their hold over their traditional areas of activity.

Ben Bagdikian (2004) has documented the rapid contraction of the number of the world's major media companies. Today it is estimated that nine transnational corporations dominate the global media market. These corporations present themselves as supranational entities – according to the then CEO of AOL-Time Warner 'we do not want to be viewed as an American company. We think globally' (McChesney and Schiller, 2003, 9). However, of the nine, five are US firms and the others have core operations in the US. Many see them as promoting commercial at the expense of public service values, emphasising profit over service and encouraging US ways of business and media practice, including a US style of journalism (McChesney and Schiller, 2003: 6). According to Walter Cronkite, legendary CBS anchor and a leading foreign correspondent of his day:

> Today we have the mega-mergers, the mega-ownerships and these people are solely in business for profit. As such (news departments) are directed to make higher ratings, greater profits, cut costs and this is not the way to produce the best news ... (Walter Cronkite, quoted in Shanor, 2003: 76)

At a regional level a similar trend can be observed as a smaller number of companies emerge as market leaders. Some large corporations have surfaced in the Third World such as Brazil's TV Globo and Mexico's Televisa, but these 'second tier' companies have grown in collaboration with the major players, often adopting their values and approach (McChesney and Schiller, 2003). Fewer players means a decline in diversity and a reduction in the quality of journalism, according to critics.

> The global commercial media is radical in that it will respect no tradition or custom, on balance, if it stands in the way of profits. But ultimately it is politically conservative, because the media giants are significant beneficiaries of the current social structure around the world, and upheaval in property or social relations – particularly to the extent that it reduces the power of business – is not in their interest. (McChesney, 1999: 16)

As part of these global media conglomerates news organisations have undergone a transformation in their operating practices as well as the product they deliver. The growth of these conglomerates has been at the expense of public service media whose decline has major implications for the production of foreign news. Commercial broadcasters do not reflect the social commitments that characterise public service media, and with foreign news perceived as low down in the interests of audiences they have cut back on their provision of international news. There has been a drop in political, government and policy related news at the expense of life style, celebrity, sport and human interest stories (Thussu, 2007b). A survey of the content of US news media found that between 1977 and 1997 celebrity, scandal, gossip and similar stories increased from 15 to 43 per cent of total coverage (cited in Shanor, 2003: 27). To make profits the boundaries between news and entertainment are becoming more blurred. By 2007 Reuters Television provided sports and showbiz news ('from Hollywood to Bollywood') in addition to their general news and financial information services, and also a digital service directed to the needs of web-casting (Thussu, 2007b: 64). What is sometimes described as the 'Murdochisation' of the news media has increased the pressures on correspondents to produce different kinds of news stories and more entertainment oriented stories; the centralisation of ownership and control of global media has ensured these pressures are more effectively brought to bear. It is in this context that the growth of alternative news agencies seeking to educate citizens about international affairs should be understood.

Alternative news agencies

Since the NWICO debates of the 1970s and early 1980s a number of alternative news agencies have been established with a commitment to serving those parts of the world under-reported by the INAs. These agencies and the kind of journalism they practice have not received the scholarly attention they deserve (Rauch, 2003). They have sought to provide audiences with a different way of understanding global events. Perhaps the most successful has been the Inter Press Service (IPS), which started in 1964 as an 'information bridge' between Christian Democratic political parties in Europe and Latin America (Giffard, 1998: 191). It was formed as a cooperative of primarily Latin American journalists and, with the growth of the Non-Aligned Movement, the focus of the agency was on developing news and information exchange between Third World countries in order to assist the development process. The focus on cooperation between the countries of Asia, Latin America and Africa inevitably linked the agency with calls for a NWICO, and as the debate between the West and the Third World intensified it expanded into 'the largest international agency specialising in Third World news' (Giffard and Rivenburgh, 2000: 12). By the mid-1980s it had offices in around 60 countries including 23 in Latin America, 16 in Europe, five in the Middle East and four each in Asia and North America (Giffard, 1998: 191). IPS was committed to providing in-depth stories about the fundamental issues of the day; it rejected the focus on breaking news and entertainment of the INAs, whose coverage 'careers from crisis to crisis, disaster to disaster and, increasingly scandal to scandal' (Giffard, 1998: 192). It focuses on human rights and democracy, the environment, natural resources and energy, population, health and education, food and agriculture, international finance and trade, politics and conflict resolution, culture, arts and entertainment, science and technology, and regional integration and sustainable development (1998: 192). In line with the aims of those calling for a new order, IPS was committed to a 'balanced' coverage of world affairs. Its service is delivered in two main languages, English and Spanish, but it also provides a selection of news in 14 other languages including minority languages such as Urdu, Nepali, Tamil and Kiswahili (Bielsa and Bassett, 2009: 51). It is not surprising that two-thirds of IPS subscribers are located in developing countries (Giffard, 1998: 200).

Like its mainstream rivals, IPS has undergone financial troubles over the last couple of decades. Unlike its rivals it has always been run as a 'shoestring operation', obtaining revenue from the sale of its news service, projects for third parties and carrier services (1998: 198). These three sources have all shrunk with a consequent contraction in the IPS network. Today its global network is composed of 250 journalists, mainly stringers, 14 full-time bureaux and a presence in 150 countries (Bielsa and Bassett, 2009: 51). This represents a significant reduction over the last few decades: in 1994 there were 44 permanent bureaux (2009: 51). However, the subscription list has not been so adversely affected; it can still claim to be 'civil society's leading news agency, an independent voice from the South and for development, delving into globalisation for the stories underneath' (quoted in Thussu, 2006: 241). Besides serving newspaper and broadcasting outlets and news agencies, it is also subscribed to by a large number of non-governmental organisations, 549 in 1996. Projects for these organisations have played their part in enabling the network to survive in the face of its inability to establish commercial viability. In recent years there has been a 'levelling off' in the support from intergovernmental and NGO institutions (Boyd-Barrett, 2000: 9).

Despite its precarious finances IPS has managed to keep operating. This distinguishes it from many other of the enterprises that were set up to report and reflect the voices of the Third World. Depthnews, Gemini News Service and the South–North News Service are examples of alternative agencies which came and went relatively quickly (Hatchen, 1996: 38). Started by concerned journalists in the North, who made a commitment to work with colleagues in the South to provide local perspectives on world events, such agencies struggled with funding and finance during their short existence. Gemini News, for example, started in 1967 as a non-profit, features agency which sought to promote the 'decolonisation' of news (Thussu, 2006: 241). It folded in 2001 when funds eventually dried up, eventually becoming part of the international non-governmental organisation, PANOS. The regional news agencies set up by Third World governments have fared little better. PANA, CANA and NANAPOL as well as the Asian-Pacific Network News (ANN) and the Middle East News Agency (MENA) are examples of regional agencies that floundered as a result not only of a lack of funds but also on the quality of the product and the professionalism of the service offered. National news agencies were the backbone of PANA in its early years – unfortunately only five of the 52 member states paid their full contributions in 1991 (Forbes et al., 1998: 156). Inaugurated in 1983 the agency sought to exchange news and information among African states as well as provide a service to disseminate African news to the world (Hatchen, 1996: 168). Political factors impaired its operations and news would often not be reported to avoid giving offence to governments and their allies on the continent. Sometimes, sensitivities led to a delay in getting the story out and much of what was reported was dismissed by western critics as 'protocol news': 'news involving the mere reception, greeting, honouring, visiting, and seeing off of officials or delegations from inside and outside the country' (Hjavard, 1998: 213). Unlike IPS and the other independent agencies the regional agencies of the Third World relied to a considerable extent on the western international news agencies for copy. Research found these agencies had a high degree of dependency on Reuters, AFP and AP for many of their stories and often their coverage replicated that of the INAs (Musa, 1997). Reporting western news was one way of avoiding the potentially difficult and dangerous problem of covering domestic and regional politics. Regional agencies – like national agencies – tended to act as 'gatekeepers' on stories, for example, changing the term 'terrorist' to 'freedom fighter' when it was used in relation to national liberation movements in the Third World (Musa, 1997: 128). They did not possess the resources, networks and personnel to gather much of their own material, and government involvement impaired their credibility, independence and ability to find solutions to the challenges that faced them (Boyd-Barrett, 2003: 374). For critics they tended to 'consolidate' the old international order with their reliance on the international news agencies for the 'greater part' of their foreign news (Musa, 1997: 145).

Financial pressure saw the whittling away of the operation of these agencies. CANA, for example, was rescued when it went into partnership with Reuters, acquiring new technology and marketing Reuters financial data across the Caribbean. This helped to reduce the deficit and allow the agency to limp along as the Caribbean Media Services (CMS). New technology also provided some relief as email and the internet promised to reduce costs. Attempts were made to revive PANA in 1994, making use of the new technology. The agency was privatised in 1999 and a board of trustees representing the 'good and great' of Africa was set up to guarantee the agency's independence (Boyd-Barrett, 2003: 375). Stakeholders included telecommunications companies, national news agencies, NGOs, financial organisations, private individuals (usually in the business sector) and private media. The changes did not result in an increase in the usage of PANA's news service (2003: 375). IPS also made efforts to develop online but again the efforts failed to attract a significant increase in subscribers.

For most of the post-war period the international news system within which foreign correspondence took place was dominated by the INAs. They alone – with perhaps the exception of a few large national media outlets – determined the gathering and dissemination of reports on international events and issues. Today their monopoly has waned as new sources of international news have emerged. The 24-hour news channels represent a mainstream challenge to the INAs while the internet has produced competition from non traditional sources, including the individual citizen. The distinction between wholesaler and retailer has broken down. The agencies not only find themselves in competition with retailers such as CNN and the BBC who also supply international news, but also with their own clients who subscribe directly to global news sources or disseminate news themselves; they also act as retailers in delivering news on the net (Rantanen, 2004: 303). New technology and commercialisation have transformed the institutional arrangements under which international journalism is practised.

Note

1 For a discussion of the broader complexities of the changes in the agency's operations inside and outside of China see Xin Xin, 2008.

4

'OUR MAN IN HAVANA': THE OCCUPATIONAL CULTURE OF INTERNATIONAL JOURNALISM

Tradition has it that an effective journalist need only know a little about a lot. Tough minded-ness, rugged individualism, a commitment to what passes for objectivity and an ability to ask good questions commonly serve as adequate substitutes for thorough-going knowledge of a country, its political and cultural history and even its language. (Dorman, 1986: 421)

The foreign correspondent is, and always has been, the envy of his or her peers ... the despair of his or her family, the model of every aspiring young journalist, the rock or sinking sand, on to or into which a foreign editor will climb or sink. With rare exceptions, success-ful foreign correspondents are prima donnas and workaholics, selfish loners who are either pushy or cunning ... (Victoria Brittain, *The Guardian*, quoted in Marr, 2004: 334)

Popular culture presents a romantic image of the foreign correspondent. Films,[1] novels, TV dramas and plays portray him as a glamorous hero strug-gling against difficulties and dangers to bring us the news from obscure and alien environments. The emphasis is on the rugged individualism of the hero in overcoming the vicissitudes that are placed in the way of 'getting the story'. He – and it is usually a 'he' – has to fight against the unpredict-able nature of what may confront him in the field as well as the demands, often unreasonable or ill-informed, of the 'resident geniuses', the editors at home. This image is cultivated by correspondents themselves. Many accounts include colourful stories of dodging bullets, stumbling through snake-infested waters and defying hostile 'natives' (for example, Behr, 1982; Harriman, 1987). Even critical, anti-establishment correspondents are not immune from playing up their role in world events. John Pilger's book *Heroes* provides many insights into the problems of foreign reporting but still appears to add to the perception of the foreign reporter as a loner who is the main protagonist of the piece (Pilger, 2001). Foreign correspondents, in their accounts of their work, life and times, tend to 'celebrate the unpre-dictable'. They also cultivate an image of a community which is 'of a tightly knit group, largely male, coming together wherever there is trouble in the world, congregating in bars after a day's work is over, drinking and swapping stories' (Hannerz, 1998: 553).

The reality is less glamorous and more mundane. International journalism, like the rest of the profession of journalism, is dull, repetitious and often desk bound. It is mostly a matter of logistics: meeting deadlines, filing stories, attending briefings and press conferences, gaining accreditation, finding translators, drivers and guides, providing editors with what they want and ensuring it is all done within budget (Goodman and Pollock, 1997). In other words international journalism is subject to a number of routines and practices – it is a bureaucratic activity. The foreign correspondent 'is not a loner but an organization man' (Bogart, 1968, quoted in Cole and Hamilton, 2008: 806). Stephen Hess (1996: 47) notes that 'there is a distinctive culture, an amalgam of attitudes, practices and ideas that informs the behaviour of all those involved' in gathering foreign news.

This chapter examines the occupational culture of the foreign correspondent and the way they work. Who are foreign correspondents, what do they do and what are the newsgathering routines they follow? The increasing emphasis on the foreign correspondent as a 'generalist', as someone who can empathise with his or her audience, is explored. This is an important relationship. For audiences the foreign correspondent is a familiar face or cultural landmark in a strange and unknown setting. He or she acts as a cultural intermediary between the story and the audience. The growing importance of the generalist approach is highlighted by the decline in the long-stay correspondent and the rise of the 'parachute' or 'fire-fighter' reporter. The argument that the new breed of globe trotting correspondents, who touch down in the world's hot spots in large numbers for shorter and shorter stays, are producing a more impressionistic and uniform coverage of the world is examined. For many it is the internet and other forms of new media technology that are 'redefining' the way in which foreign correspondents work (Hamilton and Jenner, 2004). The proliferation of news and information outlets brought about by technological change has had the most profound impact; it is seen as marginalising the traditional foreign correspondent, making him or her simply another source among a variety of sources of international news.

A vanishing species

International journalism since 1945 has witnessed the decline in the number of men and women representing national news organisations based abroad. The international news net has shrunken from a high point at the end of the Second World War. The disappearance of the foreign correspondent is most noteworthy and most noted in the world's great power, the United States. CBS producer Scotti Williston (2001) writes of the 'vanishing' foreign correspondent as she documents the decline in CBS's foreign news-gathering capacity since the early 1980s.

> In the late 1970s and early 80s, CBS had 14 major foreign bureaus, 10 mini foreign bureaus, and stringers in 44 countries around the world ... Now, CBS and the other networks have just a handful of foreign bureaus. Paris is gone, Frankfurt is gone, Cairo, Rome, Johannesburg, Nairobi, Beirut, Cyprus, all gone. (Williston, 2001)

Williston's experience is reflected by that of correspondents working for the print media. Pamela Constable (2007) relates what happened at her newspaper, the *Baltimore Sun*, which had correspondents from Mexico to Beijing when she worked there in 1978, but today has none. Today only four American newspapers – the *Wall Street Journal*, the *New York Times*, the *Washington Post* and the *Los Angeles Times* – maintain a team of foreign correspondents abroad (Constable, 2007).

A similar picture emerges in Britain and other European countries. British newspapers have gradually reduced the number of reporters they station abroad. The most dramatic cuts in newspaper foreign staff took place in the 1970s. The 1977 Royal Commission on the Press identified a 30 per cent decline in the number of British newspaper staff correspondents based overseas (Boyd-Barrett, 1977: 16). Certain parts of the world have virtually disappeared off the global map of foreign news coverage. Colin Legum has drawn attention to the decline of the number of reporters covering Africa in the UK press:

> In the 50s, when we still had serious newspapers in this country, I was appointed Africa correspondent of *The Observer*. We built up a group of 12 well informed Third World correspondents. We had an Africa circle, correspondents, editors and people from the BBC used to meet monthly at the Reform Club, looking at and discussing Africa. There was then a real and serious interest in it. Even the *Daily Mail* had an Africa correspondent. (Quoted in Harrison and Palmer, 1986: 82)

Declining numbers is associated with the concentration of staff in certain parts of the world. By the mid-1970s more than 80 per cent of full-time foreign correspondents for British media outlets were based in North America and Western Europe (Boyd-Barrett, 1977: 21). The Dutch quality newspaper *De Volkskrant* closed its operations in India and Africa in 2004 (Tuinstra, 2004), an experience shared by many other print outlets in recent years. As their presence disappears in certain regions, the number of correspondents based in other regions increases. Brussels is one of the fastest-growing news beats. The number of reporters covering the EU doubled between 1976 and 1987 and by 2004 had reached just under 1,000, many of whom were representing countries outside the EU, including 43 from the US and 17 from China (Raeymaeckers et al., 2007: 105). The importance of the beat is highlighted by AP having six permanently accredited correspondents and Bloomberg 11, an indication of the EU as an economic world power. Some question whether many of these journalists are really *foreign* correspondents, as much of the news they file out of Brussels is domestic European news – dispatches about developments in the EU which replace reports from the respective capitals in Europe (Tuinstra, 2004).

Some argue that the resources devoted to foreign newsgathering reflect short-term financial considerations and the state of international relations (Tunstall, 1996: 341). Foreign news goes through stages of coverage and 'the period 1940–70 offered a unique collection of big stories' (1996: 342). Moments of huge interest in foreign affairs such as the collapse of the Berlin Wall and the attacks on the World Trade Center do not hide the long term, gradual decline of the capacity of news organisations to gather their own foreign news. After 9/11 nearly every American agreed they would be better off if they knew more about the world. International news coverage as a result picked up but by 2004 the percentage of articles related to foreign affairs published on the front pages of American newspapers had dropped to 'the lowest total in any year we have ever studied'; according to the Project for Excellence in Journalism it was 14 per cent, down from 21 per cent in 2003 and 27 per cent in both 1987 and 1977 (Hiatt, 2007). The urgent necessity of knowing more about what was happening in the world did not prevent American newspapers and television networks returning to steadily cutting back the resources devoted to international news gathering. Between 2002 and 2006, the number of foreign-based newspaper correspondents shrank from 188 to 141 (excluding the *Wall Street Journal*).

The long term decline is attributed to a variety of economic factors. The changing commercial circumstances facing the news media from the late 1970s onwards is emphasised by some commentators. Subjecting broadcasting to market forces is seen as a decisive moment in the decline of foreign news on US television screens. Prior to deregulation in the late 1980s and early 1990s stations were required to do a certain amount of public broadcasting, and news was classified under that banner. International news benefited from such obligations and with the scrapping of these regulations it was no longer seen as profitable to cover foreign events in as much detail. Growing competition brought about by the expansion of channels and outlets led to cost cutting. News bureaux across the world were closed as network television resorted to 'pooling resources'; a single camera crew often provided every network with the same footage. Technology facilitated such arrangements with the advent of the ENG camera and the shift to videotape (Williston, 2001).

The disappearance of foreign correspondents is also attributed to a declining interest in international news. Given the central role attributed to the reader, viewer and listener in the determination of what is news in a market economy, there is limited research into audience knowledge of and interest in international affairs (Bilteryst, 2001). Much of the research that has been done relates to studies of US listeners, viewers and readers. Notorious for their ignorance of geography, it is possible to argue that American consumers as an audience for international news are atypical. A comparative international study of public knowledge of foreign affairs shows that Americans had 'the least knowledge' (Bennett et al., 1996). Some of this research draws attention to a gap between journalists' expectations of their audience and the actual interest and engagement of ordinary people with international news. A Harris poll in 1978 found that while US journalists polled believed that only 5 per cent of the public was greatly interested in foreign news, the actual percentage of the audience saying they were deeply interested stood at 41 per cent (cited in Rosenblum, 1979: 55). A study of international news in several media systems found that 'there is little relationship between what the news covers the most and how important audiences think it is to them' (Tai and Chang, 2002: 259). For some correspondents it is their professional duty and responsibility to report the news whether their audience wants it or not. As one US foreign correspondent puts it:

> Do they care two hoots about the elections in Pakistan, the Palestinian National Congress meeting in Algeria or turmoil in Albania? Ninety-eight per cent probably couldn't care less. That doesn't mean we shouldn't do these stories, since we have an editorial duty to inform. (NBC London Bureau chief, quoted in Wallis and Baran, 1990: 251)

There is an inference in professional and scholarly circles that there is a greater demand for international news from online audiences. Media companies are sometimes keen to stress 'there's a real thirst on the internet for international news, something you don't see among television audiences' (quoted in Smillie, 1997). This is not supported by research which has shown that the level of interest in news on the internet is generally lower than in the traditional media (Elvestad, 2009). Even in a world we describe as 'global' it is worth pointing out that there are hundreds of millions of people, primarily in Asia, Africa and Latin America, who have little or no contact with the media: 'a large part of humanity still lives beyond the reach of the media and has no reason to worry about media manipulation or the bad influence of television' (Kapuściński, 1999).

Not all commentators see the foreign correspondent as a 'vanishing species', preferring to describe what is happening in terms of a transformation in the nature of foreign correspondence. New technology – and especially the internet – is seen as compensating for declining numbers by producing new kinds of international news gatherers. New types of correspondent are emerging who 'are neither so elite nor so easily defined in their personal characteristics, outlook or work habits' (Hamilton and Jenner, 2004: 312). The types of journalist who gather international news are changing, with the long stay specialist correspondent one among a vast array. The ability to download foreign news is seen as representing a fundamental shift in the balance of power, away from the elite correspondents of the traditional media to the ordinary citizen. The 'unaffiliated and often untrained *de facto* journalist' who reports on international events is seen as the face of the new international information system (Hamilton and Jenner, 2004: 314). For veteran correspondent Ryszard Kapuściński (1999) the consequence is that: 'Today there are countless people practising journalism who feel no identification with the profession, let alone deciding to devote their life to it'.

The background of foreign correspondents

In his examination of British foreign correspondents Boyd-Barrett (1977) identified three types of foreign correspondent. There is the *staff correspondent* based abroad who works exclusively for a single news organisation. There are *general reporters* who are sometimes flown out to cover major news stories abroad. Finally there are *stringers* who fall into two categories: those who have a special relationship with one or two news organisations which pay them a fee to retain their services, and are the most regular users of their copy, and those who are paid on the number of lines used, generally selling their services to those willing to pay. The majority of the men and women employed full time as foreign correspondents have roots in or close ties with western countries. Boyd-Barrett (1980) in his study of the INAs found that nearly three-quarters of the bureau chiefs of the major agencies were westerners, primarily North American, British and other Europeans, Australian and white South Africans. According to Geoffrey Nyarota (2009) western news organisations rely on western correspondents to file stories, as they want the story reported through the lens of western interests; the presupposition is that there must be a western angle conveyed in reporting events, without which there might be no coverage.

Men are disproportionately represented – although studies indicate that the number of women correspondents has increased over the years (Morrison and Tumber, 1985; Hess, 1996). More women tend to be stringers (Hess, 1996: 72). Stringers are cheaper to employ and prior to the 1980s women were three times as likely to be employed as stringers as men (Hess, 1996: 18). Since the 1980s they are twice as likely to be freelancers. Stringers are also likely to be younger and in an environment in which cost is an increasingly important part of the decision about the deployment of correspondents; many young and inexperienced reporters are travelling to dangerous places independently to establish their reputation, earning a living by working piecemeal (1996: 19). These people are often dismissed as 'flingers', as they are usually embarking on a short-term adventure rather than a career in journalism. They have been criticised by full-time correspondents for endangering the credibility and lives of the professional (1996: 69–70).

The lure of danger has figured prominently among the reasons why correspondents say they are attracted to the job. For veteran war reporter Peter Arnett 'what I learned to love [was] the thrill of covering wars, for which there was no substitute' (quoted in Hess, 1996: 58). The bang-bang action that can accompany foreign tours of duty is regarded as exhilarating, a compensation for the long moments of boredom that characterise the job. Nora Ephron has commented on the fascination of violence and danger for many reporters in the field: 'the awful truth is that ... war is not hell. It is fun' (quoted in Knightley, 2003: 448). As a *New York Times* reporter in Sarajevo put it: 'It seems so indecent to say we are having the most tremendous amount of fun in the midst of all this misery. It's not fun but it's an experience I would not want to miss' (Hess, 1996: 58). Photographers and camera workers have been particularly attracted to capturing the most riveting moments of the big news stories of the day. This has implications for the kind of stories that are covered: 'the attraction of excitement biases news gathering in favour of certain institutions and certain types of newsmakers' (1996: 59).

One of the traditional characteristics of the long stay correspondent is the independence he or she is supposed to have from the home office and the organisational imperatives that weigh on the newsgathering process. Many reporters aspired to a foreign posting as a result of the freedom it gave them to make their own decisions and follow their own instinct as the man or woman 'on the spot'. The former foreign editor of the *Guardian*, Victoria Brittain, talks of foreign correspondents prior to the age of the satellite having 'life on their own terms' (quoted in Marr, 2004: 332). Surveys of foreign press corps highlight the attraction to foreign correspondents of 'the independence offered by communications distance' (Morrison and Tumber, 1985: 457). Going 'off-base', that is, not telling the news desk where you are, was an appeal of the posting. You had the space to follow up your own stories and explore your beat. James Cameron, a doyen of foreign reporting, covering Asia, Africa and the Pacific for British media outlets such as the *Picture Post*, the *Daily Express* and the *News Chronicle* in the decades following the Second World War, describes the 'cat and mouse' nature of his relationship with his editors. They would 'devise for me abrupt and intricate changes of location all over the world involving logistical problems of great complexity and expense', while Cameron gained pleasure from accomplishing them 'as often as not to no greater end than our mutual gratification at the solution of a problem (quoted in Hannerz, 2004: 148). Leading foreign correspondents of yester-year describe their relations with the home office as 'tenuous' and 'distant', accepting their editors' authority while paying limited attention to their directives. Today, new technology has further enslaved the man or woman in the field to the home office. You are 'more likely to have to call in on the satellite phone to discuss the next live insert' (Franks, 2005: 98). The editorial gatekeepers exert considerably more influence over determining what the story is about. The news desk often dictates the story to the correspondent, limiting the correspondent's ability to input his or her on-the-spot knowledge. In broadcasting, the script of the reporter in the field is often vetted by the home office to ensure it conforms to the editorial line of the day (*The World is Watching*, 1988).

Specialist knowledge

The specialist knowledge associated with the long stay foreign correspondent appears to be valued less and less by the news organisation they work for. Today many foreign correspondents have relatively little relevant knowledge or skills related to the area or region to which they are assigned – with the exception of some of those posted to the major beats such as Washington. William Dorman and Mansour Farhang (1987: 195) note that only one of the 300 or so western correspondents who flew into to Tehran in the late 1970s to cover the fall of the Shah spoke the local language, Farsi. With breaking stories of this scale perhaps it is understandable that reporters would not be totally prepared for the assignment. But it is also apparent in the posting of many long stay correspondents. According to Andrew Torchia, who covered Africa for AP in the 1970s:

> Most foreign correspondents, in my experience, arrive unprepared for Africa. I certainly did. We may lack language skills. We almost certainly lack a relevant cultural back- ground. It may take us two or three years to make one swing around our beat … by the time we begin to understand a little of what is going on, we are exhausted, frustrated, and probably about to be reassigned out of Africa. (Dorman, 1986: 422)

For some editors and reporters, speaking the local language is sometimes seen as problematic. Such is the strength of the commitment to the notion of objectivity that speaking local languages could impair the ability to take a 'balanced view'. As one AP reporter put it:

> … if a correspondent speaks such languages as Urdu or Lao, used only in a single country, it usually means that he has a close personal association with the culture that might affect his overall objectivity. (Rosenblum, 1978: 123)

The strange attitude that any learning or knowledge could weaken your objec- tivity was manifest among the ranks of the reporters who went to Vietnam: one refused to read a single book about Vietnam before taking up his assignment because 'I didn't want to clutter up my mind' (Mercer et al., 1987: 236). But such professional prejudices do not detract from the capabilities and compe- tence of many long stay correspondents in reporting their patch of the world.

Assessment of the quality of the coverage of the Middle East in general and the Iranian Revolution of the late 1980s in particular compares favourably the reporting of specialist correspondents with that of the generalist reporters who dropped in to report on breaking events (Said, 1997). According to Edward Said (1997: 107–8) 'no matter how gifted the individual, he or she cannot hope to report places as complex as Iran or Turkey or Egypt without some training and a lengthy residence in the place'. He contrasts the Iranian coverage provided by itinerant correspondents whose work profile included moving between countries as different as Lebanon, Portugal and Turkey in relatively short periods and whose tour of duty in Iran was less than a year, with the long term specialist reporters such as Eric Rouleau of *Le Monde* and David Hirst of the *Manchester Guardian*, who not only spoke the local languages but had between them nearly 50 years' experience of covering the country (1997: 108).

Rapid rotation has become a feature of the way in which western news organisations deal with foreign assignments: there is an assumption that 'going stale' or 'going native' is an occupational hazard. According to one American veteran correspondent: 'The first year you are learning, the second year you are on your feet and can give more texture to stories, the third year you are getting tired' (quoted in Hannerz, 1998: 551). The BBC's concern about the partiality of long stay correspondents was at the heart of the decision of their man in India, Mark Tully, to leave the organisation when asked to move to another posting. The BBC had lost one of the internationally recognised authorities on the country.

A sceptical attitude to specialist knowledge and skills is deeply ingrained in the occupational culture of international journalism, which has come to place considerable emphasis on the 'generalist'. He or she is supposed to represent the audience they are reporting for – which usually means in foreign coverage an audience that is often unaware. Speaking to them is as important, if not more important, than getting the story right. The way in which the focus on 'generalism' can prescribe the work routines of foreign reporters is illustrated by the experience of Paris bureau chief of the *New York Times*, Flora Lewis. In 1980, during the hostage crisis in Tehran, she was asked by her editors to undertake a special assignment on the upsurge of Islam.

> They had a meeting in New York, and someone said, 'Jesus, nobody knows what the hell is going on in Islam. Let's send Flora'. So they called me up and I went. It was crazy; I wasn't even sure how to use the material I would gather ... I had to make arrangements frantically ... I started off in Paris and London. Then I went to Cairo, because that's where the Islamic university is located, and also to Algiers and Tunis. Then I came back with twenty notebooks and ten pounds of paper and sat down to write. (Quoted in Dorman and Farhang, 1986: 197)

Lewis's hastily-thrown-together articles were published in the *New York Times*, a newspaper of record, which many would expect to produce well researched and carefully considered assessments of their subject matter. Edward Said (1997: 91) comments on the sweeping generalisations – for example, the Islamic mind was described as unable to employ 'step by step thinking' – that appeared in such reports. Newspaper men and women are expected to work on several stories simultaneously – and often drop everything to respond to a breaking story. Flora Lewis describes what she was doing when asked to turn her attention to the 'Islam project'. She was working on a number of stories:

> One was a music piece about a young American composer over here. And I had been following through the NATO missile decision for some time; and although New York wanted me to drop that ... I was eager to take time out for the NATO meeting. (quoted in Dorman and Farhang, 1986: 198)

The wide variety of stories Lewis was working on highlights a chronic problem of spreading yourself too thin. Lewis sums up what she does in this way:

> I dabble. I'll write about a gastronomic binge, I'll write a piece about NATO, I'll do an interview with Nureyev, I'll do a political piece. I don't know a hell of a lot about anything.

The generalist approach is defended by many in the profession; generalists are able to represent more effectively their audience, seeing the world through their eyes, which specialist knowledge might impede. However, as Dorman and Farhang note, such an approach coincides with the profit-making objective of the media. Specialists cost money and training correspondents to become expert is a costly and time-consuming activity.

The foreign beat

Covering foreign news abroad varies according to the medium one works for. Print, radio and television correspondents have different problems and pressures to struggle with. However, the daily routines of all foreign correspondents are dominated by common features. Most bureau correspondents are responsible for vast areas. Labels such as the 'Middle East Correspondent' or the 'Africa Editor', or today the grandiosely entitled 'World Affairs Correspondent', indicate that foreign correspondents are responsible for reporting vast areas that are characterised by a diversity of countries, cultures, peoples and languages, to say nothing of political and social systems. The geographical distance that correspondents have to cover simply to get around their beat is daunting in places like Africa, which are beset with a variety of natural, man made and infrastructure obstacles (see Boafo, 1992).

During the 1980s most American and European TV news channels covered Africa from Johannesburg in South Africa. Not only was this as geographically remote from many parts of the continent as they were from

Europe, it was also the only African country run by whites only. Robert Terrell (1986) noted that the 'overwhelming majority of US journalists stationed in South Africa are upper middle class whites' and as a result 'isolated from South Africa's majority due to class, cultural, economic, racial and political factors' (Terrell, 1986: 23). Living in separate housing, immersed in white society and unable to converse with many black people owing to their inability to speak the languages used by black and coloured South Africans, they were subjected to 'procedures of assimilation'. Those who resisted were 'ostracised' and US editors seemed unwilling to post black journalists in South Africa. The appointment of African-Americans to postings on the continent did not necessarily produce a better state of affairs. Keith Richburg, who was based in Nairobi for the *Washington Post*, expressed relief that he was American and his ancestors had found their way to the US (cited in Hannerz, 2004: 34). Restrictions on reporting are not only a matter of geography and distance. They are also a product of 'culture, class, color and consciousness which are harder to detect' (quoted in Rosenblum, 1993: 138).

Most foreign correspondents are based in capital cities. Full-time foreign correspondents cover the United Kingdom – and Europe in some cases – from London which for many years had the second-biggest concentration of foreign correspondents after Washington DC (Morrison and Tumber, 1985). This is mainly for practical reasons. Capital cities in most countries offer the comforts that most correspondents demand, particularly after a long day in the field. Capital cities also supply correspondents with what they need to keep their editors at home happy – a regular supply of particular types of stories. London is the main hub of information about what is happening in the UK, with a thriving media and communications industry and a government machine which pumps out press releases, organises regular briefings and provides sheaves of official handouts and documentation. For the most part there is no need to travel outside the M25 beltway, read provincial newspapers or access regional television and radio. It can all be done in London – and today the internet makes this simpler. This capital city bias is confirmed in numerous studies of foreign reporters. Chu and Gross's (1988) study of the foreign press corps in Taiwan found that only two out of the 11 full-time correspondents stated they travelled outside the capital city Taipei more than once a month. Hess (2005) discovered that many Washington based foreign correspondents rarely travelled to the mid-West or Southern states of America. The result according to one commentator in the 1970s was that 'in the main therefore they don't see and talk to Americans who dine at McDonalds, bowl on Tuesday evenings, attend stock car races, guzzle beer at the Legion Hall or shoot baskets in a ghetto schoolyard' (Hess, 2005: 21). They are less in touch with Main Street America than what is happening inside the beltway of Washington politics.

Not all foreign correspondents are equal – some are more important and influential than others. Some postings are clearly more important: London, New York, Washington and to a lesser extent Paris and Rome and perhaps today Brussels. These traditionally have been the world's major news hubs or centres and with their air-conditioned buildings and appealing lifestyle they are often considered as the pinnacle of achievement within the profession. Other bureaus vary in importance according to events; Johannesburg was a major centre during the years of apartheid but with the demise of the racist system interest declined and the number of international journalists located there dwindled. Jerusalem, at the centre of one of the world's longest-lasting conflicts, remains a major news operation. Within foreign press corps there is a 'pecking order'; there are star correspondents whose on-screen or page talent has produced an audience following that distinguishes them from their colleagues and competitors. It is often said in Britain that an international crisis wouldn't exist unless Kate Adie or John Simpson had arrived on scene. The hierarchy on foreign beats is also differentiated in terms of the status of the news organisation. Mark Pedelty's A Team, covering El Salvador during the civil war, consisted of staff reporters for outlets such as newspapers of record, the international news agencies and the major TV news channels (Pedelty, 1995: chapter 4). These reporters would get additional, often intimate briefings from the embassy (1995: 71). They were trusted and part of an ongoing relationship based on the exchange of information. Confidences can be entered into as each needs the other in order to do their job. Freelancers and stringers who make up the B Team are treated with suspicion, primarily as they have to 'sell' their stories and in the eyes of officials embellish and take risks in order to talk up what they have got. The power to define the newsworthiness of an event rests in the hands of the bureau chiefs and the 'star' reporters who parachute in; a decision by these journalists about which events to attend 'often influenced the stringers' reporting schedules' (1995: 83).

The daily grind

Like most journalists the daily grind of the work of foreign correspondents revolves around deadlines. Time and space are major constraints under which they work. The BBC's World Affairs Editor, John Simpson, complains about the time limitations and recurrent deadlines under which he has had to work during his broadcasting career.

> The room is hot and airless ... the picture editor besides me stirs slightly and looks at his watch. We have an hour and a half to turn the raw video of whatever experience we have just undergone into something coherent, understandable and roughly two-and-a-half minutes in length, record a commentary to go with it, and expedite the entire package to London by satellite ... I have watched the slow business continue, hands

damp and stomach tightening, in the knowledge that at any moment the power might be cut and the edited version locked irrevocably in the machine until hours after our satellite booking. The one thing that I have never had is quite the amount of time I needed to complete the job. (Simpson, 1988: 14)

The limitations of time within TV news bulletins – a US nightly network news bulletin is 22 minutes long excluding the advertisements – have traditionally worked against the efforts of correspondents to provide a comprehensive picture of world events which does not rely on narrow stereotypes and crises. An ABC news producer covering Nicaragua in the late 1980s compared TV news reporting to trying to 'shoe horn a size twelve foot into a size eight shoe' (*The World is Watching*, 1988). An average report from an overseas TV correspondent contains 'half a minute from an interview or speech and around 330 words' from the reporter and is 'more interested in the filmable effect than the hard-to-film cause' (Knightley, 1988).

Foreign correspondents have always been required to provide a regular flow of news and information to their home offices, and logistical considerations have always figured prominently in their daily routine. This was particularly apparent in the days of the telephone and cable. According to one old Africa hand:

Our primary concern in those days was not so much to get the story as to get the story out. The correspondent's main pre-occupation on arrival at any given dateline was to secure the most reliable means of communication with London, Paris or New York. A colleague of that era had calculated that we spent up to 70 per cent of our working time trying to 'file' – or transmit – our copy. (Munnion, 1999: 65)

New technology may have alleviated some of the pressures of filing but it has also created its own logistical headaches. Robert Fisk, the *Independent*'s Middle East correspondent, draws attention to how 'dangerously reliant' the foreign reporter is on the computer and email. Trained to take apart, mend and reassemble a telex machine, Fisk was able to operate in the most difficult and obscure terrain; but confronted by 'total disk failure' he is unable to repair his computer (cited in Marr, 2004: 340). Television reporters complain about the restraints imposed by mobile phones, satellite dishes and fast turnaround editing systems. According to the BBC's Kate Adie:

Increasingly hacks are tethered to the satellite dish always on hand to deliver the 'live spot' in a curious belief that rabbiting on live is a more relevant and informed kind of reporting: in reality, someone stuck next to a dish for hours on end is the last creature on earth to have learned anything new, and probably unaware of a corpse twenty yards away. (Adie, 2002: 415)

Technology has not necessarily made correspondents' lives any easier but simply tied them down in different ways. Adie's comments are reminiscent of concerns expressed by Simon Hoggart in the days of telexes and telephones.

> The main task of the real foreign correspondent is not finding out where the bullets are flying and standing in front of them but getting to a phone or telex line. I spent almost a whole day after Papa Doc Duvalier fled Haiti, sitting in the Port-au-Prince exchange trying to get a line to London. When I emerged I found that two men had been shot dead in the street outside, and a curfew had been declared. Since I'd sent my story, I was entirely indifferent to these events, which might as well have occurred on the planet Neptune. (Hoggart, 1988: 16)

Whether it is the satellite dish or the telephone, the telex or email, technology can become a handicap to witnessing the unfolding news story.

The demands of time and technology have traditionally been most heavily felt by agency reporters and television crews. Speed is of the essence in the dissemination of financial information when 'a few seconds can mean a loss of millions of dollars for a client' (Boyd-Barrett and Rantanen, 2001: 139). The acute pressure of deadlines and the technical considerations in getting the story have meant that these reporters tend to have had less autonomy in developing their own stories and more dependence on the home office for their agenda. Simpson (1988) argues that the 'pressure of time is by far the greatest' on the television foreign correspondent. In addition to uncovering the story, 'he or she then has to organise the shooting of the pictures which illustrate that story' as well as overcome the technical and logistical difficulties of getting the pictures home. Boyd-Barrett (1977) notes the high frequency of contact between the agency bureaus and the home office: copy is filed around the clock and this often elicits an immediate response, congratulating and asking for more of the same or criticising and requiring a new 'angle' on the story. With more space and airtime to fill in the 24-hour news culture the pressure on the correspondent in the field has increased. Often during wars and crises, working 16 hours a day with no respite for months at a time is typical (quoted in *Standard Techniques*, 1985).

Feeding the contemporary news machine has become a daunting task. In the days following the Second World War, correspondents such as Christopher Serpell, the BBC's man in Rome from 1945–52, could spend up to a week preparing his coverage of events and would be expected to file twice a week (Fox, 1988). At times of crisis the pressure would mount; thus elections or disasters could lead to a large number of dispatches in a relatively short time. Today what was crisis coverage has become the routine; immediacy is everything. Correspondents are worried about the effects of this on the quality of their reporting. Kate Adie (2002: 415) bemoans that reporters are 'moving *into* the story: popping up on screen to chat to newsreaders, walking around and frequently asked to explain how they themselves "feel" about the situation'. The emphasis on personal emotions, part and parcel of the efforts of television to make news more accessible, is seen as a shift in the culture of international journalism and an obstacle to the ability to tell the story. For others it is the correspondent's lack of time that is the problem. According to a Canadian TV correspondent who was based in Washington: 'It's like a treadmill; you don't have the chance to think about what you're doing that much anymore before they throw you on live to talk about it' (Bivens, 2008: 124).

The result of this time and deadline-dominated culture is that the correspondent has less time to find things out. Boyd-Barrett's survey of agency work in the late 1970s found that 60 per cent of the time of the bureau chief was spent in the office (Boyd-Barrett and Rantanen, 2001: 138). The 'increased dependence on the internet for information will cause journalists to spend more of their time behind a computer screen instead of getting out of the office to properly report stories' (Wu and Hamilton, 2004: 529). In addition to administrative tasks, he or she was involved in writing stories, reading local news sources, editing and filing copy. Most of the news sent out was spot news – 75 per cent of the bureau's words were devoted to this. Maintaining their competitiveness is crucial to wire reporters and many are tied to the television sets in their office to keep abreast of breaking news. Print correspondents are allowed to 'take a more subjective and analytical viewpoint' and have 'greater length in which to explain opposing outlooks and to expound on what might be considered gratuitous criticism if stated briefly' (Rosenblum, 1978: 112). However, with more editions, earlier filing times, pressure on space and additional requirements made of reporters such as blogging and interacting with their readers, newspaper reporters are also facing limitations on the time they have to investigate things.

Technological change has had the greatest impact on the pressures faced by TV news. Kate Adie (2002: 402) notes how TV news selection is 'vulnerable to both commerce and intellectual fancy, and to fashion and technology'. No longer are TV crews scrambling to overcome obstacles such as non-existent transport links, ruined roads and the lack of electricity to be first on the scene. With news agency camera crews on the spot, pictures of unfolding disasters or crises today are being broadcast as the reporter is on her way out to the front line of foreign news. Western camera crews are ceasing to dominate as 'young people in even the poorest countries acquire the skills and scraped up money for professional equipment' (2002: 410). The result is that today we have more non-westerners reporting, covering and supplying news for the western media. 'Going native' is less of a problem as 'the natives' take on the role of the reporter. They cost less and 'travel in buses rather than limos and will not need "fixers" or translators'

(Shuster, 1988). However, the capacity of these non-western correspondents to influence the nature of the reporting is limited by the organisational constraints within which they work. The increased capacity of the home office to exercise surveillance over their men and women in the field ensures a high degree of compliance to the established occupational routines and rules.

Competing international news gatherers

Changes in the way in which foreign correspondents are doing their jobs have been accompanied by competition from new types of international news gatherers. Competition between gatherers of international news has always been apparent: the main competition for space and air time, besides fellow foreign correspondents, has traditionally been diplomatic correspondents. Foreign news at home has been primarily the 'beat' of the diplomatic correspondent although other specialist reporters such as defence and today security correspondents act as domestic based foreign reporters. Briefed by the Foreign and Commonwealth Office (FCO), British diplomatic correspondents often had more credibility in the eyes of the news desks as well as the capacity to get their stories back more quickly (Cohen, 1988). Often, correspondents in the field found themselves having to challenge and question accounts produced from official sources by their colleagues at home. In recent years the concentration of power in the hands of the executive branch of government has increased the power of the political correspondent – whether based at the White House, Number Ten Downing Street or the Elysée Palace. The parameters within which foreign stories are reported are increasingly set by domestic correspondents: hence the tendency to mis-read foreign events through domestic concerns (Fallows, 1997: 197). New technology is blurring the already porous division between news beats and providing the opportunity of marshalling expertise on a new basis, with some editors seeing the possibility of organising international reporting on a transnational basis with 'global beats' on topics such as democracy, human rights and the environment (Erickson and Hamilton, 2007: 142). Bureaus located geographically would be replaced by home based correspondents who would roam the world as required in an operation described as 'parachuting plus', which is something that has been attempted by smaller publications such as the *Irish Times* (Smyth, 2009).

Technology has led 'newsgathering abroad to be moving towards a system of multiple models co-existing and collectively providing information' (Cole and Hamilton, 2008: 806). The emergence of an environment hostile to the 'bureau-based foreign correspondent' has been 'fecund for others' (Hamilton and Jenner, 2004: 313). This includes not only a new type of international news gatherer but also a return to older methods of international information provision. In their typology of foreign correspondents, Hamilton and Jenner (2004: 313–4) identify the 'in-house foreign correspondent' as being employees of non-news organisations or companies who provide information about activities around the world. This is a throwback to the private newsletters of the Fuggers and Rothschilds (see Chapter 2). Unlike the finance houses of early centuries, not only is the information output of modern corporations more public, it is also systematically organised in the form of public relations, the aim of which is to shape what is reported (see Chapter 5). Among the newer types of reporters are *local-foreign* and *foreign-local* correspondents: the latter work for foreign news organisations whose material is available on the web (hence *Le Monde* can be read in Los Angeles and the *Washington Post* can be accessed in New Delhi), while the former represent the increased tendency among local publications around the world to report stories which have international angles. The emergence of global pandemics such as SARS and swine flu, climate change and international migration indicates that telling a local story is increasingly part international (Hamilton and Jenner, 2004: 313).

Perhaps the most significant development is the emergence of the 'amateur' or 'do-it-yourself' correspondent who, with the internet, has the ability to distribute information to rival the reach of international news agencies. Citizen journalists take on many guises, from those who happen to 'be there' when a news event breaks to those involved in more systematic attempts to provide an 'alternative' to mainstream news reporting. The role of the 'citizen journalist' in foreign news gathering often reflects a positive disposition to the liberating dimension of new technology. Computers, camcorders and mobile phones enable ordinary people to become foreign correspondents – to go out and cover international events in their own pictures and words, upload them onto the net and with the click of a button distribute them to the world. Citizens can also cover the world without leaving home and without having any direct experience of the sounds and smells of the streets and fields in which the events being reported take place.

> Many chroniclers of the foreign scene 'travel' without ever leaving home, literally as armchair blogsters or figuratively as hyper-connected correspondents glued to their cellphones and laptops. In either case, the source data, the substitute for raw experience, comes mostly from the same place, the virtual universe of the internet. (Viviano, 2007)

Whether we see amateur reporters as 'active' or 'passive', their activities have increased the amount of international information available. This compensates for the decline in international reporting by the mainstream media. However, there are questions about the quality of this information. In contrast to the claims made about citizen journalism bringing about diversity of accounts, some complain about the 'incestuous' nature of international news on the net.

> The vast majority of those stories are clones of each other, with mind-numbingly scant differences in the range or content of what's reported in Beijing or Moscow, Buenos Aires or Chicago, Bamako or Riyadh. The scope of our potential interests is trimmed down to the barest of common denominators: what we already know, and more alarmingly, what we already think about it, endlessly repeated. (Viviano, 2007)

International news on the internet is also accused of being riddled with 'error, rumour and disinformation that is often difficult to sort out from the authentic and factual' (Hamilton and Jenner, 2002: 18). Assembling contemporary accounts from others on the net is the basis of much amateur foreign correspondence. The anonymity of the information posted calls into question the authenticity of what is reported and of the reporter. Citizen journalists and bloggers argue that internet news is less reliant on official spokespersons and experts, representing the 'voices' of ordinary people. Yet – like their mainstream colleagues – citizen journalists have to negotiate the miasma of sources that push their account of events either on the net or in other ways and, as many traditional journalists would argue, without the skills, experience and training to interrogate them properly.

Sourcing stories

The search for sources of information that enable foreign correspondents to provide a regular supply of news to their home office is crucial. Boyd-Barrett's seminal survey of the INAs found that the local press is one of the most important sources of news for foreign correspondents. Nearly two-thirds of the reporters surveyed identified the local press and media as their main source of information (Boyd-Barrett, 1980: 97). A study of the London foreign press corps in the 1980s found that 53 per cent of those asked claimed the British media as their most important source of information, with the overwhelming majority singling out the press (Morrison and Tumber, 1986: 466). Foreign correspondents traditionally have exercised 'lifting rights'; they take stories direct from the local press and often file them with only a change in the by-line (1986: 466). The local press has been and remains a common and convenient source of news: 'a rule of foreign reporting [is] that a correspondent is as good as the local media' (Hess, 2005: 22). The level of language proficiency, however, determines the ability and capacity to use the local press. The English language press or editions of newspapers around the world are accessed more frequently than their vernacular counterparts. Rosenblum (1978) draws attention to the distorting effect of the inability to speak local languages, noting that agency men and women in Asia make heavy use of the local newspapers in English and tend only to talk with those Asians who speak English or French.

> This can eliminate major streams of national thought since only in the Philippines and the Indian sub-continent are the predominant newspapers in English. Also those Asians who have had the motivation to learn English or French may have an atypical approach towards the affairs of their own country. (Rosenblum, 1978: 123)

While Rosenblum may be accused of exaggeration, he does draw attention to ways in which sourcing information can influence the nature of news-gathering. Reliance on official government and political sources of information is also significant. Chu and Gross (1988) state that Taiwanese based foreign correspondents met most regularly with government officials and legislators and members of the ruling party, the Kuomintang. American correspondents abroad have traditionally relied on US diplomats and the State Department for information and analysis. For many foreign correspondents in Chile in the early 1970s covering the rule of Salvador Allende, whose government was eventually overthrown by a US-supported *coup d'état*, 'the anti-Allende US Embassy was the first stop' (Dorman, 1986: 426). Strict guidelines inform the interaction between correspondents and US diplomats. Conducted under the condition of 'deep background', quotes cannot be directly attributed to Embassy or diplomatic sources – hence the use of phrases such as 'it is generally understood ...' or 'it is widely believed ...' (Pedelty, 1995: 85).

Stringers and freelancers often complain about the close connection between full-time representatives of the mainstream media and their local embassies. They are envious of the special access they gain to information but also draw attention to the uncritical way in which staff correspondents use the information they are fed. This is reinforced by officials who are much more cautious about talking to stringers, as they are likely to deal with information in a more 'critical or at least idiosyncratic fashion' (Pedelty, 1995: 71). Dependence on the embassy in the field is reinforced by what is labelled 'Beltway blindness' (Rosenblum, 1993: 206). Editors at home tend to be more attuned to Washington's reporting of international affairs than the reports of their men and women on the spot. One foreign editor bemoans the reliance of the major US media outlets on Washington's definition of international news stories.

> I think there's an evolution in the wrong direction with the definition of the story increasingly happening in Washington. Great newspapers spend ... $450,000 a year for a correspondent, and then they allow the problems to be defined in Washington more and more. (Rosenblum, 1993: 222)

This dependence has implications for the ability of government and officials to influence the international news agenda (see Chapter 5).

Ways of seeing

The disproportionate reliance on official sources, the daily pressure from the home office for particular stories and story lines and the cultural and social values which shape their perceptions lead some scholars to conclude that the foreign correspondent's working routines correspond with certain ways of seeing the world (Dahlgren and Chakrapani, 1982; Ibrahim, 2003). With correspondents' spending less time in their regions familiarising themselves with the background, history and culture, they are increasingly unable to question or challenge the ideological values or stereotypes that underpin the processes by which news is produced. Dahlgren and Chakrapani distinguish between two ways of interpreting the world: mythic and historical. The former provides meaning to events and issues by referring to the eternal and recurrent aspects of the human condition. They emphasise 'essences', that is, the qualities that are seen as inherent in the nature of people, groups and societies. This contrasts with historical ways of seeing which explain social reality in terms of social, political and economic factors from the past and present. Whereas the historical approach provides the possibility of transition and change, the mythic ossifies the world order in what is, or appears to be, the here and now. TV news, they argue, is dominated by the mythic approach, eschewing historical context. For example, in the reporting of the Third World:

> ... it is not to be expected to remind the audience that the instability of the Third World is at least in part due to the West's role over several centuries. The news merely draws upon and contributes to a convenient cultural amnesia that it did not create. (Dahlgren and Chakrapani, 1982: 54)

Dina Ibrahim (2003) examines the variety of ideological, organisational and personal factors that shape the reporting of correspondents based in the Middle East. She draws attention to the personal baggage that correspondents carry with them, their own individual background and experience and the preconceived notions they bring to understanding the country they are covering. For many, their 'fleeting and superficial exposure to Middle East history and culture ... confirms inaccurate stereotypes of the Arabs' (quoted in Ibrahim, 2003: 92). Nobody would deny that individual perceptions can inform reporting – journalists themselves are aware of this and tend to guard against it as much as possible. However, the cultural and national mindsets that shape understanding are more insidious. Said (1997) emphasises the restricted cultural lens through which reporters cover the Middle East and Islam. He attributes their ethnocentrism to the Euro-centric or 'Orientalist' representation of the Arab World stemming from the interaction with and studies of the region in the eighteenth and nineteenth centuries. Journalists are 'locked ... into their own national mindsets and into the sense of the needs and the comprehension of their audiences' (Smith, 1983: 423). Despite the commitment to objectivity and the deployment of practices designed to cut out personal bias and subjectivity in the reporting of news, journalism operates within a particular worldview, the product of life-long conditioning. This, according to Dorman (1986: 428), shapes not only the news agenda but also what qualifies as news. The performance of western media and western journalism in reporting the world 'is but one of a number of historic processes that cannot be dealt with by lecturing a few journalists or denouncing their employers' (1986: 428).

The failure of western journalism and diplomacy to comprehend and interpret the Third World stems from an in-built, historical set of assumptions of these countries and their relations with the West. There is a limited realisation of how their own cultural background shapes their understanding of events in other cultures. This is manifest in the statement of an editor of one US media outlet during the 1984 Ethiopian famine who stated that 'starving kids in Africa, that's not news, that a way of life' (*Consuming Hunger*, 1988). The doyen of twentieth century realpolitik, former US Secretary of State, Henry Kissinger, summed up the problem more starkly when he said:

> Nothing important can come from the south. History has never been produced in the south. The axis of history starts in Moscow, goes to Bonn, crosses over to Washington and then goes to Tokyo. What happens in the south is of no importance. (Quoted in Dorman and Farhang, 1987: 224)

The motif within which the world is reported is shaped by news values and practices rooted in the cultural understanding journalists and their audiences bring to the part of the world that is reported (see Chapter 6). TV news in the West, and the western media in general, has 'an implied commitment to a particular international order' and reinforces specific 'dispositional orientations' to the various regions of the world grounded in specific political and historical perceptions (Dahlgren and Chakrapani, 1982: 62, 48). This has particular implications for the coverage of Africa, Asia and Latin America, which has for many periods in the post-war years been reported on TV news in terms of violence and disorder.

> Devoid of social, political and historical causation, the manifestation of disorder and violence take on the quality of eternal essences which define the nature of those countries. 'That's just the way they are.' (Dahlgren and Chakrapani, 1982: 53)

The limitations of time and space have traditionally meant that context becomes a taken-for-granted aspect of international news coverage. What is happening to five billion people in more than 200 countries speaking thousands of languages has to be condensed into a highly limited amount of time and space in the world's media. The process of selection 'inevitably distorts' and 'the process of selection … is bound to confer on a few items a huge importance and relegate other matters, people, places and problems to a secondary level of reality, and perhaps oblivion' (quoted in Adams, 1982: 3). Cultural assumptions about the balance of international power and history underpin this process of selection which is 'anchored in particular social locations, both in terms of class relations and hierarchies within a society and between societies' (Dahlgren and Chakrapani, 1982: 62).

This, according to Dahlgren and Chakrapani, leads TV news to foster a mythic approach to the Third World that is 'congruent with the global relations which characterise imperialism' and 'evidences an implied commitment to a particular form of international order' (1982: 62).

Journalists are often limited by the priorities and perspectives of the news organisations they work for. The domestic or national filter appears to be a crucial organisational consideration in determining international news. Broadcasting networks produce news that is largely consistent with the foreign policy of their government (Paterson, 1999 quoted in Nossek, 2004: 347). Most newspapers are national entities which seek to project to their audience a world view compatible with their national outlook of world affairs (Skurnik, 1981: 101). Journalists often have to defer to notions of national morale, national image and national interest (Nossek, 2004: 348). This is particularly true at times of crisis or war involving one's own country when the correspondent's duty as a citizen is more acutely felt. This is often not seen as conflicting with professional goals; in fact the opposite may be true as the 'domestic filter' is considered as incumbent on journalists seeking to address their particular audience (Nossek, 2004: 347).

The natural way in which cultural and national perspective underpin international news can be seen in how reporters often provide the 'foreground' to events, the background of which lies in the taken-for-granted assumptions of the audience which allows the viewer to locate the story and give it meaning. This applies to what the press produces as well. While perhaps not as acute a problem, news and feature stories as well as analysis pieces in the mainstream press often cater to what is assumed to be the cultural understandings and prejudices of their readers. Specialist reporters may try and challenge these assumptions, understandings and prejudices. The 'generalist' approach not only leads to greater dependence on certain sources but also encourages an acceptance of the received wisdom. The ability and capacity of news desks and home editors to ensure they impose national, domestic considerations on their men and women in the field is enhanced in the 24-hour news culture. But even then star reporters have the ability to resist the demands of the news desk – the increased surveillance exercised by news desks in the digital age has to be seen alongside the pulling power of names such as CNN's Amanpour in an increasingly commercial market. Perhaps the most important means by which shared ideological assumptions are reinforced is pack journalism.

Pack journalism

Today the international press corps appears to operate as a pack that continuously moves from one breaking crisis to another. Stanley Karnow, who worked for the *Washington Post* for much of his career, draws attention to the camaraderie of such reporting:

> Show up in Tel Aviv or Srinagar during a crisis and you encounter colleagues who reach back to Kabul or Kinshasa. American, British, French, Russian – you belong to an exclusive international fraternity. The mood is familiar, perhaps a bit boisterous, as you catch up over drinks and dinner, or trade rumours and sources. (Quoted in Hess, 1996: 58)

The effect of this is to make foreign correspondents inward looking and likely to share the same mindsets on the issues they are covering. According to the *New York Times*'s Harrison Salisbury:

> The world of foreign correspondents, diplomats and intelligence agents is parochial. They trade in the same kinds of goods, move from one capital to another, frequent the same bars, go to the same cocktail parties, have the same interests. They know each other. They talk together. We all feed at the same trough. (Quoted in Walker, 1982: 21)

Long stay foreign correspondents find ways of institutionalising their routine interaction through foreign correspondents' clubs which are located in most of the major news centres of the world. The most famous is the Foreign Correspondents Club in Hong Kong, which was founded in the 1940s. Many have their offices in the same building or the same part of town: for example, the *Yomiuri Shimbun* building in Tokyo, the Richmond suburb of Johannesburg and Beit Agron in Jerusalem (Hannerz, 2004: 156–7). Some correspondents have been made to stay in the same compound in certain countries, such as Beijing prior to liberalisation. However, it is the 'roving reporters' who parachute into crisis situations who find themselves under greatest pressure to conform and cooperate with their colleagues. Finding themselves in conditions of ignorance, insecurity and unfamiliarity, the pressures to seek the 'reassuring comfort' of the group are intensified. Dorman and Farhang (1987: 195) describe the pressures on the press pack covering the fall of the Shah in Iran in the 1980s.

> Thrust into a revolutionary situation in an alien culture, lacking a coherent understanding of the historical forces at work, confronted with the intense pressure of successfully

outdistancing equally eager and beleaguered competitors working under similar deadlines and limitations, the typical reporter can only fall back on what appears to be the safe path.

Pack journalism not only provides greater protection but also allows for a far more efficient sharing of resources (Pedelty, 1995: 32). Logistical considerations weigh heavily especially on stringers and freelancers and many reporters, in spite of their awareness of the problems of pack journalism, share in group activities with their fellow press corps colleagues to minimise costs of travel and resources. Even the most independently minded journalist will participate in a pack activity if he or she feels they might be scooped.

Parachute journalists or 'fire-fighters' are forced to make instant judgements based on first impressions, and their colleagues are the first point of call in an environment that is unfamiliar. Simon Hoggart of the *Guardian* emphasises the importance of his 'fellow hacks':

> In real life your fellow hacks are the only people who will tell you what is happening –
> or, more important, what they say is happening. You need to know the received wisdom
> since, if you write anything too different your editor will neither believe it nor print it.
> (Hoggart, 1988: 16)

Hoggart draws attention to the unusual nature of pack journalism – a unique combination of competition and collaboration. The classic objective of the reporter is the scoop. Journalists seek the exclusive story, beating out their rivals sometimes only by a matter of minutes in breaking the news. For scoops to work it is vital that all other reporters in the pack file the story along similar lines. If they do not follow suit then editors, the news desk and the home office may assume there is something wrong with the story. What is defined as newsworthy is largely decided by a story's acceptance by other journalists. The dangers of becoming part of a 'hermetic' group of journalists have been described by several commentators (Crouse, 1972; Gitlin, 1980; Pedelty, 1995).

> Reporters covering the same event find it convenient (and prudent) to borrow angles, issues
> and questions from each other. Borrowed frames help them process a glut of facts – on
> deadline. Especially when reporters are in unfamiliar social territory, and when enough
> of them are clusters in that unfamiliar territory to constitute a social group, they are liable
> to become a *hermetic* group, looking around the circle of reporters, rather than outward
> to the event for bearings. (Gitlin, 1980, quoted in Dorman and Farhang, 1987: 195)

The dangers of this can be that some aspects of a story or event are given disproportionate attention. Rosenblum (1979) provides the example of the reporting of riots in Jamaica in 1975 when hundreds of journalists were visiting the island to attend a meeting of the International Monetary Fund (IMF) at the height of the organisation's dispute with the Third World. One of the leading critics of the IMF was Jamaica's Prime Minister Michael Manley. The visiting journalists played up the riots in their reports, appearing eager to hype up the story of a 'Caribbean isle in flames'. Rosenblum (1979: 12) suggests that such coverage distorted what a correspondent based in the country would have seen as a more commonplace and less significant event. Gathering together in the same cities to cover the same story, staying in the same hotel and socialising together can lead to the emergence of 'a kind of consensus press view' which sometimes can be 'badly adrift' (Walker, 1982: 11).

The comforts, cosiness and convenience of pack journalism can detach reporters form the realities of what is going on around them. They become inured against the suffering and pain that surrounds them. This dislocation is reflected in the comments of some of the correspondents who covered the Biafran civil war in the late 1960s. Looking back on the conflict, Angus McDermid of the BBC made the following observation:

> You had a very heady atmosphere of revolt. Biafra was fighting for its existence. This was a very romantic situation, really nothing like it had occurred in African politics before. It was an excellent news story. (Harrison and Palmer, 1986: 12)

His colleague in the foreign press corps in Nigeria, Michael Leapman, recalled visiting a hospital in Biafra:

> It was the pictures that really made that first story, some marvellous pictures of kids in great distress ... It was very moving stuff. I'd never done much of the heart throbbing, sob-story before: I'd been mainly in diplomatic reporting. (Leapman, quoted in Harrison and Palmer, 1986: 29)

Dealing with the trauma of war, coups and famines, the staple features of international news is a matter for all correspondents. Cynicism, alcohol and denial are part of the way in which many reporters deal with the horrific moments that punctuate the boredom and routines of their job. Camera workers use the lens to distance themselves from what is happening: '... you squint through your lens and it's like watching TV; you don't think it could affect you' (Hoggart, 1988). Another way in which the foreign correspondent can distance themselves from events is to focus on the story. As Simon Hoggart puts it:

> ... what matters in journalism is not 'the truth', whatever that might be, but the 'story', an artificial creation which is fashioned with reality as its raw material. Your true foreign correspondent is an artist, who in the end is hardly more concerned with the facts in front of him than a chef with the vegetables he's slicing. (Hoggart, 1988)

It is deeply ingrained in journalistic culture that journalists are not, or should not, be affected by the stories they cover; it is also presumed that by distancing yourself from events you are able to build sufficient defence against emotional trauma and injury (Brayne, 2004: 280). Cynicism, however, can make journalists more accepting of – or even colluding with the execution of – traumatic acts. Mark Brayne (2004: 281) cites the example of a reporter in Africa who paid a young girl to sit and pose with a baby, placing some dead flies on her face to enhance the dramatic effect. The most famous example of perceived callous indifference is the case of AP photographer Kevin Carter whose picture of a vulture hovering next to a starving child in the Sudan won a Pulitzer prize in 1993. Carter later was to commit suicide, and some associate his death with his failure to help the child in the prize-winning photograph (see Moeller, 1999; Marinovich and Silva, 2001).

Competition and technology appear to have coincided to make news producers become 'less squeamish' about "live" death' (Knightley, 1988: 13). There are political and economic pressures to produce more graphic and vivid pictures. Aid and humanitarian agencies have indirectly relied on the compassionate realism of photojournalists such as Robert Capa and Don McCullin and in latter years on dramatic TV reports to gain public support and attention for their activities (Benthall, 1993: 178). In today's media-saturated world, in which a tsunami of images can overwhelm consumers, the struggle to gain attention is acute. For certain parts of the world deemed less important or for stories considered of a 'second rank' a pictures become all – without dramatic images to fill the story line they will not be covered (*Consuming Hunger*, 1988). These are usually stories from the Third World – sensational or inappropriate images are a matter of concern for non-governmental organisations who, in 1989, issued a code of conduct on images and messages relating to the Third World (Benthall, 1993: 182).

Not all correspondents experience the camaraderie of foreign tours in the same way. John Simpson (1988) believes that 'newspaper correspondents tend to group together – check the facts, agreeing the line, exchanging quotes – but the television correspondent and his crew are on their own'. This he attributes to television news being the 'most competitive medium in modern journalism'. Some print correspondents emphasise the 'loneliness of being a good foreign correspondent' (Marr, 2004: 333). One example is Ryszard Kapuściński, who spent most of his 40 years working for the Polish National Press Agency. Much of this time was spent in Africa where his ability to travel around the continent was hampered by his employer's lack of funds. He often had to cut deals with contacts to hire transport so that he and other journalists who did not have sufficient funds could reach the scene of the latest drama (Brittain, 2007). Travelling on local transport brought him into close contact with local Africans. 'Being alone and lost' was a feature of his working life; for example, he was the only foreign journalist in Luanda during the chaotic and fearful summer of 1975 when the Portuguese left their former colony of Angola. His agency was grateful for his copy, although when his reporting contradicted the official perspective that 'everything happening in Africa was progressive and everyone there was our friend', he was recalled.

It was not Kapuściński's agency copy that enabled him to gain the reputation as a leading foreign correspondent. He was critical of this kind of journalism: 'I knew what I was doing was superficial. The way in which Africa was often reported: "President of Togo went to visit President of the Ivory Coast." It's totally meaningless' (BBC World Service, 2001). He used two notebooks: one allowed him to earn his living with the bread and butter of agency reporting of facts and the other was filled with personal accounts of his travels to remote areas and his experience of living with people. This was published in several celebrated books, such as *Another Day of Life* (1976), *The Emperor* (1978) and *The Shadow of the Sun* (1998). Kapuściński justified the 'literary reportage' he practised on the basis that it conveyed the deeper emotions and feelings that lay behind the events that appear in the news. News journalism was superficial; anyone, he believed, can learn how to report surface truths and statements. The essence of the stories lies in the people, the background and the context within which they take place. This requires 'the experience of being there, lots of reading and lots of your own reflection'.

> I don't belong to the group of journalists who visit a place for one day, or one week, and write about it. I prefer to stay longer to adjust; only then I am able to feel something and write about it. I need time. Empathy is very important. (Quoted in BBC World Service, 2001)

According to Kapuściński (1999), the lone individual searching the world to convey the truth of events has been replaced by 'a mass of media workers who are more or less anonymous'. They 'move in a pack', sweeping across the world to drop in to cover one event at the expense of other equally important occurrences that are taking place. The foreign reporter in the modern world has become 'a pawn to be shifted around the world', no longer the heroic individual who commits him- or herself to bearing witness and unearthing the underlying truths of the world. Kapuściński's approach has been criticised, with his view of foreign correspondents as 'heroes of journalism' dismissed as overly romantic. But his sense of a loss of independence and the growing conformity of international reporting is a view shared among more experienced foreign correspondents.

For many correspondents the most important members of the pack are the local interpreters, translators, guides and drivers, often collectively known as 'fixers', without whom they would not be able to work (Tumber and Webster, 2006: chapter 8). 'An interpreter embodies the adventure of reporting abroad ... he becomes your voice and ears, your cultural advisor in a foreign land, smoothing over your faux pas, offering tips ... (Working, 2004). The importance of these 'local contacts with reality' is not simply assessed in terms of their linguistic or communication skills; they are valued for 'their ability to navigate through tricky situations' and 'willingness to share their background knowledge and views on a situation' (Susanne Goldenberg, quoted in Tumber and Webster, 2004: 106). The intensity of this relationship emphasises the importance attached to 'on-the-spot' reporting as well as the multi-tasking expected of today's foreign correspondent, who has become a 'Jack or Jill of all trades', responsible for a variety of technical and editorial duties previously done by others.

Being 'on the spot'

The decline of the long stay correspondent is usually juxtaposed against the rise of the parachute journalist. The latter is seen as compensating for the former in spite of the many limitations that are attributed to the ability of parachute journalists to gather foreign news. This distinction is misplaced. The 'roving reporter' is not a new invention. The nineteenth century was an era in which the great men and women travelled the world to cover crises and wars. More recently, celebrated reporters such as James Cameron and Martha Gellhorn moved from 'trouble spot' to 'trouble spot' without putting down roots anywhere. Kapuściński covered at least 27 coups and revolutions in Africa alone. The work of these reporters is not usually seen as having suffered as a result of their peripatetic schedule; rather it was often regarded as supplementing the output of locally based reporters. Erickson and Hamilton (2007) believe that the criticism of parachute journalism is often 'misconceived'. Not only do roving reporters provide news organisations with flexibility, they also address the real problems created by the rising costs of international news gathering. The net allows roving reporters to 'keep up with events without being abroad permanently' (2007: 138) and while the worst kind of 'hit-and-run reporting' has its limitations, the experienced parachute journalist can add to the quality of international news.

Perhaps the more pertinent discussion is between the 'on the spot' and 'armchair reporter'. Citizen journalism can produce images and accounts of 'being there', as the reporting of the 2004 tsunami indicate. The vividness and immediacy of their reports enhance the coverage of major breaking news stories. It also makes international news gathering less costly, more efficient and more accessible and open to more people. However, it is changing journalism, making it 'much more visual ... where images are an increasingly dominant part of the news landscape' (Pavik, 2005: 253). In the midst of technological transformation 'something crucial has been lost along the way, something essential to our ability to find meaning in a confusing universe' (Viviano, 2007). The 'technology-driven withdrawal from the lonely, insistent pursuit of direct experience' has impacted on the quality of the information. Investment in journalism has been much more 'in disseminating the news, not the collecting of it' (Pavik, 2005: 261). We may have more ways of finding or accessing news about foreign events but this does not mean that international news gathering is more efficient.

Note

1 A study of film portrayals of foreign correspondents indicates that the 'romantic image' of the correspondents has slowly faded to be replaced by the image of an angst-ridden individual struggling with and often questioning the responsibilities of the job. This is attributed to the growing limitations placed on the freedom of reporters working for mainstream media outlets to make decisions about where to go and what to cover. See Cozma and Hamilton, 2009.

5

'STANDARD TECHNIQUES': NEWS MANAGEMENT AND INTERNATIONAL JOURNALISM

When the President of the United States calls you in and says this is a matter of vital security, you accept the injunction.

AP's General Manager (quoted in Boyd-Barrett, 1980: 149)

PR firms and communications departments operate with impunity because the mainstream media continue to pretend they are not really there.

Joris Luyendijk, *De Volksrant* (2009: 239)

International journalism operates within an environment in which information control, public diplomacy and news management are used to shape the messages and images citizens around the world receive. Propaganda has been a feature of international relations since the birth of the nation-state. However, from the beginning of the twentieth century, governments have attempted to organise their propaganda efforts in a more systematic and structured fashion. The end of secret diplomacy and the advent of mass media technologies coincided to provide the impetus for this development. While propaganda campaigns were waged prior to the First World War, it was during this cataclysmic struggle that governments in the West laid down the components of news management and spin that we recognise today: news departments, press officers, press releases, press conferences, public relations officials and techniques of persuasion and psychological warfare emerged at this time. Propaganda joined military force, economic pressure and diplomacy as the basic instruments by which foreign policy objectives are pursued. Cultural relations became a vital component of the conduct of international politics, with agencies such as United States Information Agency (USIA), Alliance Française, the Japan Foundation, the Goethe Institute and the British Council playing an integral role in the promotion of national policy. International radio has been, and continues to be, in the world of the internet and satellite, a key instrument of diplomacy, persuasion and even intimidation. In some countries the lack of a domestic radio infrastructure means that international radio stations are their main sources of news and information.

Propaganda, secrecy, censorship and political control confront the work of foreign correspondents. This was never more apparent than during the Cold War. While it sometimes broke out into 'hot wars', usually fought on the territories of the Third World, the Cold War was primarily a 'struggle for men's minds', an ideological battle to convince people of the value of two sets of ideas (Foreign and Commonwealth Office memo, 1951 quoted in Taylor, 1999: 227). A range of 'standard techniques' were deployed by state agencies, such as the Central Intelligence Agency (CIA) and in Britain the FCO's International Research Department (IRD) and the British Information Services (BIS), to manage the news and manipulate international journalism. Journalists either served as innocent dupes or active participants in this struggle. During the Cold War there was a thin dividing line between journalism and espionage, fuelled by revelations in the 1970s that the CIA had infiltrated western and foreign news organisations and used stringers as part of its disinformation campaign (Boyd-Barrett, 1977: 26). One of the Soviet Union's most celebrated double agents – Kim Philby – worked as a correspondent for the *Economist*, the *Observer* and *The Times*. William Dorman (1985) argues that US journalists during the Cold War were 'accustomed to accepting the dictates of "national security" and Washington's view of the world'. Since the end of the Cold War the national security state has been replaced by the PR State. PR plays a central role in the cultivation of national images in international relations. Governments, including many from the Third World, have employed PR agencies with some success to change coverage of their countries in the world's media. Traditionally, the attempt by Third World governments to influence the way in which their countries have been reported is discussed in terms of the harassment, physical threats and the badgering and bullying of foreign correspondents. Today, image management and information control are increasingly resorted to.

This chapter traces the evolution of international media management, from initial attempts to coordinate international propaganda through the days of the Cold War to the contemporary efforts of PR agencies to shape how and what foreign correspondents report. The impact of new media technology on the ability to set the international news agenda is explored. Some governments fearful of the new technology have responded in traditional ways: banning satellite dishes, making agreements to restrict access to the internet and vigorously prosecuting and pursuing those who 'hack' into privileged information systems. Their efforts can be seen as 'Canute-like' in the face of the transformation that is taking place. It is simply not possible to roll back the 'information society'. Incorporating information and propaganda into policy planning and making is a feature of contemporary foreign policy. Part of this is the increasingly sophisticated use of the techniques of persuasion to influence the practice of international journalism. Journalism has adapted in two broad ways: collusion and confrontation. These responses will be compared and contrasted in different societies.

International public relations

International public relations activity is associated with the contemporary forces of globalisation. American PR companies, however, have acted for overseas governments since the 1930s; during this decade they worked for the Czechoslovakian, German and Cuban governments (Alleyne, 1997: 55). Many of the techniques of persuasion that pervade the contemporary world were developed in the early twentieth century. We can trace these back to the First World War when the British government established several mechanisms to manage information, the news media and international journalism. The News Department of the FCO was set up at the start of the war with the dual responsibility of the projection of Britain overseas and the release of information to the British and foreign press about events happening abroad. Unlike the rest of the wartime propaganda apparatus it was not dismantled at the end of the conflict. The FCO recognised the growing importance of publicity and press relations to its operations. As one official wrote in 1925:

> The era when it was possible either to lead opinion in foreign politics by mere authority or tradition, or to ignore it from Olympian heights, has long since vanished, and once modern contact, however vulgar, has been established, it is not possible to confine it to an intermittent dispensation of tit-bits of news at the will of one or two minor officials ... It has now become, and must be, practically a never ceasing intercourse with the publicity world. (Taylor, 1994: 324)

Establishing a regular supply of information about international politics to the press became a goal of most liberal democracies during inter-war years. Diplomatic correspondents were used to further the aims and policies of the FCO. It was realised that 'with a certain degree of openness and flattery diplomatic correspondents could be welded into a cohesive body which could be relied on always to put the Foreign Office point of view in the press' (Cockett, 1989: 16). The function of the News Department was 'not only the supply of day to day news but to educate the different organs of publicity along the lines of the foreign policy pursued by the government' (1989: 17). Rex Leeper, the head of the News Department for most of the inter-war period, insisted it was 'a highly important duty of His Majesty's missions (abroad) to assist British correspondents', although he was not successful in convincing many in the diplomatic service at this time that they should embrace the press. It was in the 1930s that the value of publicity was recognised by government and the power of propaganda deemed important in the prosecution of international relations.

It was the struggle between capitalism and communism that galvanised the international propaganda war. The Russian Revolution in 1917 sparked a major PR campaign against Bolshevism and Soviet Russia. Whipping up the 'Red Scare', a coalition of corporate, media and government interests in the US was responsible for the 'implantation of the Bolsheviks in the American mind as the epitome of all that was evil' (McNair, 1995: 161). Soviet propaganda sought initially to spread a class based ideology which did not recognise national boundaries: 'Workers of the world unite, all you have to lose is your chains.' Lenin and other Bolshevik leaders recognised the power of radio to promote their message of change to workers around the Soviet Union and throughout the world: he described the medium as 'a newspaper without paper ... and without boundaries' (Lenin, quoted in Taylor, 1995: 205). By the mid-1920s Moscow was home to the 'most powerful radio station in existence' broadcasting in English to the rest of the world (Jowett and O'Donnell, 1999: 130). Radio played an essential role in international politics in the 1920s and 1930s. By the early 1930s most of the world's powers were disseminating their worldviews by radio to the rest of the world, and the centrality of the medium to international communication was cemented in 1932 when the League of Nations set up its own station broadcasting in three languages, French, Spanish and English (1999: 131).

The rivalry between the US and the Soviet Union was suspended to engage in the all-embracing struggle against Fascism that consumed the 1930s and culminated in the Second World War. Central to the struggle was the Spanish Civil War, a dress rehearsal for 1939–45, in which propaganda techniques and methods were deployed in what is described as 'the major battlefield in the international propaganda war of the 1930s' (Taylor, 1995: 207). Portrayed as a struggle between 'good' and 'evil' by both sides, nearly 1,000 newspaper correspondents went to Spain (Preston, 2008b: 15). Among them were some of the great names of journalism and literature, including Ernest Hemingway, George Orwell, Antoine de Saint-Exupéry, André Malraux, Martha Gellhorn, John Dos Passos, Arthur Koestler, Sefton Delmer and Herbert Matthews. They were subjected to an unprecedented degree of control, censorship and manipulation. Correspondents were expelled, their output rigorously scrutinised and their reputations vilified if they were deemed wanting. One correspondent believed that the war 'ushered in a new and more dangerous phase in the history of newspaper reporting' (2008b: 17). Correspondents were targeted and several were killed, including Reuters' star reporter of the day, Richard Sheepshanks (Preston, 2007: 234). Character assassination accompanied death threats. The Roman Catholic Archdiocese of Brooklyn organised a campaign against *New York Times* correspondent Herbert Matthews and his reporting, which led to the newspaper losing readers (2007: 235). Matthews and many of his fellow reporters working for American papers complained about news desks changing copy, editing out material sympathetic to the Republican side or simply not using their material. Matthews criticised editorial policy at the *New York Times* thus:

> The publisher laid down a mechanical, theoretically impartial, plan of operation – print both sides, equal prominence, equal length, equal treatment. This often meant equality for the bad and the good – the official handouts hundreds of miles from the front lines with the eye witness stories, the tricky with the honest, the wrong and the right. I say that not only I, but the truth suffered. (Matthews, quoted in Deacon, 2008: 404)

Many in the field believed the home office was more susceptible to accounts sent by Franco's propaganda machine, and this was compounded by the unwillingness to let the reporter in the field apportion blame or make judgements about the claims and counter claims. Draconian censorship and the rigorous policing of access by the Nationalist side also meant that the activities of Franco's forces were not subject to the same degree of scrutiny. Those who did not convey Nationalist propaganda uncritically incurred the disapproval of the Generalissimo's news managers and could expect 'rough treatment' (Deacon, 2009).

Following the end of the Second World War the importance of propaganda and information management was recognised by the establishment of several key agencies. The Voice of America (VOA), which was founded in 1942, was converted into the radio arm of the US State Department in 1948 as part of an international information strategy designed 'to promote a better understanding of the United States in other countries' (Taylor, 1995: 34). In 1950, as the Cold War developed, the Campaign for Truth, later re-designated the Crusade for Freedom, was launched following the outbreak of the Korean War with the objective:

> to generate world wide confidence in American leadership of the free world, counter misrepresentation and misconceptions about US intentions, reassure the international community of American aspirations for peace ... and to undermine confidence in Communist regimes. (1995: 35)

In 1953 the United States Information Agency (USIA) was set up to coordinate this campaign and to oversee activities such as student exchange schemes, international broadcasting and the cultural activities of the diplomatic attachés (Snow and Taylor, 2006: 394). It was the task of Radio Liberty and

Radio Europe – set up in the same year under the direction of the CIA – to disseminate the message to the peoples of Eastern Europe and the Soviet Union. Clandestine radio was a feature of the Cold War world of the 1950s and 1960s (Boyd, 2003). By the mid-1960s USIA employed over 10,000 people and had a budget of $200 million, four times more than was spent on official domestic broadcasting, and was transmitting radio broadcasts to countries on every continent (Schiller, 1973: 45). Among those who sat on the Board overseeing the USIA's work was a former head of CBS News, the editor of the *Reader's Digest* and the pollster George Gallup (Schiller, 1973: 46). Journalists and editors also participated in USIA programmes – most significantly one of America's leading broadcasters, Edward R Murrow headed up the agency under President John Kennedy. The pull of serving the nation in the international arena appeared in the eyes of many reporters to have less of an impact on their professional commitment than political associations in the domestic sphere would have.

The budget of USIA grew six-fold between 1963 and 1993 but the staff declined by 25 per cent (Nye, 2004: 104). The resources devoted to waging the information war against the Soviet Union dwindled with détente and the thawing of US–USSR relations and the eventual collapse of Communism. Spending on official information services fell by 10 per cent in the decade following the end of the Cold War and in 1999 USIA was incorporated into the State Department (2004: 104). The number of cultural exchanges dropped, cultural centres around the world were closed and the number of radio hours broadcast internationally collapsed. Only after 9/11 did the US government start to reinvest in information and propaganda activities and then to such an extent that surveillance, control and information warfare became more pronounced in the 'war on terror' than they ever were during the Cold War.

The decline in official government information activity since the 1990s must be seen in the context of the rise of corporate PR around the world, and in particular its deployment in campaigns on behalf of Third World governments. Herb Schiller (1973: 133) noted in the 1970s that the migration of American capital overseas ensured that PR became an 'international phenomenon'. People around the world became aware of the PR activities of US firms in their countries, 'to create a favourable climate for products, services and the corporation itself' (1973: 134). Within a decade governments and business around the world were employing PR firms to promote their political and commercial interests as well as improve their image in the US. One study showed that after Argentina, Indonesia, South Korea, the Philippines and Turkey hired American PR firms, positive coverage of each country in the *New York Times* increased (Albritton and Manheim, 1985). The global PR agencies' business in 2006 was estimated to be worth US$7 billion and employed more than 50,000 people (Sriramesh and Vercic, 2007). A study of the South Korean press indicated that 'news events selected by government public relations are more likely to be covered in international news' (Kim and Yang, 2008). A highly successful PR campaign was conducted by Hill-Knowlton for the Kuwaiti government during the first Gulf War. The creation of Iraqi atrocity stories such as the plucking of babies from incubators in Kuwaiti hospitals and throwing them to the floor was instrumental in mobilising public opinion in the US in favour of Operation Desert Storm, the intervention to liberate Kuwait (Moorcraft and Taylor, 2008: 156).

Embracing PR methods represented a shift in many countries, from attempts to directly control the correspondent to the manipulation and management of his or her information environment. The harassment of reporters has been a feature of international journalism. Expulsion, imprisonment, arrest, detention, violence and death have figured among the means by which governments have attempted to restrict the reporting of their societies. During the height of the Cold War, foreign correspondents working in Moscow and Eastern Europe were subject to surveillance, questioning and expulsion. Kelly (1978: 19) describes the threat of expulsion as a 'fairly global phenomenon', which often leads to reporters censoring themselves. The threat is more acute for freelancers or stringers who do not have the backing of a news organisation. It is possible for news organisations to replace their correspondent. However, according to the *Washington Post*'s David Ottaway, who was expelled from Ethiopia in the late 1970s, every correspondent has to balance 'telling it as it is' with the need to deal with the sensitivities of local governments (1978: 20). Western correspondents have been critical of the way in which many Third World governments have treated them (Meisler, 1978). At the most extreme end is physical intimidation, such as the public beating dealt out to an AP correspondent by Emperor Bokassa of the Central African Republic in late 1970s. More recently the destruction of Al-Jazeera's office in Kabul by Coalition Forces in 2001 could be seen as a warning to those whose reporting is deemed to threaten western interests (Gowing, 2003: 234).

The use or threat of physical violence and other direct methods of harassment are usually seen as crude and counterproductive. Direct censorship is also inefficient at controlling foreign reporters. Correspondents could always get around direct censorship of their copy by going to a neighbouring country to file or asking someone else to take their report out of the country. Today mobile telephony enables reporters – as well as ordinary citizens – to get pictures and reports to the outside world. The recent riots in Tehran were seen throughout the world via the mobile phones of the ordinary citizens caught up in the demonstrations. The government eventually responded by closing down the mobile telephone network inside the country. Direct methods of containing correspondents are taking a back seat to other forms of control over what correspondents do. Four forms of indirect censorship have been identified as prevailing in most societies: censorship by visa, customs, access and use of facilities (Stone, 1980: 222). Governments have regularly denied visas to correspondents to prevent coverage. Delaying equipment clearing customs can also impede the reporting, and often the facilities necessary to edit and transmit stories can be denied or suddenly fail. During Mrs Ghandi's state of emergency the Indian authorities cut the telephone and tele-printer lines of several foreign agencies in Delhi (Rosenblum, 1981: 231). Denial of access to events and personnel is also used. With no-one available to talk on the record or an inability to gain access to meetings or areas where events are unfolding, the work of the correspondent is made more difficult. This has led some correspondents to argue that practising journalism according to western standards in dictatorial or semi-dictatorial societies is an impossible task (Luyendijk, 2010). Joris Luyendijk, who reported the Middle East for many years for the Dutch newspaper *De Volkskrant*, notes that many of the facts and statistics emanating from government sources and the indigenous media in the Middle East are 'unreliable or falsified', and human interest stories are almost impossible to write as the 'man-in-the-street' is 'afraid to talk' and women are not allowed to speak at all (Luyendijk, quoted in Kester, 2010: 55). The inaccessibility and unreliability of sources is 'one of the most important restrictions correspondents are met with when working under dictatorships' (2010: 55). In the post-9/11 world the integration of information and communication at the heart of government strategy has accentuated the difficulties international journalism has had to confront in using sources in democratic societies.

Total information control post-9/11

The launch of the global 'war on terror' following 9/11 brought about a significant re-arrangement of the 'architecture' supporting the communication infrastructure deployed for international information warfare (Winseck, 2008). The rise of a 24/7 global communication environment, the advent of new and more powerful information technologies and the all-embracing threat of global terror have combined to extend information operations and put them on a par with military power as a means of exerting American influence and pursuing US foreign policy objectives. Robin Brown (2003: 90–2) describes three different approaches to using communications as a tool of influence: public diplomacy, news management and information operations. Aspects of all three approaches have been used in the 'war on terror' but the deployment of information operations is seen by many scholars as a qualitative change in the history of propaganda (Brown, 2003; Miller, 2004; Winseck, 2008).

The objective of information operations is 'full spectrum dominance', which implies – in the words of the Pentagon – 'that US forces are able to conduct prompt, sustained and synchronised operations with combinations of forces tailored to specific situations and with access to and freedom to operate in all domains – space, sea, land, air and information' (quoted in Miller, 2004: 7). Information is an 'element of combat power', and waging the information war today goes beyond the traditional conceptions of propaganda and PR, in which a message is crafted and disseminated via the state or private media (2004: 8). David Miller (2004) identifies two new elements that differentiate information operations from previous propaganda efforts: the 'integration of propaganda and psychological operations into a much wider conception of information warfare' and the incorporation of information as the 'core of military strategy'. It includes 'surveillance, control or destruction of communication networks, psychological warfare and propaganda and more routine methods of public affairs and media relations' (Winseck, 2008: 420).

The news media and journalism have been more systematically integrated into the US government's 'total information strategy'. Embedding journalists with military units in combat zones was a feature of the 2003 Gulf War. Putting journalists in uniform has antecedents: the British correspondents who covered the First World War were given the rank of major and became part of the military command (Knightley, 2003). Western reporters have increasingly covered Afghanistan embedded with NATO forces, two losing their lives in attacks by the Taliban in early 2010. Information deemed 'unfriendly' is regulated by the ability to 'deny, degrade and destroy ...' (Miller, 2004: 11). This has involved both the attacks on Al-Jazeera offices in Kabul, Basra and Baghdad in which journalists have lost their lives, and attempts to discredit critical journalism.

The incorporation of the independent media into the propaganda efforts around the reconstruction of Iraq is another example of the blurring of boundaries between the media and the PR state. The major US networks, ABC, NBC, CBS and Fox all joined in, supplying programmes, expertise and know-how to the service that initially replaced Iraqi state television, something the President of CBS deemed the 'patriotic thing to do' (Miller, 2004: 12). The US news media had become 'cheerleaders' (Schechter, 2004: 27) with the exception of CNN whose status as a 'global news organisation' made it 'inappropriate to participate' in a United States government video transmission.

The ability to keep the US media 'on team' has waned as the 'war on terror' has proceeded and international public opinion and domestic opinion in the US have hardened against the interventions in Iraq and Afghanistan. According to CNN's Christine Amanpour the US media 'got its spine back' in 2007 (quoted in Moorcraft and Taylor, 2008: 199). However, as veteran reporter Nik Gowing (2009: 20) notes, the environment in which international reporting has taken place since 9/11 is characterised by a 'shocking official intolerance by some in power' to journalism and information gatherers; 'the price of truth has gone up grievously' with the large number of reporters killed since 2003. It is not just journalists who have suffered; individual witnesses whose access to new technology has enabled them to record events others do not want shown have been in the firing line (Gowing, 2009: chapter 4).

Institutional intolerance towards the media, journalism and independent witnesses covering international events is apparent with governments around the world. Concerns about this development led the UN Security Council to pass a resolution in 2006 asserting the right of journalists to work freely and safely in conflict situations (Gowing, 2009: 20). Terrorist organisations have also targeted journalists, kidnapping and in some cases – such as the *Wall Street Journal*'s Daniel Pearl – killing them, in order to seize the news agenda. Al-Qaeda has used new technology and the media to broadcast their message across the world. Hezbollah has its own TV station, Al-Manar, which has served to rally the organisation's own supporters and communicate its views to the world: repeated attempts by the Israeli air force in 2006 failed to put the station out of action. Such acts attest to the centrality of the media and journalism to contemporary public diplomacy. The branding of countries as tourist destinations or investment opportunities as well as promoting cultural events, attaining foreign policy objectives and managing international public opinion have widened the information activities of governments. They have become more sophisticated at using the media and targeting journalists. Reporting and interpreting international relations has never been more challenging (Kendall, 2009). The relationship between foreign correspondents and government has become more complicated with the blurring of the boundary between peace and war following the trauma of 9/11. The 'war on terror' has produced a perpetual state of information warfare, the intensity of which has made the foreign correspondent more vulnerable to physical threat and psychological manipulation. Add to this new international information sources such as human rights groups and humanitarian organisations, as well as new information channels such as the internet, and it is clear that the international information environment has never been busier. The efforts of reporters to make sense of what is happening are more problematic than ever – a situation made worse by the 24/7 news culture which demands instant judgements.

Global propaganda machines

National governments and multinational corporations are powerful actors in the production of global information and propaganda but, during the postwar years, there has been an unprecedented growth of other international information producers. International organisations and non-governmental agencies (NGOs) have expanded and developed their 'news machines'. Cultivating the international media and in particular their reporters on the ground has become a feature of their operations. Perhaps the most significant global actor is the United Nations system. The specialised agencies of the UN such as the World Health Organization (WHO), UN High Commissioner for Refugees (UNHCR), the International Labour Organization (ILO) and the World Bank are major news and information providers. At the heart of this 'global information machine' is the Department of Public Information, which in 1999 employed more than 700 people with a budget of US$135million (Alleyne, 2003: 34). This vast 'international information service' generates a huge amount of material on a variety of topics in several languages every year. For many years the organisation paid several major newspapers around the world – including *Le Monde* in France, *El Pais* in Spain and *Asahi Shimbun* in Japan – to publish a 'World Newspaper Supplement' (Alleyne, 2003: 67). The publication was seen as a guarantee of 'the best coverage of the realities of the Third World in the news media of the developed countries and in order to avoid the risks of trivialisation, sensationalism or insufficient journalistic coverage' (Alleyne, 2003: 69). However, it caused controversy, and some major donors from the West looked on it as promoting propaganda, especially in the support provided for a NWICO. The effectiveness of the UN's information effort is a matter of debate. For some the effort is an antidote to the failings of a global news system that neglects many parts of the world and many issues that are crucial for large numbers of people. For others it is a vast bureaucracy that generates a huge amount of paper that piles up in the corridors of its Department of Public Information in New York.

One means by which the effectiveness of the UN's information operation could be judged is as a source of information for international journalism. The UN beat has never developed as a major source of international news. The more than 200 correspondents accredited at the UN in New York tend to report on the activities of their national delegations and the set piece debates in the Security Council during major crisis events such as the Gulf War. New media, such as OhmyNews, have UN based reporters but bodies such as the General Assembly gain little coverage – unless it is reporting the speech of a leading international political actor, usually at the height of an international crisis. Similarly, UN conferences are subject to coverage that stresses national angles and frames the events in the context of the host nation. Anthony Giffard's study of the reporting of the 1995 Beijing Women's Conference by the INAs found that America and China dominated the references to nations in the coverage (Giffard, 1999). China's approach to human rights, its policy on Tibet and its government's logistical organisation of the conference were the main themes in the agency copy filed. The size of the UN 'beat' contrasts with the Brussels press corps, which has grown rapidly with the expansion of the EU and NATO. Most of these correspondents believe that EU press officers support their own nationals (Morgan, 1995; Gavin, 2001: 303). Reporting of the EU is framed through national perspectives – successive studies of the British media have shown how national attitudes, interests and prejudices shape the coverage of Europe (Anderson and Weymouth, 1999). Supranational bodies such as the UN and EU struggle to gain coverage that moves beyond national perspectives in spite of the efforts they put into news management and public information provision. Research has shown that national identity plays a crucial role in the selection of foreign news and the media 'tend to project a world view compatible with their nation's outlook on world affairs' (Skurnik, 1981: 101), primarily in circumstances in which a foreign news item is defined as 'ours' (Nossek, 2004).

Since 1945 supranational agencies have been joined on the world stage by a large number of international non-government actors. The number has increased enormously; the UN in 1998 accredited 1,550 such organisations (Alleyne, 2003: 127). They vary from the larger, better resourced and more well known organisations such as Oxfam, Save the Children, Médecins Sans Frontières (MSF), World Vision and the International Red Cross to smaller resource-poor groups, many of whom struggle inside the Third World. Much of the attention has focused on the larger, well-known western NGOs who have been able to take advantage of the opportunities provided by new media technologies and devote resources to developing their information-gathering and news dissemination activities (Fenton, 2009). They are involved more than ever in the gathering and dissemination of international news, using the growing variety of communication technologies available. This is both in cooperation with and competition to mainstream media outlets. In some cases they act as their own news agencies or use new media technology to speak directly to audiences (Abbott, 2009). Their motivation is twofold: to ensure that they 'brand' their organisation and to redress the imbalances in mainstream media reporting. Simon Cottle and David Nolan (2009) argue that 'the increasingly crowded NGO aid field produces a situation where more organizations are now chasing public and government funds' and are as a result more concerned with promoting their own organisational profile.

Aid agencies have generally been critical of the international news media, accusing them of offering sensational coverage and exploitative images and paying limited attention to the problems of poverty, disaster and suffering in the Third World (Benthall, 1993). Journalists have responded by criticising the failure of NGOs to alert the international community to impending crises such as the 1984 Ethiopian famine, which took considerable time to become a story in the international media (Gill, quoted in *Consuming Hunger*, 1988; see discussion in Philo, 1993; Franks, 2006). Using the media has become crucial to the operation of NGOs to the extent that:

packaging information and images in conformity to the media's known predilections has now become institutionalised inside aid agencies, whether this means putting a number on death tolls, featuring celebrities or 'making it visual' because 'nothing sells a story like a good picture'. (Cottle and Nolan, 2009)

Working closely with western reporters has been a feature of the news operations of NGOs and aid agencies. Some western reporters have had their trips to the Third World sponsored by international NGOs. This has been described as 'beneficent embedding' (Cottle and Nolan, 2009). Today aid agencies prepare, pitch and produce their own stories for the mainstream media. Many perceive a 'trend of NGOs filling in for journalists'. One reporter relates an example of this when, following elections in East Timor, his editors pulled him off of the story and instead instructed him to 'just leave the [phone] numbers for key NGO [staff], and if we needed something we would get it from them' (Abbott, 2009). A clearer example of this development occurred during Cyclone Nargis in Burma, when a package filmed by Jonathan Pearce, a press office at the aid agency Merlin, led the BBC Ten O' Clock News on 18 May, 2008. The item was re-voiced by a BBC correspondent but with the exception of 32 seconds all of the two-and-a-half minute report was filmed by Merlin (Cooper, 2009). The benefits are apparent: news organisations receive content at little or no cost while aid agencies are able to reach larger audiences. More aid agencies are employing journalists to manage their information operations. NGOs are adapting the content of their information output to fit pre-established journalistic norms and values, and according to Natalie Fenton (2009), this media logic has led to 'news cloning'. They provide news that 'mimics, or indeed matches' the requirements of mainstream news media. The larger NGOs cooperate with the mainstream news on a daily basis, attempting to provide ready-made copy to help the news organisations fill the ever-expanding space for news in the digital age. This has consequences for the NGOs and the news media.

The relationship between the mainstream media and NGOs has always been close; journalists have always used NGO experts for news tips, quotes, and access (Abbott, 2009). The decline in foreign correspondents and foreign bureaus has encouraged the growth of the media operations of the NGOs. They are today:

... doing even more: researching and pitching stories, sharing contacts, developing content and providing logistics, guidance, analysis, opinion and, in some cases, funding. Put simply, without the help of these groups, many foreign news stories would not be told at all. (Abbott, 2009)

They 'can and are helping to address the foreign news gap' but while this may appear beneficial to some, reservations are expressed on both sides (see Cooper, 2009). One Africa correspondent has communicated her wariness at the new set-up, expressing the concern that it produces an abundance of tragic images for the audience back home (Hogge, 2007). As with being embedded with the military, many reporters worry that such arrangements compromise editorial integrity and impair credibility. Often, news organisations and individual correspondents have to weigh these concerns against the benefits that are presented in terms of access and funding. Conscious that producing international stories is an increasingly expensive venture, there is a blurring of professional boundaries. In their search for the story, editors and correspondents are increasingly subject to pressures that force them to make compromises. These pressures have always been present: for example, Michael Buerk was only able to reach Tigray to film his reports of the 1984 Ethiopian famine because the NGO World Vision provided a plane for him (Franks, 2010: 79). World Vision complained to Buerk's BBC employers that their contribution had not been fully and adequately acknowledged, highlighting the dynamics of the relationship between aid agencies and media organisations.

Standard techniques

Corporations, governments, international bodies and NGOs around the world are adept at using the media and managing information for their own ends. The manipulation of news by official bodies and by intelligence agencies has only been documented in recent years – and then only partially and selectively – owing to the lack of transparency surrounding these operations in most countries. The Freedom of Information Act in the US has enabled scholars to examine some of the CIA's disinformation practices. The term 'standard technique' is used to describe the practice most other people would label as 'disinformation'. The Agency has, over the years, deployed a variety of covert strategies of information management to influence the reporting of major international events. Christopher Hird, in a documentary for the British TV network Channel Four, identified some of these strategies in relation to US intervention in the Angolan civil war in the late 1970s and in Central America in the 1980s (*Standard Techniques*, 1985).

Angola gained independence from Portugal in 1974 and, following a left-wing revolution, it was selected as a target for a covert action operation using some of the hundreds of CIA 'covert action' specialists who had been re-deployed back home from Vietnam and Cambodia following the end of US intervention in Southeast Asia. It was estimated that a third of the CIA personnel working on the 'Angolan campaign' were assigned to 'disinformation duties'. Operating from London, Lisbon, Lusaka and Kinshasa the primary role of these operators was to invent stories about the war in Angola that discredited the government of Agostino Neto and his ally, Cuba, which had sent troops to support him. Hird describes how working from the US

Embassy in Lusaka, CIA operatives concocted stories that were fed to the Reuters correspondent, who in turn passed the material on to London for dissemination. The Reuters correspondent explained how it was impossible to check or verify what appeared to be 'official' communiqués emanating from Angola, even though it was later shown that many of these CIA- inspired stories about the war were pure fabrications. He describes the pressure that agency correspondents are under and which are exploited by those who seek to manage the news. First, all that was wanted by the news organisations subscribing to Reuters was a flow of information, the more sensational and dramatic the better. Stories that fitted this bill tended to move more quickly through the newsgathering and -processing system. Second, the correspondent was working long hours and had little time or resources to check the veracity of the vast amount of information passing through the Reuters office in Lusaka for transmission worldwide. At the time it was difficult to get reporters into the country and hubs such as Lusaka were crucial sources of news about the war. The reason why many stories, especially those from 'official' sources, are taken on trust by the agencies is the intense competition to be first with the news. The news organisations that are the clients of the INAs have little or no opportunity themselves to check what they are told: the agency is their only sources for many international stories and without their own correspondents on the ground they cannot check the accuracy or veracity of what is reported. Some argue that it is not their job to do this. The then diplomatic editor of the *Daily Telegraph* argued that it is not the job of a newspaper to decide what is true or not but simply to reproduce what it is told and acknowledge the source.

The ability of the disinformation specialist to succeed relies on exploiting the routine practices of international journalism. Disinformation techniques depend for their effectiveness on being first with the news. It does not matter that the stories are later shown to be false. As one ex-CIA analyst tells Hird: 'It's the initial charge that makes the headline – people tend not to notice a retraction published days or weeks later on the inside pages.' As well, the predisposition of news rooms to certain stories is a crucial factor in the success of such operations. One of the fabricated stories that appeared in the pages of many of the world's newspapers during the Angolan civil war was about Cuban soldiers who had raped young Angolan women and after their capture were executed by a firing squad made up of some of the same women. Western newsrooms were receptive to stories about 'Cuban rapists' as they fitted the 'news frame' better than stories about Cuban troops in Angola behaving well and gaining the confidence of the local population.

The selection of news, what is left out as well as what appears, is often filtered by the stereotypical assumptions that are held of the people and the part of the world they emanate from. Thus western news accounts of Africa are often shaped by western perceptions of the continent. In 1983 independent film-maker David Kline brought back the first pictures of the major famine that was developing in Ethiopia – this was nearly a year before the BBC's Michael Buerk and his cameraman Mohammed Amin broke one of the biggest post-war international news stories in October 1984. Kline could not get the US news networks interested in the story because the pictures were not deemed 'strong enough'. Most editors saw starvation as commonplace in Africa and hence not newsworthy; as one editor told him, 'starving kids in Africa, that's not a story – it's a fact of life' (*Consuming Hunger*, 1988). The lack of interest can be attributed to notions of what makes good television but it was also shaped by the stereotypical perceptions of Africa shared by many editors.

Reliance on official sources is central to the ability and capacity of spin doctors to shape the nature of international news. Getting the story out is the primary function of the foreign correspondent – although the pressure to be first with the news varies according to the media the reporter works for. A regular and reliable source of news is vital to this activity, and finding sources in a foreign country and foreign environment is a major challenge. The most reliable source is the correspondent's own eyes (Rosenblum, 1993: 105). Audiences are encouraged to believe correspondents gather their own news stories and witness the events they are describing – terms such as 'eyewitness' figure in the titles of news programmes, especially in the US. However, few correspondents are fortunate enough to witness the events they are reporting and many of the stories they report are not subject to such coverage. Even being there does not guarantee you are able to understand what is going on – getting a full picture of a disaster and its aftermath is often not within the purview of one reporter. Correspondents have to rely on 'well placed' or 'highly reliable' sources or 'sources close to ...' an event or an actor in an event. Most of these sources are unnamed and official. Preserving the anonymity of sources is a feature of all journalism. In many parts of the world preserving the anonymity of sources is crucial; the consequence of providing critical information to the foreign media in a closed society can be fatal. Rosenblum (1993: 131) describes the importance of local journalists in these societies and the dangers under which they work. However, unnamed sources have their disadvantages in that they:

> ... covered laziness and sloppiness, and they allowed politicians to float ideas or take pot shots from safe cover. In foreign dispatches, editors had few means to weigh their true value. (1993: 108)

More crucially, they build up a dependency. Official sources are best organised to meet the demand of a regular news flow. New technology, financial problems and dwindling media resources have strengthened international journalism's dependency on official sources – governments and corporations are feeding information directly into newsrooms around the world, bypassing traditional channels. For example, the US Department of Defense's policy of embedding reporters with the military in the field has been accompanied by the growth of operations such as 'The Pentagon Channel' and the US Army's Digital Video and Imagery System (DVIDS). According to a DVIDS spokesperson, 'we provide a pipe, a trough of products for national, local and military media' (Zewe, 2004). The Pentagon Channel serves, in the words of a deputy assistant secretary for defence, as 'the megaphone for the Pentagon' and looks like any other cable channel in the US with the exception that the anchors are in uniform (2004). A mixture of what is described as C-SPAN-style current affairs and cable news is offered free of charge to the US domestic media. One of the most celebrated ways in which government-produced material entered the mainstream media was the rescue of Private Jessica Lynch from an Iraqi hospital in 2003.

Saving Private Lynch was choreographed by the US military. A mainte-nance clerk in the US Army, Lynch's rescue had been staged for the cam-eras (Tumber and Palmer, 2004: 132). Many aspects of the story of Lynch's liberation have been challenged. Doubts have been cast on the injuries she received, the circumstances surrounding her capture and detention and whether Iraqi troops were present. The footage of the operation was supplied by the Pentagon; it had been edited by the military and had been shot on a night-vision camera in a way more comparable with Hollywood than news channels (Shah, 2007). It was packaged for cross platform pro-motion, news, talk shows, magazines and books and satisfied the require-ments of news organisations for drama that would have audience appeal (Reese, 2004: 249). The BBC's John Simpson summed it all up: 'It was all the creation of US Army spinners, and a credulous press desperate for some genuine heroics in a war which seemed disturbingly short of gal-lantry' (Allan and Zelizer, 2004: 8). The 'mythical version' of the story was reported around the world and it was only after critical investigative reporting by the Canadian Broadcasting Corporation and the BBC that the story was queried (BBC, 2003); even then the 'mythical version' appears to have been 'largely accepted' in the US media while the UK media 'largely accepted' the BBC account (Tumber and Palmer, 2004: 133).

While the US attempts to influence the international news agenda were not always successful during the wars in the Gulf, several commentators and reporters have attested to the growing effectiveness of international information control (Knightley, 2003). Some governments are believed to be more successful than others. The Israeli government has gained consider-able recognition for its ability to manage the flow of international news. This stems from an information policy that has been tried and tested in several conflicts since the state of Israel was founded in 1948. Studies have found that most correspondents believe that Israeli media relations are 'more accessible and more professional in releasing information about the Middle East' than their counterparts in Egypt and other Arab countries (El-Nawawy and Kelly, 2001: 105).[1] Given the precarious situation in which Israel has found itself in the region, the military and political authorities have always been 'sensitive to outside opinion and particularly attentive to the European and US media' (Mungham, 1987: 264). As a perennial 'hot spot' the country has been a major posting for foreign correspondents, with the core of regular reporters estimated at between 200 and 300 with an approximate tenfold increase at times of conflict (1987: 264).

Accreditation distinguishes between different kinds of correspondents. Those on long term assignment, more than a couple of years, usually receive considerable help from the Israeli government, from finding accommodation to introductions to ministry spokespersons. Making correspondents 'feel grateful' is part of the pressure on those on long stay assignment. Other pressures come from the monitoring of the output of all foreign television by Israeli embassies, a system of military censorship that must be adhered to and mechanisms of controlling access or minding reporters which are tightened at times of major tension. This web of connections in which long stay correspondents are enveloped ensures that they have a strong interest in maintaining good relations with the authorities as well as local sources and contacts. It is the parachute journalists, particularly those working for television, who are deemed 'harder to control or hold accountable' (Mungham, 1987: 267). These reporters feel fewer obligations to accede to ground rules and arrangements and are less concerned about incurring the disapproval of the local authorities. Of the long stay reporters the Israeli authorities have traditionally been most focused on the output of the wire services or news agencies, as their accounts can be accessed in a matter of minutes by people in other countries. Acutely aware of the time pressures these reporters work under, the authorities exploit the deadlines that they confront. It is to the authorities' advantage that the constant pressure to be first encourages wire service correspondents 'to grab the official communiqué and wire it off. No Checking. No Nothing' (1987: 274).

The success of the Israeli PR operation has gradually been blown off course by the development of new technology, and in particular the emergence of 24-hour news broadcasting. Real time information presents problems for minders, censors and press officers. The long-established state procedures to control the foreign media as well as international public perceptions have been confronted with circumstances they had not been trained to tackle. Soldiers, civilians, reporters and witnesses of all kinds are today equipped with mobiles phones and small cameras that can instantly communicate events on the ground to the mainstream media. The structures put in place to control both the information flow and the media messages during the invasion of Gaza in 2008 proved inadequate in the face of the degree of media transparency that operated there – video and eyewitness evidence contradicting Israeli claims about the impact of their bombardment on civilians emerged quickly from the Hamas-controlled territory (Gowing, 2009: 58). Relations with the foreign media deteriorated all independent media coverage was 'shut down' by Israel; foreign correspondents were prevented from entering Gaza and like many governments who have lost control of the agenda, attacks were launched on the professionalism of foreign reporters. The Israelis had previously struggled to counter the propaganda and psychological warfare launched by Hezbollah in 2006 in the face of the invasion of Southern Lebanon by the Israeli army. The extent of the problems the Israelis faced was indicated by having to resort to primitive propaganda techniques, namely the dropping of leaflets from the air (Otte, 2009). The failure of the Israeli news machine to respond to what Gowing (2009: 59) describes as the 'real time media tiger' raises questions about the effectiveness of information control in the digital world.

The internet and information control

The internet has been characterised as an 'antidote to state dominance', a 'tool whose possession, or ability to access, allows individuals, opposition parties and NGOs to escape the control the state can exercise of TV and radio channels, and the press' (Fossato et al., 2008: 1). It is seen as making it more difficult for propagandists and PR agencies to manipulate the information the public receives. The proliferation of sources of information impedes the ability of those in power to control the provision and flow of information while the increased speed of international communication stymies their capacity to shape the international information environment. The institutions of corporate and political power are deemed to face a 'new vulnerability'; there is 'a fragility and brittleness of power which weakens both the credibility and accountability of governments, the security organs and corporate institutions' (Gowing, 2009: 6). Some commentators draw attention to official unwillingness to face up to the challenges of the new media environment (Gowing, 2009), while others articulate the view that the capacity of governments and international agencies to exercise information control is severely diminished in the real time media environment (NcNair, 2006). There is also a counter-view, that the new media technology enhances the ability and capacity of governments and international agencies to propagate their view of the world. New technology, according to Yoel Cohen's survey of 300 foreign correspondents in Israel, has an impact on governmental public relations: 94 per cent of correspondents surveyed said they received more government-sponsored material in the email era than in the pre-email era and 64 per cent said that governmental sources had, as a result, greater impact upon them (Cohen, accessed 12 June 2009).

Much of the discussion of the impact of the internet on information control has concentrated on how totalitarian or closed regimes have sought to rein in the information blizzard generated by the new medium. The efforts of governments such as those in Iran, China, Russia and Kenya to clamp down on the use of the internet and social media have received considerable attention. Technically it is possible to shut down the new media; the plug can be pulled on the internet and the mobile telephony system can be closed down. China closed down the entire internet in July, 2009 after riots leading to the deaths of nearly 200 people. This is an extreme solution which has only been used in a state of crisis. Controlling the flow of information on the net is more problematic. It requires an agreement between the companies controlling the servers and government. Such agreements have been forthcoming, as in the case of China and Google, but they are fraught with tensions and are precarious – as Google's withdrawal from China in 2010 indicated. The collusion of western interests in attempts to control the net is also shown in the efforts of software companies in the US, Germany and Australia to develop programmes to facilitate this (Tuinstra, 2009). The US Committee on International Relations 'chastised' Cisco, Google, Yahoo and Microsoft for 'tailoring their technologies, search engines and web services to meet the Chinese government's demands' (Winseck, 2008: 423). In addition to agreements to filter material, the Chinese government has adopted policing and punitive action to control what appears on the net. However, the capacity of some users to get around barriers is considerable and Chinese netizens have shown inventiveness in ensuring their continued participation in cyberspace.

Unlike 'the army of censors and watchers' deployed by China, the ability of Russia to defy the logic of the internet is attributed to the country's political culture (Fossato et al., 2008: 9). As foreign correspondence has had to adapt to local cultures, so the internet has to take into account the political and social context in which it operates. Russian bloggers and users are 'far more free' from regulation, imprisonment and persecution, and 'Russian internet sites offer a range of opinions' (Oates, 2008: 180). However, this has not been translated into political activity; the growth of online information has not acted as a catalyst to greater freedom of speech or democratisation. Many governments have developed their ability to use the internet to their advantage. Both the Chinese and Russian governments have launched sites to deliver services:

> which help to increase citizen satisfaction with the government and perhaps to provide a form of legitimacy that somewhat replaces the representative process ... such efforts will also help to strengthen state capacity from within, (while) propaganda organs are benefiting from internet use, helping the government to reach a new, younger audience. (Fossato et al., 2008: 9)

It is not only authoritarian or closed governmental systems that have sought to use the net to promote their interests and manage information to their advantage. Israel's foreign ministry is reported to have set up a special undercover team 'to surf the internet 24 hours a day spreading positive news about Israel' (Cook, 2009). Posing as ordinary net surfers and citizens their task is to 'provide the government line on the Middle East conflict' and play up good news about Israel. A Ministry official stated that during the Gaza bombardment they concentrated their activities on 'European websites where audiences were more hostile to Israeli policy', targeting sites such as BBC Online (cited in Cook, 2009). To counter charges of killing civilians the Israeli Defence Force started a video channel with around 40 videos on the internet platform YouTube (13 January 2009) to show that every effort is made to be as precise as possible in targeting Hamas activists (Otte, 2009).

The potential of the internet as a tool for propaganda was recognised by a range of political groups around the world in the early 1990s. The Zapatistas, a liberation movement in the Chiapas region of Mexico, used the web to promote their cause against the Mexican government when they were denied access by commercial media in 1994 (Russell, 2001). They posted communiqués which were sent out over an array of internet networks such as Peacenet and Usenet groups. NATO's intervention in Kosovo in 1999 is described as the first web war (Taylor, 2000; Keenan, 2005). The Serbian government was able to infiltrate and hack into the internet, not only enabling them to bypass traditional journalistic gatekeepers but also allowing them to plant information that discredited NATO's 'humanitarian justification' for going to war. They also used the web to challenge NATO claims about the impact of the bombing campaign on the civilian population (Hall, 2000). Foreign correspondents for established media outlets often took up this information to examine NATO's accounts of events (Uhlig, 1999).

The quality of what is on the net is highly dubious and the anonymity of the source of what is posted makes assessment of the credibility and accuracy of what appears problematic. The net is more susceptible than offline media to the dissemination of distortion and misinformation, as spam emails, hate mail and corporate and political propaganda hurtle across the web. Many blogs are 'faked, hidden or hacked' and become the tools of corporations, propagandists and identity thieves (Keen, 2005: 84–5). It is estimated that nearly 56 per cent of active blogs are splogs: faked blogs designed to trick advertisers and search engines. There are also 'flogs' which are in the pay of a sponsor while claiming to be independent. Web blogs have been described as 'the ultimate vehicle for brand-bashing, personal attacks, political extremism and smear campaigns' (Allan, 2006: 174). Hate propaganda has proliferated. Atrocity stories have always been a component of international reporting at times of conflict (Read, 1941), but the unregulated high-speed technology of the internet has allowed many disaffected groups and individuals not only to spread their messages of hate but also to make connections with one another (Allan, 2006: 17). Besides having to surf through all this material, foreign correspondents have been the objects of directly targeted hate. Their work is scrutinised, criticised, poured over for 'inaccuracies' and the reactions are often delivered to them immediately. Orchestrated campaigns were waged against reporters such as Robert Fisk, whose reporting of the Middle East incurred not only the disapprobation of the US administration but also the attention of those bloggers intent on identifying 'liberal propaganda' – the verb 'to fisk' was coined to describe the act of minutely picking apart on the internet factual reporting for signs of bias (Hammersley, 2009: 247).

The growth of the internet, with its provision of instant access to databases and information around the world, reinforces the 'stay at home tendency' of modern foreign reporting (Franks, 2006: 97). Susanne Franks describes the growth of 'an office based editorial culture', which has been made possible by new technology and facilitated by 'the massive global PR industry … available through every national hack's laptop' (Marr, 2004: 383). In a world increasingly conscious of the costs of news gathering, international reporting is more 'vulnerable' to the provision of packaged information (Franks, 2006a: 97–8). Less able to check out what is happening in the field, foreign editors are more reliant on their online sources of information. Pinning stories on sources is traditionally what characterises the work of the agency correspondent. Attribution is valued and correspondents are not encouraged to express their own opinion or interpret what they are told (Shanor, 2003: 41). This makes the international news agencies more dependent on their sources and more open to news management. The autonomy of the man and woman in the field is further undermined by the multi-platform approach demanded by news desks. Ben Hammersley (2009) describes his experience of 'doing' new media reporting of elections in Turkey. Sharing the TV shot with a producer, he was also 'writing a blog, posting pictures to Flickr, sending a running commentary to Twitter and uploading behind-the-scenes footage to YouTube' (2009: 250). His experience led him to worry about the impact on the quality of journalism of the many demands that result from working across a range of platforms. The amount of time devoted to checking information is significantly reduced, further enabling sources to present their views of events unchallenged or unquestioned. The net in this sense has speeded up a trend that was noticeable in the pre-digital era – the history of foreign reporting shows that increases in the speed of the transmission of news and information have weakened to the capacity of the individual reporter to identify, interpret and explain events as they unfold in the field.

Note

1   El-Nawawy and Kelly criticise Egyptian press spokespersons for their lack of professionalism. They argue the Arabs are 'at least partly responsible for misconceptions about themselves in the western news media ...'. But the 'slick' and 'sophisticated' attempts by the Israeli government to manage news are also described as 'counterproductive', as they can lead to 'more scrutiny, more fact-checking and more critical attitudes' as well as making correspondents 'more suspicious'. While it is important to draw attention to the failings of the Israeli and Egyptian PR systems, it is worth noting that successive Israeli governments have been able to determine the news agenda in the Middle East over the years.

6

WINDOWS ON THE WORLD: INTERNATIONAL JOURNALISM AND THE NEW MEDIA

The one-way flow in communication is basically a reflection of the world's dominant political and economic structures, which tend to maintain or reinforce the dependence of the poorer countries on the richer. (MacBride report, 1980: 148)

... despite technological advances that enable us to access the remotest places, many parts of Africa are less understood and less well reported in this period than they were several generations ago. We may have access to sophisticated satellite communications that enable reporters to broadcast live or to file stories from the middle of a desert or jungle, but that has not led to equivalent understanding and explanation of what is happening in remote and faraway places. (Franks, 2010: 72)

What kind of coverage is produced by international journalism is a question that scholars have asked and systematically attempted to answer since the 1930s. Their answers about the contemporary state of affairs have not deviated much since Wilbur Schramm explored a 'day of crisis' in 14 of the world's great newspapers in 1959. A pattern emerged in which some parts of the world and some people across the planet receive disproportionate coverage. Much of our international news since the Second World War has been dominated by events and people in one country, the United States of America. The extent of this domination led one African leader, Julius Nyerere of Tanzania, to comment that as his people were so well informed about US politics they should be able to vote in Presidential elections. The geography of foreign news is overwhelmingly skewed to elite nations and elite people (Galtung and Ruge, 1965). It is also about certain topics – politics and 'hard' news have featured prominently as international stories. What happens in relations between nations and the political events that take place within nations have constituted the major portion of international news stories. Certain parts of the world are noticeable for the absence of coverage; despite containing most of the planet's population and resources and making up more than two-thirds of the world's land mass, the Third World, Asia, Africa and Latin America are under-represented in international news coverage. When they do appear it is often in a negative context, framed by what has been referred to as the 'coups, wars, famines and disasters syndrome'. Routine and ordinary everyday life stories rarely emerge from Third World countries, which only feature at times of crisis when they are the 'hot spots' of the international news agenda. In some cases, a major crisis in the form of a war, famine or disaster is not sufficient to gain coverage – the war in the Democratic Republic of the Congo has claimed nearly 5 million lives. Analysis of a 15-month period of network news coverage in the US found that nearly 5,000 stories on Iraq were broadcast by NBC, CBS and ABC compared to only four on the Congo (Fahmy, 2010: 149). Some conflicts only fleetingly make it onto international television screens and into the pages of the world's press.

This chapter examines the pattern of international news in the world's media in the wake of the development of new media and technological change. It explores the extent to which the pattern of international news that has dominated the output of the traditional media in the West and the rest of the world is a feature of the digital age. Claims that online news is counteracting the inequalities and limitations of international journalism practised by the 'old media' are central to this discussion. For some, the net offers an opportunity to attain some sort of equality in the global information flow (Deuze, 2003), while others talk about changing journalistic practices leading to 'a different presentation … of international news' (Wu, 2007). According to Hamilton and Jenner (2002: 21) 'the ability of the public to get foreign news for itself may offer one of the best solutions to dwindling foreign reporting by traditional media'. To what extent is international news online different from what has constituted international news since 1945? Is the evolution of the new media producing a picture which allows for a greater and more diverse range of international voices and a more complete representation of the world? How true is the claim that new media are redefining international journalism to produce a truly global perspective on world events?

Where is foreign news from?

Studies of the image of the world in international news indicates a 'bias' – a bias towards certain regions and countries and certain kinds of stories. George Gerbner and George Marvanyi's study of a week of foreign coverage in the world's press in the early 1970s found that North America and Western Europe dominated the pages of news devoted to international issues and events (Gerbner and Marvanyi, 1983). Some parts of the world were noticeable only for the limited attention paid to them in the world's newspapers. Africa, a continent today of over 922 million people, received little coverage in all the media systems examined. Even in the pages of 'some Third World newspapers' only a small percentage of the foreign stories were located in Africa. The only parts of the Third World that appeared in any sustained coverage were Vietnam and the Middle East – the 'hot spots', the big news stories of the day during the period of the study. These were countries on whose soil the Cold War was being fought.

The geography of international news has not changed much since the early 1970s. A large scale study conducted for UNESCO in the early 1980s by academics in 29 countries found a similar geographical spread of international news stories in the world's media. North America and Western Europe still dominated the output, although this time the study was able to point out that much foreign news in all media systems was about neighbouring countries (Sreberny-Mohammadi, 1984). Geographical proximity plays a crucial role in determining the value of a news story. Stevenson and Cole (1984) stress the importance of news emanating from local geographic regions in their study of the world's press. The importance of neighbourly proximity is emphasised by the studies of foreign news in non-western media outlets. An examination of the content of Nigerian and Ghanaian newspapers found that 52 per cent of foreign news stories were about Africa (Obijiofor and Hanusch, 2003). African stories received more prominence than other parts of the world. However, the sources of many of these news stories about neighbouring countries were the INAs. In neighbouring countries, such as Chile and Peru, news of events was often communicated via dispatches sent back to London, Paris or New York by agency men and women on the ground, edited and then returned to the countries. Neighbourhood news had to travel a long way and be filtered though newsrooms and news editors remote from the region in which it happened.

The UNESCO research has been followed by many studies which reiterated the finding of geographical proximity as a determinant of international news. These studies have not always acknowledged the problematic nature of 'proximity', which can be different for large and more powerful nation-states. The economic and political power of the US extends its global reach to many more parts of the world, making it proximate to more countries than smaller, less powerful nations. There is a hierarchy of nations in international news, with the core countries of the international system receiving more coverage than smaller, less developed and less powerful peripheral nations (Chang, 1998). This inevitably means that what happens in the US is more newsworthy in the media of other countries. Newsworthiness is not a product of size of territory, population or resources but of political and economic influence. Location is not the only variable that determines the international flow of news. Close cultural ties also determine coverage. Cultural affinity can take many forms: shared language, ethnic similarity, migration and travel are all reasons put forward to account for international news coverage (Golan, 2008: 45). For many countries the ties fostered by colonialism ensure greater attention; the disproportionate reporting of Indonesia in the Dutch media (d'Haenens and Verelst, 2002) or East Timor in the Portuguese media (Monteiro, 2002) or India and Africa on the BBC are examples of the legacy of colonialism.

International news is tied to the level of economic interaction between nations. Studies of US and Western European newspapers have found that trade is positively linked to the amount of coverage countries attain (Rosengren, 1974; Ahern, 1984). A survey of more than 30 countries in the 1990s found a strong correlation between news flow and trade; the links between trade and news were 'high in the majority of countries studied' (Pietilainen, 2006). This confirmed the finding of a similar study conducted at roughly the same time that trade is 'the principal predictor of news coverage about foreign countries in both developed and developing countries' (Wu, 2003). A correlation has also been found between the level of international aid and news coverage (Soo Lim and Barnett, 2010). However, with some exceptions the pattern of trade of individual countries depends on 'geographic, political and cultural proximity' and 'historical connections' (Pietilainen, 2006: 226). A cross-cultural study of the importance attached to news events found that the media in every part of the world 'display provincial biases of their own' and are 'myopic' to those stories that are culturally, geographically, psychologically and economically close (Tai, 2000: 351).

What is foreign news about?

The most celebrated, as well as most cited, study of foreign news was undertaken by Johan Galtung and Mari Ruge in 1965. Galtung and Ruge's examination of how international events did or did not become news in the Norwegian press provided a taxonomy of values which have come to be seen as the basis of the selection of news in the media ever since. A combination of their 12 news factors was crucial in determining the newsworthiness of events. Galtung and Ruge's list – a list of what they acknowledged were 'deductions' – has become the definitive study of what makes news (see Harcup and O'Neill, 2001). Studies of journalists have tended to 'confirm' the hypotheses put forward by the two researchers. Sophia Peterson's (1979) study of the criteria reporters on *The Times* used to select news suggests 'strongly that news criteria shape a picture of the world's events characterised by erratic, dramatic and uncomplicated surprise, by negative or conflictual events involving elite nations and persons' (1979: 124). She did, however, also conclude that there were differences in ranking the importance of foreign news between news gatekeepers based on their cultural backgrounds. Scholars have re-evaluated Galtung and Ruge's criteria of newsworthiness to take account of contemporary developments (Harcup and O'Neill, 2001). Other scholars have expressed more fundamental reservations about Galtung and Ruge's approach, which are relevant to understanding the nature of foreign news reporting. They take issue with the assumption that news is always about events – there are many news stories which have nothing to do with 'occurrences in the real world which take place independently of the media' (Curran and Seaton, 1997 quoted in Harcup and O'Neill, 2001: 265). There is also an objection to the assumption that journalists 'report' on events – for critics, reporters make news; they 'construct' reality according to ideological factors (2001: 265).

Examination of the content of international news coverage indicates that foreign news is more likely to be about 'elite people' and 'elite nations'. Herbert Gans's study of US news shows that 'knowns' as opposed to 'unknowns' are more likely to appear in the news media (Gans, 1980). Political leaders have generally figured more prominently among the ranks of the 'known', while 'unknowns' tend to be made up of protestors, violators, deviants, voters and victims. Power, influence and status are determinants of who is reported within media systems around the world. What governments do, say and believe is an essential ingredient of international news. Even in the old Soviet system the state-controlled broadcast media sought to get pictures of the second permanent undersecretary getting out of the car to participate in an opening ceremony. Foreign news is no different; the comings and goings of leaders are deemed highly newsworthy, despite much of international politics being conducted behind closed doors and pictures of prime ministers and presidents getting in and out of planes, trains and helicopters being of little note.

Who constitutes an elite person has changed with the growth of 'soft news'; celebrities, their activities and visits have come to figure more prominently in attracting news stories about certain parts of the world. One version of this that singles out foreign news in Britain is the 'royal tour'. A trip by a member of the Royal family guarantees even the smallest African country some newspaper column inches or air-time in the British media. The focus on celebrities reflects the competitive nature of foreign news gathering. Confronted with the unprecedented competitive environment of the digital-age broadcasters, net news aggregators and the press have recognised that human drama attracts larger audiences (Baum, 2002). In what managing editor Walter Isaacson acknowledged was an effort to 'chase ratings' against rivals Fox and MSNBC, CNN moved toward more entertaining, provocative talk about the news, as well as increased 'soft news' (quoted in Shaw, 2001). For some critics, the news media 'by following Bob Geldof and

Bono, Angelina Jolie and Madonna as tour guides to world problems … offer comic book versions of world problems and relief …' (Pieterse, 2009: 64). Live Aid's Bob Geldof himself has supported calls for more serious news and documentaries about the developing world: 'People want to see reality on TV, rather than yet more reality TV' (Geldof, quoted in Franks, 2004: 428).

Research shows a shift in recent years in the nature of foreign coverage on British television. While the total hours devoted to foreign programming has not changed significantly, serious news and current affairs accounts of the world have been replaced by reality TV formats: what is dubbed as factual entertainment (Glasgow Media Group, 2000; Dover and Barnett, 2004; Franks, 2004). The largest category of factual international programming broadcast on British television in 2003 was 'travel shows', and much of the serious documentary reporting was shown on minority digital channels such as BBC 4. In such shows the lives and conditions of the peoples in the Third World are rarely commented on – other than the odd taxi driver, tour guide or hotel receptionist (Franks, 2004: 425). They are simply part of the service industry or used as the backdrop to the activities of the traveller or tourist. An example of such programmes is *Worlds Apart* on the National Geographic Channel, which followed American families on a '10 day survival camp among indigenous groups in remote Third World villages'. It emphasised 'self-discovery' as well as a 'renewed appreciation for family and nation' (Roy, 2007: 572).

The representation of the Third World

Galtung and Ruge (1965) emphasised the importance of drama, conflict and negativity in determining the newsworthiness of foreign events. There is, however, a distinction between stories about western countries and other parts of the world. It is possible to see news stories about the non-western world as located in a second division of news in which visuals, drama and conflict are the only determinants of coverage. Coverage of these parts of the world is 'episodic' and in the absence of regular reporting there is little engagement with on-going politics and everyday life in these countries (Franks, 2010: 72; Martin-Kratzer and Thorson, 2010: 172). As a result there is a tendency to reinforce simplistic explanations, stereotypes and clichés. Peter Elliott and Peter Golding (1973b) identified five components to the image of the Third World in the western news media. The first is of nations subject to *recurring political or military crises*. They stress that the distortion arises not because coups and wars do not happen but because they are often the only context within which certain countries are reported. Smith (1980: 27) argues that the western media represent the Third World as a series of 'moral shocks' such the Biafran civil war, Pol Pot in Cambodia, Idi Amin in Uganda and Emperor Bokassa in the Central

African Republic – and today one could add Darfur, Rwanda, Somalia and Burma. These often serve as 'evidence for the failure of Third World leadership'. Alexander Cockburn (1987: 357) makes the same point in a more sarcastic manner when he quotes from an article on the Knight Ridder news service in the US:

> *Orderly challenges to leadership are not culturally accepted in Africa. In Independent Africa, power has changed hands most frequently as the result of coup or assassination. Thus, the Nigerian experiment with democracy was tremendously important.* Translation: Africans are a bunch of bloodthirsty savages. They always will be. (Italics in original)

Smith points out that any African country is vulnerable to a coup d'état by a small group of armed men, but this is not a manifestation of inherent instability as much as a function of the problem of government's attempting to create national entities out of territories which were crudely carved out of the geography of the previous colonial regimes. The contribution of colonialism, Europeans and western commercial and political interests to creating and accentuating division, resentment and instability across Africa and other parts of the Third World is only rarely mentioned (Philo et al., 1999). The BBC newscaster and former Africa correspondent George Alagiah (1999) regretted that he had 'done Africa a disservice, too often showing the continent at its worst and too rarely showing it in full flower', and pleaded with his colleagues to drop the historical baggage that led to the reporting of Africa being 'infected with the prevailing wisdom of the nineteenth century' (see also Ankomah, 2008).

The second component of the image of the Third World is the focus on *western interests and concerns* – to the extent that news stories from Africa, Asia and Latin America concentrate on the political and/or economic impact on the West at the expense of what may be other, far more important issues. A study of the reporting of disasters between 2003 and 2005 in a variety of western countries found that there was a 'clear correlation' between the impact of the disaster on western political and economic interests and the amount and nature of media attention paid to the disaster (CARMA, 2006). It concluded that 'western self-interest' is the 'precondition for significant coverage of a humanitarian crisis'. Economics is 'a better guide to press interest than human suffering' and 'politics determines the timing, level of interest and story angle, not the humanitarian issues'. For example, one in six stories about the Asian tsunami in 2004 was about the impact on the tourist industry, and 40 per cent of the coverage concentrated on the impact of the disaster on westerners – out of the estimated 175,000 people who died around 900 were westerners. A significant proportion of the coverage of disasters concentrates on the relief operation and the donors – focusing on how the West helps the Third World. Examination of the coverage of the

Rwandan refugee crisis in 1996 found that the 'biggest story' in the *Mirror* during the period of study was the 'Please Save Me' appeal launched by the newspaper, which praised readers for their 'caring hearts' (11 November, 1996) and carried headlines such as 'Saved by Readers' (18 November, 1996) (Beattie et al., 1999). For some critics the focus on western interests rests on the assumption that the Third World should aspire to western political and economic standards (Woollacott, 1976). According to a Filipino official:

> It is as if Western reporters feel their job in any developing society is to identify that society's weakest points and biggest problems and then make them worse by exaggeration and unremitting publicity. (Woollacott, 1976: 13)

The dynamics of superpower relations were an important element in determining coverage of some parts of the world. Elliott and Golding's third component – *Cold War-ism* – was instrumental in determining why some parts of the world were covered and others ignored. For example, the Soviet press paid considerable attention to Africa as a result of the international rivalry of the Cold War years (Quist-Adade, 1990). With the collapse of communism and the end of the Cold War, Africa disappeared from the pages of the post-Glasnost newspapers as there were no longer ideological points to be scored at the expense of the West (1990: 175). Africa's marginalisation in the Russian newspapers was accompanied by increasingly negative stories about the continent. The Soviet newspapers had not been free of such stories but tended to attribute the continent's backwardness and political instability to the influence of western capitalism. In a world without Cold War rivalry Africa and other parts of the developing world has fallen back into relative obscurity. There are exceptions – the media fanfare surrounding the release of Nelson Mandela and his eventual inauguration as President of a multiracial South Africa was a good news story. However, as Susanne Franks (2010: 73) notes, this rare good-news story about Africa drew resources away from other major stories happening on the continent at the same time – in particular the genocide in Rwanda which was 'ignored by most of the foreign media' (Melvern, 2001).

The Cold War provided a 'clear narrative to world events' (Franks, 2006: 98) and with its collapse the ability to tell the story of global events and provide an explanation of what is happening is more difficult. Today's world is more complicated, demanding more knowledge and understanding to make sense of what is happening for viewers, readers, listeners and surfers. In the post-Cold War world the selection, reporting and interpreting of events present a greater challenge for international news organisations and their correspondents. The problem of identifying which events in the developing world are today newsworthy has led to some notable – and some would say unforgivable – omissions. The failure to report Rwandan genocide, the limited coverage of the war in the Congo and of Hurricane Stanley, which killed nearly as many people as Hurricane Katrina, are examples (CARMA, 2006).

The fourth component is the tendency towards the *simplification* of economic, social and political structures in the Third World. Elliott and Golding (1973b) emphasise the attention given to national leaders in these countries and the way in which large-scale political upheavals are often reduced to explanations that concentrate on 'religion' or 'tribalism'. An example of this is cited by Cockburn (1987: 188), who quotes from an article by one of the *New York Times*'s most celebrated foreign correspondents, CL Sulzberger:

> Africans are accustomed to dwelling in tribal societies and respect authority … the greatest question for the next generation of leaders is: Can nation-states in the future be maintained over the disintegrating thrust of ancient tribalism?

The conflict in Rwanda between Tutsis and Hutus has been a feature of the country's history in the post-war period. Tribalism has been a term used by the West to interpret the tensions, grievances and bloody violence that have erupted. The label was used in 1959 to explain the war between the Bahutu majority and the Batutsi aristocracy in what was seen by some experts as a peasant revolt similar to what had happened throughout European history (Hatchen, 1971). Colonial intervention, class conflict, land reform and the unequal distribution of resources have all been seen at one time or another as central to understanding the complexities of Rwandan politics. However, the 1994 genocide was again reported through the frame of 'ancient ethnic hatreds' and a continuation of an ongoing cycle of bloodletting and tribal savagery (Seaga Shaw, 2007: 363). Presenting war, conflict and political violence in Africa as 'tribal' reinforces a notion of these events as 'irrational', 'primitive' and 'savage'. This fits comfortably with traditional stereotypes of Africa and Africans as backward and bloodthirsty, grossly oversimplifying our understanding of these events.

Clutching on to clichés and well trodden stereotypes is often how journalists attempt to make sense of situations and societies with which they and their audiences are unfamiliar. Robert Fisk (1988: 8) has expressed his concern about what he sees as a feature of international news reporting:

> I have a suspicion that the clichés which are now governing our news reports and headlines are becoming a real danger to our task about telling the truth of what is going on in the world.

Fisk was commenting on his beat, the Middle East and in particular the Lebanon, the coverage of which he describes as subject to 'a dead language of easy parallels and simplistic allusions which help neither the editor nor the reader understand the great tragedy' of that part of the world. Several commentators have provided whistle-stop tours of journalistic clichés, recommending a handy range of terms to sum up in a nutshell vast tracts of the world, their peoples and cultures (see Cockburn, 1987; Wainaina, 2005). In his satirical essay on 'How to be a Foreign Correspondent', Cockburn (1987) extols the maxim, 'never shun the obvious'. Touching down in New Guinea he writes:

> This is simple stuff: head-hunters *face-to-face* with the Twentieth Century ... Speak of the *menace of the modern world* for these simple, yet unpredictable tribes which are usually coated with white clay ... Indonesia, first of all, is a *teeming archipelago*. It is still shaking itself free of the confused yet charismatic leadership of Sukarno. There was a massacre, but the *wounds are healing* (or schisms still run deep and *much bitterness remains*). Wealth *coexists uneasily* with desperate poverty. There are Moslems (a growth subject). (Cockburn, 1987: 188)

In a similarly acerbic style Binyavanga Wainaina (2005) tells us 'how to write about Africa':

> Always use the word *Africa* or *Darkness* or *Safari* in your title ... Also useful are words such as *Guerrillas, Timeless, Primordial* and *Tribal* ... Never have a picture of a well-adjusted African on the cover of your book, or in it, unless that African has won the Nobel Prize. An AK-47, prominent ribs, naked breasts: use these. If you must include an African, make sure you get one in Masai or Zulu or Dogon dress. In your text, treat Africa as if it were one country ... Don't get bogged down with precise descriptions. Africa is big: fifty-four countries, 900 million people who are too busy starving and dying and warring and emigrating to read your book ... Make sure you show how Africans have music and rhythm deep in their souls, and eat things no other humans eat ... Taboo subjects: ordinary domestic scenes, love between Africans (unless a death is involved), references to African writers or intellectuals, mention of school-going children who are not suffering from yaws or Ebola fever or female genital mutilation. (Italics added)

Satirical accounts may exaggerate but they come close to identifying the reality of much foreign reporting of the Third World. They expose the fact that cultures and countries – like individuals – can be 'imprisoned inside the misrepresentation and misunderstanding of others' (Smith, 1980: 27) which can inhibit if not distort international relations. Today the perceptions of Islam and the Muslim world in the West can be seen as particularly problematic.

Prior to 9/11 western media accounts of Islam and the Muslim world were framed by a narrow range of stereotypes. A series of distinct events such as the OPEC oil crisis, the revolution in Iran, the Soviet incursion into Afghanistan and the subsequent war and the terrorist attacks perpetrated by organisations supportive of the cause of Palestine had been bundled together under recurring themes such as the 'Islamic revolution', 'the arc of instability', 'the crescent of crisis' and the 'return of Islam' (Said, 1981: 15).

Such accounts were also apparent in the press in the non-western world (Vilanilam, 1989). Since George W Bush's declaration of the 'war on terror', crude and exaggerated images of Muslims have become more prominent in the world's media. Accentuated by the wars in Iraq and Afghanistan, some of the coverage of the Muslim world has been labelled as 'Islamophobic'. The most extreme example of this form of representation is found in America's great patriotic TV channel, Fox News, and the British tabloid press, which present a 'menacing image of Islam' (Vultee, 2009; Poole, 2002). Distinction is sometimes made between the reporting of 'domestic' Islam and international Islam. In a study of a leading Dutch newspaper it was found that coverage of Islam abroad tended to be more unbalanced and hostile than of the Muslim community within the Netherlands (D'Haenens and Blink, 2007). International news is characterised by less diversity of opinion and viewpoint. This was also the case with US network news in which the peaceful portrayal of American Muslims contrasted with 'visuals of violent, gun-carrying Muslims' abroad (Ibrahim, 2010). Having been defined as a threat to US security, the network news has 'mostly framed' Muslims around the world 'as fanatic, irrational, America-hating and violent oppressors of women' (Ibrahim, 2010: 122). The wide range of political grievances in the Muslim world has been oversimplified into 'an inherent conflict between Islam and America'.

How the world's media represent developing countries, Islam and the world's 'hot spots' has been fairly well researched. Less academic study has been made of the images of the West and in particular the US in the world's media. During the Cold War, research highlighted the 'negative' image of the US and the West in the press of the communist world; in the late 1950s America was represented as 'an imperialist constantly meddling with the internal affairs of other nations, seeking subversion and control of the once-colonial states' in the Chinese press (Lee, 1982: 63). Images of the US only shifted with *rapprochement* between the US and China following President Richard Nixon's overtures in the early 1970s. Much of the coverage of the US has a 'disproportionate emphasis on US official institutions' focusing on what the government in Washington does at the expense of a 'more holistic' picture of the American way of life (Lee, 1982: 60). As mentioned, in the immediate post-Maoist period, Xinhua, the Chinese national news agency, based all of its US correspondents in Washington and New York, often neglecting the Mid-West (ibid.).

The final component identified by Elliott and Golding (1973b) is that foreign news reporting, like domestic coverage, follows what they describe as *pre-existing news cycles*. When a foreign news event is breaking there is fragmentary information available, and the tendency is to interpret what details there are in terms of previous, apparently similar events in the country or region in which it is located. Thus a coup in Ghana is reported in terms of the advent to power of 'another Nkrumah'. This appears akin to what Steve Chibnall (1977: 34) describes as 'conventionalism', that is, 'a tendency for new events to be cast as well known scenarios'. The correspondent's role is seen as organising the chaos of events and the 'normalisation of the potentially problematic'. This linking of disparate events results in distortion.

> The news process therefore establishes its own links between situations, links not at the level of underlying structures and processes but at the level of immediate forms and images. Situations are identified as the same if they look the same. In this way news rewrites history for immediate popular consumption. (Chibnall, 1977: 34)

The story cycle can continue even if considerable changes take place in the situations and locations they describe. Recent changes in the economic and industrial situations of India and China provide a challenge to international reporting. Mark Tully, for many years the BBC's man in India, remarked that many in the West cannot see beyond the poverty and 'backwardness' of the Subcontinent (quoted in Twitchin, 1988: 21). Today the story of economic success cannot be ignored but it is still contextualised in familiar frameworks. Globalisation is represented as the West bringing economic benefits to the rest of the world, and the mainstream media 'underestimate and under-represent the rise of the rest' (Pieterse, 2009: 65–66).

Underlying Elliott and Golding's components that make up the image of the developing world in the western media is a particular image of helplessness. Africa, a 'whole continent in distress' as Harrison (1986) puts it, is the extreme example of this perception of the peoples of what we now label as the Global South. Angela Barry shows how images of helplessness have come to symbolise and reinforce the 'dependency myth' that prevails in the coverage of much of the developing world. She shows how it works at a number of levels:

> The starving child can be seen as Africa itself, unable to get beyond childhood, looking to Europe for its salvation, even though independence has severed the umbilical chord. From another angle, the starving child can be seen as the populations of Africa, suffering from mismanagement and indifference of African leaders who are willing to allow things such as starvation to happen ... the dependency myth neutralises the political debate and makes all intervention and aid appear to be acts of disinterested generosity. It also strips the continent of its dignity. (Barry, 1988: 90)

For one African journalist, news reports of his continent 'show outside white people feeding and helping black people' (Makunike, 1993). Coverage of the Ethiopian famine in the early 1980s focused on various westerners such as Bob Geldof, Michael Buerk and Robert Maxwell 'saving Africa from disaster' (Harrison and Palmer, 1986: 98). An example of the 'mercy mission' approach was found in the headline of the British newspaper the *Daily*

Mirror: 'The Smiles and the Horror: Mirror Brings Aid to Tragic Families' (Van der Gaag and Nash, 1988: 35). The extent to which Ethiopia was given support by other African countries during the famine was neglected. It also downplayed the broader context of famines and their causes. A drought or crop failure may be the immediate cause but the fact that millions of people live at subsistence levels – which means their very survival can be threatened by a lack of rain – is more difficult to explain. The role of the international economy in perpetuating economic deprivation in Africa and other parts of the developing world is often omitted from coverage of famines and underdevelopment.

There is also an exotic side to foreign news reporting of the developing world which evokes the *National Geographic* travelogue (Dahlgren and Chakrapani, 1982). Descriptive colour is an important component of the international news story. Describing the scene to convey to audiences the nature of the place, landscape and culture provides some kind of background to the events and reactions of the people involved. It is an essential element in making the unfamiliar accessible to audiences – programmes such as the BBC's *From Our Own Correspondent* deploy this device to convey the 'feel' of where they are to the audience. This reflects the 'dualism' in the coverage of the Third World in which the exotic and the barbaric co-exist side by side. Western perceptions of the non-western world are steeped in colonial interactions which stressed the 'naturalness of the natives' and the savagery of their lives (1982: 60). The juxtaposition of geographic beauty and natural habitat with barbarity and violence was apparent in the coverage of Rwanda. For example, the highly respected veteran Africa correspondent Richard Dowden began an account for the *Independent on Sunday* of the genocide in Rwanda thus:

> The land is twisted and folded in on itself. Volcanoes thrust up from the horizon. Grey rivers of lava scar the plains. Earthquakes are common. Flying over this region you quickly pass from rolling hills to lava fields to plains of scrub and grass, over lakes of brilliant blue and dark rivers in tropical jungles. The plane is thrown about by air currents from the jagged landscape. It is as if the heart of Africa is in turmoil. (*Independent on Sunday*, 10 April 1994)

Such coverage is anchored in the particular ways of seeing the Third World in the West as a product of the legacy of colonialism (see Chapter 2).

Recent studies confirm the basic truth of Elliott and Golding's taxonomy – the coverage of the Third World is dominated by the 'coups, wars, famines and disasters syndrome'. A content analysis of British television in 2000 found that 80 per cent of the coverage of the Third World was accounted for by the following categories: conflict/war/terrorism; politics; sports; natural disasters or accidents; and western visitors (Glasgow Media

Group, 2000). Doom, death, devastation and distress characterise much of the reporting of the developing world, and without any context within which to place these events the international reporting of the nations and peoples of Asia, Latin America and Africa is deemed narrow and negative.

Victims

This 'negative' reporting pertains more to some members of society in the developing world than others. Women are twice as likely to be portrayed as 'victims' than men (cited in Geertsema, 2009: 155). Those considered weak, helpless and innocent are seen as 'better victims' and more worthy of our compassion (Moeller, 1999; Hojer, 2004). Victims are newsworthy as they are associated with the core news values of international reporting: violence, instability and death. Women, children and the elderly fit this category; although context plays a significant role – certain forms of violence are less newsworthy, for example domestic violence. There is very little about women's lives in international news: a study of the output of mainstream news agencies in the 1970s found that less than 2 per cent of the material concerned women (Gallagher, 1981). Irma Halonen (1999) has identified the narrow ways in which women are framed. Her examination of war news photography identified women as represented according to particular themes: these include the 'crying woman' who remains at home grieving for her man; mother and child; women crying together; the woman amidst rubble; and the woman rescued by men. A study of the representation of women in 10,000 stories in the world press during 1995 found that women's presence in terms of the frequency of their appearance is still not felt in the world's press, and when they are present, they are associated more with the private than with the public sphere (First, 2002). International crises are 'no place for women' (Sutcliffe et al., 2005).

Under UNESCO and as part of the activities around the NWICO, efforts were made to establish agencies rectifying this imbalance. Five women's features agencies were established between 1978 and 1983, the first efforts to establish a 'systematic approach to cover women's issues in international news' (Geertsema, 2009: 155). The advent of such agencies has not necessarily resulted in significant changes in the coverage of women in international news. The growing number of female correspondents has also had limited impact on coverage. Women have acted as foreign reporters for a long time; Flora Shaw was a relatively well known foreign reporter in the late nineteenth century, who became colonial editor of *The Times* (Simpson, 2010: 13). However, it is only recently that the US TV networks have appointed full-time women foreign correspondents – CBS designated its first full-time woman overseas in 1974 while NBC had made an appointment a few years earlier (Chambers et al., 2004: 58). Women are now attaining prominent positions on screen and behind the screen. Some commentators speculate that the growing number of women on foreign assignments helps to 'spice up the drama of war reporting in a market-driven profession' (Chambers et al., 2004: 197). Others believe that more female correspondents reflects the increasing focus on celebrities and human interest stories in international news – the term 'feminisation' of news has long been used as a short hand for describing the rise of the human interest story. Women correspondents traditionally have been seen as writing differently about international events and crises. The desire to expose the horrors and suffering of war and its impact on those caught up in the fighting rather than detail the weapons, strategy and deployment of troops on the battlefield has been attributed to the female reporter. Research shows that female correspondents are more likely to file victim-based stories than their male counterparts (Kennard and Murphy, 2002). Some female correspondents, such as Kate Adie and Christine Amanpour, have a high profile and are sometimes able to exert some influence over the kinds of stories they report and how they report them. However, most women reporters are subject – as are their male counterparts – to the rigours and editorial demands of the newsroom and as such there is a 'broad consistency in male and female reporting' (Sutcliffe et al., 2005).

Reporting death from abroad is subject to differences, often determined by cultural attitudes. Some people's deaths are considered more newsworthy than others; the old adage in newsrooms is one death in the same street is equivalent to ten in the next town, 100 in the next country and 1,000 in a distant place, albeit expressed in a more crude national stereotypical turn of phrase. The further culturally removed victims are, the 'more gruesome photographs can be and the less detailed written accounts are' (Sontag, 2003 quoted in Hanusch, 2008: 342). The more viewers, listeners and readers can identify with victims, the more likely it is that newsrooms and reporters will be interested in the story. Nationality is 'an important selection criterion in stories about death', emphasising that audiences tend to care most about those closest to them (Hanusch, 2008: 350). A study of US television found that earthquakes, typhoons and floods in the developing world 'received disproportionately less coverage (Adams, 1986). Comparisons of hurricanes Katrina and Stanley, which took place within months of each other and caused similar amounts of death, destruction and displacement, found a significant imbalance in the way in which they were reported – Katrina received significantly more coverage while there was little or no coverage of Stanley outside the first days of the disaster (CARMA, 2006).

The graphic representation of death, dying and victims has been a matter of debate about international news coverage post-9/11. Al-Jazeera was condemned by some in the West for its graphic portrayal of civilian deaths and its broadcast of pictures of dead and captured US soldiers in Iraq: then US defence secretary Donald Rumsfeld criticised the coverage as 'vicious, inaccurate and inexcusable' (quoted in Johnson and Fahmy, 2010: 241). It has been shown that Arabic-language media are 'consistently … more graphic' in their visual representation of war and terrorism (Fahmy, 2010). However, there is considerable evidence to support the notion that images and photographs of victims and suffering, death and destruction are politically determined. A comparison between Arab and American newspapers found that the former published proportionately more images of the Afghan bombing while the latter published more on the 9/11 attack (Fahmy, 2010: 150). Photographs that humanised the victims of 9/11 were apparent in the American press contrasting with an under-emphasis on the victims of the Afghan war; similarly the Arabic newspapers emphasised the victims of the Afghan war while de-humanising the victims of 9/11. A study of the BBC's coverage of the 2005–6 Israeli–Palestinian conflict found that 'Israeli deaths generated more coverage than Palestinian ones'. This was replicated in the 2006 war with Hezbollah (Gaber et al., 2009). The political sensitivity of photographs was manifest in the Abu Ghraib torture pictures which contradicted and undermined the efforts of the US administration to present its involvement in Iraq as a standard bearer of freedom and democracy (Anden-Papadopoulos, 2008).

Graphic pictures not accessible in the mainstream media in the West are to be found on the internet (Anden-Papadopoulos, 2009). Besides the showing of insurgent and terrorist video, US soldiers on active duty in Iraq and Afghanistan have used the net to communicate with their families at home, pay tribute to fallen colleagues, as well as post 'personal and at times shockingly brutal views from the frontline' (2009: 17). Violent combat videos sometimes set to music and containing troops using obscene language have been uploaded onto MySpace, Google Video and YouTube. They present a challenge to the mainstream media's coverage, allowing the user to experience what some see as the 'realities of war' close up. The Bush administration sought to prevent images of dead and seriously injured soldiers appearing in the media, including a ban on pictures of body bags returning home from combat zones. This has been largely successful in the mainstream media but the videos shown on the net have exposed disturbing images to a public that may question the conduct of US foreign policy in Afghanistan and Iraq. The Iraqi War on YouTube offers insights into 'mundane, violent and even depraved faces of warfare', contradicting the clinical and heroic nature of war that pervades the mainstream US media, challenging traditional journalism's claims to authenticity (Anden-Papadopoulos, 2009: 25). For some it illustrates the more diverse and more genuine nature of the representation of world events on the net.

Foreign news on the net

The internet has generated a variety of new news sites – online versions of traditional media, new media news providers such as Google, Yahoo and

OhmyNews and personal blogs and individual sites. Studies comparing hard copy and online editions of mainstream newspapers have discovered that more international news is carried by the online version. A study of the online and hard copy versions of the *Montreal Gazette* found that there was much more international news on the newspaper's website (Gasher and Gabriele, 2004). There was also a wider range of nations and places covered; 'online editions contained more stories from more places' (2004: 320). However, many of these stories were not traditional international news stories but sports news stories, most of which were 'chiefly' taken from the INAs, and nearly 75 per cent of the content was about North America. A study of the websites of several Canadian newspapers found they 'privilege ... news about countries such as the United States, the United Kingdom and France with which Canada maintains strong and formal political, economic and military ties ... consistent with ... news flow studies of hard copy daily newspapers' (Gasher, 2007: 316). Examining the two most visited news websites in the US, Denis Wu (2007: 549) concluded that their international news output 'does not seem to deviate much from that of their traditional counterparts'. His findings show 'significant overlaps between most covered nations' and that 'Middle-Eastern countries, economic elites and military powers still dominate the news space on the web'. It is more of the same rather than different kinds of international news. A comparative study of four online papers in 2007 – *Gulf News*, the *Daily Mirror*, *Toronto Globe and Mail* and the *Guardian* – found that despite more coverage of developing nations North America and Western Europe appeared as the most covered regions (Chia, 2007). In quantitative terms the gap between the developed and developing countries was 'still evident' and news events about 'elite nations' were 'dominant in the foreign news sections of the four online newspapers'. Research into online media in Australia shows that if a nation had a strong economy and a large number of internet users then it is more likely to receive coverage – that is, the US and Western Europe (Wang, 2010). The geography of online content reflects the imbalances of the traditional mainstream media; web technology has not drastically changed what is reported as international news.

This is also apparent with the value-added components of the new technology. As we noted, the hyperlink or link allows the users to access other documents with more details about the subject matter. It assists the user to acquire more information and greater understanding of the issues in the news. In some ways it fulfils the function that current affairs used to, providing the context or background to the immediacy and foreground of the television news. Easy to establish, and as a result of more powerful search engines easy to find, hyperlinks can be seen as essential to claims that the internet expands our understanding of international relations, enables us to access a wider range of views, opinions and interpretations and provides a broader perspective on the world. Tsan-Kuo Chang and his colleagues (2009: 149) concluded from their examination of international news stories from 28 online news media in 15 countries that the use of hyperlinks to external websites in foreign news stories was 'infrequent'. Many news websites are 'disinclined to make overseas websites available and accessible in their reporting of foreign news stories', and unless users actively search out related online stories they are 'denied the opportunities to learn more about the countries involved or read different perspectives of the same story' (Chang et al., 2009: 155).

The new media technologies do not appear to have had a significant impact on the portrayal of non-western countries, which remains steeped in the 'coups, wars, famines and disasters syndrome'. Research into African press coverage of international news in the age of the internet found that the quantity of stories about events on the continent had increased but the quality of the stories was still overwhelmingly 'negative' (Obijiofor and Hanusch, 2003). Of news stories examined about Africa in the Nigerian and Ghanaian newspapers, 68 per cent were 'negative in slant and tone'. Similarly, stories about the developing world were overwhelmingly negative; just under 75 per cent of the stories focused on the 'syndrome'. The new technologies have made it easier to report stories which occur on the other side of the world but they do not necessarily change the way in which the story is reported. Traditional news values and established news angles prevail. While new technology has expanded the diversity of international news, the nature of that news is determined by a journalistic culture and reporting practices criticised by the MacBride report nearly 30 years ago. International news in the digital age appears not to have fundamentally changed; it is still embedded in the traditional news reporting genre, overwhelmingly focused on news from the United States and Western Europe and on negative stories elsewhere.

Part of the explanation for this is that the internet is highly dependent on traditional media sources for much of the information about international events and issues that appear. 'The dirty secret of internet news is that it generates a microscopic proportion of the original reporting it offers' (Viviano, 2007). The majority of online content is 'shovelware', that is, 'reproductions of content that appeared in a news organisation's primary distribution channels' (Scott, 2005: 110). It has been shown that the web is highly dependent on international news agency copy (Davies, 2007: 107; Fenton, 2010: 9). Research into the content of news portal/aggregators in 2006 found that the 'average amount of measurable verbatim news agency use for these services' stood at 85 per cent (Paterson, 2006, 2007). Many CNN stories that appeared online were 'virtually unchanged' agency stories. News agencies are increasingly supplying the most popular websites run by major news organisations such as CNN, MSNBC and ABC. This research concluded that the leading news agencies (Reuters and AP), together with AFP and the BBC, 'dominate news delivery in cyberspace' (Paterson, 2006). Tracking the influence of these news providers as sources of international news is far from easy in the anonymous world of cyberspace. The anonymity of sources on the net corresponds with the tendency of mainstream media to make greater use of unnamed sources in foreign than in domestic news (see Sheehy, 2008). Newspapers in different parts of the world copy and paste from online sources. One study identified that 80 per cent of the foreign news stories that appeared in a Ghanaian newspaper originated from the BBC, presumably from the online site (Obijiofor and Hanusch, 2003). However, the sources of many of the foreign stories in the Nigerian press were not indicated, a trend that is developing in the news media in parts of the Third World.

What about the content of blogs? Blogs are most commonly characterised by content repacking, that is, commenting on traditional news stories, articulating partisan comment and in some cases peddling 'hate' propaganda and the expression of opinion of one form or another. Examination of data from weblog search engine BlogPulse found that the nations that appear in blog-posts 'strongly correspond' to those that appears in the mainstream media (Zuckerman, 2004). According to Ethan Zuckerman (2004):

> we see roughly the same correlation between wealth and mentions as we do in media aggregator sites like Google News or Altavista News and a slightly tighter correlation to national wealth than in single media sources like the *New York Times* or the *Washington Post.*

A country-by-country comparison found that 'weblogs are more likely to name travel destinations (Caribbean Islands, some Central American and Southeast Asian nations) and far less likely to mention African, Eastern European and Central Asian nations than mainstream media sources'. Stephen Reese and his colleagues (2007: 257) describe the 'blogosphere' as heavily reliant on professional news sites and stories generated by established journalists. From their study of some of the most popular news and political weblogs they conclude that bloggers 'simply engage the facts and information carried in news accounts, accepting them at face value and using them to form their own arguments, reinforce views and challenge opponents'. News agencies again figure prominently as sources of international news. The bloggers rarely challenge accepted reportorial techniques or established news values and practices. According to one former newspaper reporter the internet 'leeches ... reporting from mainstream news publications, whereupon aggregating websites and bloggers contribute little more than repetition, commentary and froth' (Massing, 2009).

Traditional or mainstream journalism plays a significant role on the web, and a more comprehensive version of the day's news is yet to emerge. Citizens struggle to practise journalism in cyberspace in a meaningful and distinct way. Not everyone would agree that blogging is parasitical – original work is done and those with specialist knowledge or eyewitness accounts who are unable to gain access to established media have the opportunity via the net to put their views (Massing, 2009). However, at the international level the capacity, ability and means to blog are limited and blogging is embedded in a network that is dominated by an established pattern of what is international news. Examples of innovative practice exist and technology is playing a part in widening the provision of international news, but the organisational structures within which new media operate are heavily influenced by the political and corporate interests that shaped the old media. According to Paterson (2006), the internet is 'for most users, a mass medium providing mostly illusory interactivity and mostly illusory diversity'.

The new media provide the opportunity for concerned individuals, groups and organisations to bring news to the attention of the mainstream media. Ethan Zuckerman (2004) cites the example of a network of NGOs – most notably Human Rights Watch – that brought increased attention to the situation in Darfur. They had monitored human rights in Sudan for years, provided considerable information on the Janjaweed militias to major newspapers, enabling them to write their first stories on the Darfur situation. According to Zuckerman the NGOs 'did the first round of investigative journalism that news organisations failed to do'. A major report by Human Rights Watch was followed by strong statements from the United Nations and more significantly the US, leading to international media gatekeepers opening the door to stories on Sudan, which increased dramatically. Bloggers have been described as 'feeding' on news that has been 'discarded' or overlooked by mainstream news organisations (MacKinnon, 2008). On occasions these discarded subjects have attracted widespread public interest, challenging the traditional editorial assumptions and norms which shape the work of news organisations. Journalists are much greater consumers of blogs than the general public as a whole; the fear of being 'caught out' is a major reason why journalists, despite concerns about reliability, believe it is necessary to follow the output of the blogosphere (Lowrey, 2006, quoted in MacKinnon, 2008). However, the capacity of concerned individuals, organisations and bloggers to draw attention to international issues and attract public interest still depends on western gatekeepers, western news values, western interests and knowledge and western sources of information. The selection of foreign news is 'still largely dominated by classical journalistic norms and traditional news criteria' (Holm, 2001).

The emergence of global news?

Care has to be taken in generalising about the coverage of the Third World and international relations in general. It is essential to distinguish between the ways in which different media systems as well as different media outlets report international events. Individual American correspondents who cover China complain that while there is a considerable amount of nuanced coverage about the country in the print media and on public radio, it is often drowned out by the more sensational 'black and white' stories on television and in other mass media outlets (cited in MacKinnon, 2008). Several commentators have argued that the global 24-hour satellite news channels are creating a global prism for international reporting. CNN and its competitors have 'extended the narrow "national" journalistic concept by including new political contexts and enlarging the political horizon beyond a single nation-state' (Volkmer, 2002: 245). These organisations and the international news agencies set the news agenda for the smaller national, regional and local news organisations around the world. Not only do they export a particular style of journalism; they also bring about a 'homogenisation' of content. This provides for the development of a 'global public sphere', which is sustaining the growth of a form of global citizenship or cosmopolitanism.

Empirical research into the content and production of international news leads to caution in any assessment of the globalisation of news and international journalism. Studies have found that journalism and the media 'domesticate foreign news in the light of their own national interests ...' (Lee et al., 2005: 332). A comparison between American and Swedish newspaper coverage of the 2003 Iraq war found significant 'differences in tone, war framing and the use of sources', reflecting the differences between the national political elites of the two countries to the war (Dimitrova and Strombeck, 2008). The use of national narratives as the organising schemes for the coverage of the 1997 handover of Hong Kong to China in several different media systems have been documented (Lee et al., 2005). These examples confirm the view that foreign news is 'domesticated' by 'casting faraway events in frameworks that render these events comprehensible, appealing and "relevant" to domestic audiences ... and by constructing meaning of these events in ways that are compatible with ... the "dominant ideology" of the societies they serve' (Gurevitch et al., 1991: 206). While national broadcasters often depend on INAs for raw footage and sound, they often put their own spin on the story to make it relevant to domestic audiences. In increasingly resource-strapped times they – along with other media including the net providers – are more inclined to accept the agency's framing of the story. Despite these economic and financial considerations, research indicates that national media outlets play a key role in domesticating international information for national audiences (Clausen, 2003).

Scholarship has shown that by and large the representation of world events in the news has remained constant in the post-war period, suiting the political and economic interests and aspirations of a small number of actors on the international stage. This pattern remains relatively undisturbed by the emergence of new media technology. Despite high hopes that the internet would bring about change in the pattern of representation of the outside world, which characterised the traditional or old news media, evidence to support the case that new forms of representation are emerging in the internet age is limited. There is an abundance of news online, and changes are apparent in the way in which news is presented, but the content of mainstream and online news outlets is largely the same. Familiar stereotypes and a narrow geographical spread are found in the blogosphere. More significantly, the internet still shows signs of being anchored to a national dimension.

It is argued that due to technological change and globalisation, 'audiences are rapidly shifting from almost exclusively local to communities of interest that transcend geographic and political boundaries' (Thurman, 2007: 286). In transcending national boundaries, people are demanding an international journalism that is more 'global' in content and approach. Transnationalisation is bringing about a global audience for news. The extent to which audiences are freed from the boundaries of the nation-state and the constraints of national perspectives remains a matter of conjecture. It is clear that new technology is having an impact on the consumption of international news but how it is changing people's understanding of and interest in the contemporary world is yet to be fully analysed.

Research indicates that many online readers of established newspapers such as the *Guardian* and the *New York Times* are foreign. The majority of online readership of the *China Times*, the *Jerusalem Post* and the *Guardian* are overwhelming overseas. However, this does not mean their readership is global; those reading the former two newspapers are overwhelmingly drawn from the Chinese and Jewish diasporas and the latter draws heavily on users in the US and North America who make up the largest proportion of the global online audience (Thurman, 2007: 287). Similarly, African newspapers online draw a considerable number of readers from the Africans who have been flung to the far corners of the world as a result of slavery, colonisation, trade, work, exile, migration and banishment (see Ndangam, 2008). By contrast US news sites draw in a much smaller percentage of international readers. For UK news sites American readers make up the majority of the sites' international readers. The BBC news site attracts more US readers than sites of American outlets such as *Fox*, *USA Today* and the *Los Angeles Times* (Thurman, 2007: 302). Many of these readers do not find their own way to the sites but are referred from news indexes such as Google News and aggregating portals. Journalists working on these publications receive instant feedback from their online readership, which is perhaps more broadly drawn than for the hard copy – but this readership is far from representative of a global audience, skewed as it is in national terms to the main consumers of traditional outlets.

Studies of websites set up with the intention of promoting the voices of the marginalised and contributing to the broadening of the international public debate are also skewed in their demographics. For example, most of the visitors to the website magazine of *openDemcoracy* in 2006–8 were drawn from the 'affluent, English or EFL-speaking part of the northern hemisphere, with Europe and North America accounting for 83 per cent of the visits' (Curran and Witschge, 2010: 110). The typical cyberspace user is male, college educated, between 25 and 45 years old, married and earning an above average income (Smillie, 1997). There is a middle-class professional bias to the voices on the net. Conversations are dominated by professionals, interest groups or special pleaders of one kind or another. Participants from the developing world are relatively few and far between. The contribution of these sites to furthering debate is problematic. Attempts to engage readers in debate have resulted in failure with, for example the *New York Times* forced to close down its unmoderated readers forum on nytimes.com owing to the low quality of debate and the vast outpouring of expletives (Benson, 2010: 194). The extent to which online debates extend that found in the mainstream media is questionable.

The advance of a 'global audience' has to be seen in the context of the continued strength of national and local culture in the global era. Updating his landmark study of American media influence across the world, Tunstall (2008) argues that the nation-state, national culture and national media systems have proven more resilient than the globalisation thesis would have us believe. Most people around the world 'prefer their own national news, politics, weather, and football and other sports' (Tunstall, 2008: xiv). This preference is reflected in the online world where national identities and the notion of the 'foreign' retain their validity (Berger, 2009: 362). A study of 246 news websites in 48 countries in the immediate aftermath of the 2003 Iraq War found they were overwhelmingly targeted at a national audience (Dimitrova et al., 2005). They also drew heavily on the international agencies for their raw footage and text. The online media share the tendency of the mainstream media to 'domesticate' the world, emphasising a national outlook. The role of the internet in undermining national audiences is far from clear: it could be argued that the new media are fragmenting the audience into smaller and smaller communities of understanding as much as they are building a homogeneous global audience. Fragmentation is, according to Neil Postman, the price we pay for the information age. It is 'a response to the decline of great national transcendent narratives; that is, people … return to the stories of their own group, their own tribe, in order to find a sense of identity and a sense of meaning' (2004: 5).

CONCLUSION

DEATH OF THE FOREIGN CORRESPONDENT?

New technology today enables international journalism to instantaneously access multimedia communication networks, products and sources. At the same time these technologies have swept away journalists' monopoly of international news gathering, forcing a re-appraisal of the role of the foreign correspondent. For some the foreign correspondent is dead; the days of Ed Murrow and James Cameron are long gone. We are now living in a world in which almost anybody anywhere with an internet connection and a laptop can be an international reporter. Technology and the web have undermined the old model of international reporting, as a variety of manufacturers of international content are able to disseminate their product without assistance from the traditional media. People are communicating with each other across national frontiers in a direct and unmediated way. News organisations are recognising the shift; practices are changing and international news is packaged to reflect these developments. In such a world, is there a need for someone who specialises in the gathering of international news and information?

It may be an overstatement to say that foreign correspondence is dead or even in a state of crisis, but clearly the way foreign correspondents gather, interpret and transmit news from and about faraway places is undergoing a transformation. Technology is driving a great deal of change, and the impact of new media on international journalism can be seen as both beneficial and detrimental. They enable reporters to access more news sources and a broader range of information, send stories and pictures more quickly and more efficiently from the field, as well as provide on-the-spot instant reports of what is happening. However, new technology also leads to a decrease in the capacity and time reporters have to assess the veracity and quality of the information they receive.

Correspondents are becoming more dependent on internet sources. The quality of the information from these sources is problematic, not least because governments can now intervene more effectively in the news production process to place their spin on international events. Sources have more opportunity to influence the work of the foreign correspondent. Equally significant is the enhanced ability for sources to put their message directly to the audience, bypassing the news media and their correspondents. Journalists' increased dependency on official sources and a greater propensity to report what they say is facilitated by technological change, but it is encouraged by other factors.

The changing economic circumstances within which international journalism is practised are a crucial factor. Power within the international newsgathering system has become increasingly concentrated in the hands of fewer and fewer organisations whose operational imperatives are increasingly driven by commercial criteria. The number of organisations with an extensive international newsgathering operation has declined and is likely to continue to decline. The cost of maintaining correspondents and bureaus abroad is increasingly seen as prohibitive. Their operations are driven more by profit, making them concentrate on managing costs and diversifying their ventures into other information-related activities besides news gathering. International news agencies such as Reuters have become more integrated into the international economy as their enterprise has come to focus more on financial information and servicing business clients than the provision of general news. The kind of international news provided is also changing as a result of commercial pressures, which lead to the search for stories that maximise audiences. Correspondents are under pressure not only to file more quickly and often but also to generate more dramatic stories. With news organisations becoming part of huge media conglomerates, such as Disney and the News Corporation, these pressures are more keenly felt. Even public service broadcasters such as the BBC are not immune from the need to maximise audiences and minimise costs as they seek to justify the level of public subsidy they receive.

These organisational changes are accompanied by a significant shift in the occupational culture of the foreign correspondent. The opportunity for the man or woman in the field to resist the pressures from their news desk for this kind of story or that kind of picture is diminishing. Technology has increased the editorial control that news organisations exert over their correspondents as well as reducing the freedom they have to seek out stories, sources and even scoops. The autonomy of the foreign correspondent, with perhaps the exception of a few star names who still have the clout to define their own agenda, has been curtailed. Whether the contemporary correspondent has the inclination to follow his or her intuition and initiate stories has been called into question by many commentators, including some of the doyens of the profession. Ryszard Kapuściński (1999) complained about the disappearance of 'the former heroes of journalism' and their replacement by anonymous media workers. The mission, commitment and dedication of the man and woman in the field are seen as on the wane. International journalism has become a business, a corporate activity, in which 'there is less tolerance for the eccentricities you used to always see in our profession' (quoted in Cole and Hamilton, 2008: 806). In institutional terms there has also been a transfer in the balance of power from the foreign to the diplomatic and/or defence correspondent. Technology and commercialisation have consolidated the position of the latter, who are believed to be able to cover the world more effectively, reliably and cheaply from home. The decline in the number of men and women in the field is a clear manifestation of organisational and occupational change.

Some commentators point out that, in spite of the diminishing number of foreign correspondents, we are getting more information from abroad than ever before. Thanks to the new digital technology and the citizen journalist the world is awash with information about what is happening, even in the remotest places. Satellite television brings worldwide media into the living room; live coverage of international events emanates from the international as well as national news channels around the world. Internet users can look for international news on the trillion or so web pages that at the last count are found on the worldwide web, and mobile services such as Twitter deliver instant networks of global information (Harding, 2009). This is the 'new foreign correspondence' (Hamilton and Jenner, 2003), in which a variety of different kinds of international news gatherers, in addition to the foreign correspondent, are involved in 'a system of multiple models co-existing and collectively providing information' (Cole and Hamilton, 2008: 806).

Those optimistic about the changes taking place in international journalism believe the rise of the citizen journalist more than makes up for the demise of the foreign correspondent. The world is full of international reporters, albeit of varying competence and capability. Individuals have established their own newsrooms, able to produce a wide array of reports and voices. Citizen journalists have not only increased the diversity of perspectives and viewpoints in international news but also democratised international relations by opening up the closed world of international journalism and making politicians more responsive. The new correspondence is judged to be a considerable improvement on what has gone before. But there are several drawbacks to this brave new world-news order and in many aspects it is no different from the old system, suffering from the same inadequacies and failings which have merely been accentuated by technological and commercial change.

There is much hype and speculation about the impact of new technology. The internet has increased the amount of international news available to consumers. Some of these sources have added to the range of viewpoints on international events. However, the overall pattern of international news in the new media does not at this stage of its development differ considerably from that of the old media. Web versions of traditional news outlets, news aggregators and the blogosphere reproduce to a great extent the picture of the world highlighted by the MacBride report back in the 1980s. News about the US is still prevalent, reflecting a bias towards the English-speaking world. Some parts of the planet remain barely visible: South America gets very little coverage, neither does Africa. We can access more newspapers' sites and personal websites from these continents but they still remain small compared to the amount of material on the English-speaking world. What there is primarily reflects the viewpoints of elites in these parts of the world, although NGO websites sometimes provide insights into the lives of ordinary people. The same 'hotspots' dominate news in the mainstream media and in cyberspace. Global events or spectacles, such as the World Cup in South Africa or the Beijing Olympics, do draw attention to these parts of the world but it remains true that newly industrialised countries such as India and China are relatively under-reported in relation to their size and population. International news on the web reflects the same news values as the mainstream media as well as drawing on similar sources. There is a high degree of content homogeneity between the main online news websites, including a comparable level of reliance on the international news agencies. Breaking news and event-oriented news also prevail at the expense of context and interpretation. With a few exceptions it is difficult to see a new news order emerging and it is hard not to agree with the conclusion that:

> ... there is an abundance of news online, but the content of the mainstream news outlets is largely the same, with different outlets – often with a very different ethos and editorial stance – using identical sources, images and similar text. Further, the news angles provided are often similar. (Redden and Witschge, 2010: 184)

There is still a role for the specialist international news gatherer in the news order that is emerging. The amount of information as well as the variability of its quality means that audiences are going to require a professionally compiled digest of what has happened. Readers, viewers, listeners, surfers, users and tweeters do not have the desire, the time or the knowledge to do this (Harding, 2009). There is still a demand for international journalism. Shifting through and making sense of the increased flow of international information from official sources and the flood of user-generated material require the continued expertise of journalists who can be trusted. At times of crisis people continue to rely on the established news organisations for news of what is going on and it is to these organisations that members of the public send their images, accounts and videos of breaking events. Nearly all the major news organisations and news agencies solicit such material (Bivens, 2008: 117). These organisations still fulfil a gate-keeping function in the international news system, as material from the web often only gains public prominence when it appears in the mainstream media. In assessing the quality of the increased flow of information there remain advantages to having someone on-the-spot who can explain events and put them in context. According to CNN President Jon Klein, 'anybody who is there automatically knows more, has better insight than anyone sitting in an office' (quoted in Cheney, 2010). Many web correspondents do not travel; they report the world 'without ever leaving home, literally as armchair blogsters or figuratively as hyper-connected correspondents glued to their cell phones and laptops' (Viviano, 2007).

With their local experience and knowledge, citizen journalists can claim to have intimate and unique insight into local issues and events. Yet is what they produce journalism? Many commentators and practitioners have their doubts, citing the inability of citizen journalists to ask the right questions, to check what they are told, to know what to look for, to care about getting it right and to place events in context (Schmemann, 2010). Tweeting, text messaging, blogging, YouTube postings, and the variety of other inputs that new technology allows people to contribute to the reporting of international events, do not necessarily enhance understanding of what is occurring. As Livingston and Asmolov (2010: 756) state: 'technology may well be no substitute for good journalism'. Pictures and first-hand accounts through the mobile phones of those involved in breaking events do not necessarily lead to any greater understanding of those events and their wider significance in the society in which they are happening. Audiences still seem to want to see a familiar face, a trusted figure interpreting what is happening. The foreign correspondent not only provides an 'authoritative, contextualized, interpretative voice' but also possesses an intimate knowledge of whom he or she is communicating to; not all forms of international 'reporting' are seen as carrying the same weight (Viviano, 2008).

Global change is having an influence on international journalism but there is a tendency in contemporary discussion of what is taking place to exaggerate the novelty of it all. It is striking that the present debate about the impact of technology and commercial change on international journalism resonates with the deliberations that accompanied the arrival of the telegraph, telex and telephone in the late nineteenth century. This should not perhaps surprise us – the late nineteenth century could be interpreted as the 'first wave' of globalisation. Assertions that the industry and profession are facing the greatest ever upheaval characterise both eras (Standage, 1999). Suggestions that we need a new form of journalism to respond to the changes and that journalism can 'save' the world find similar parallels (Beckett, 2008; Stead, 1886). It is possible to trace the standardisation of international journalism to this earlier period, when western news agencies and newspapers were able to impose their values and practices on the rest of the world through military force and empire. Subsequent media – radio, television and now the internet – have simply speeded up this process, which has increasingly concentrated on the American media as they have consolidated their dominance of the international media system in the post-war years. However, the notion of an emerging homogeneous international journalism is problematic. It is possible to make a distinction between style and substance. Television news around the world looks similar; presentation, packages and formats resemble one another. Even the appearance of the anchors, studios and reporters is remarkably similar – and very American in style. Studies have shown that news values are similar across gender, politics, culture and societies – this has led some to conclude that they are universal (see O'Neill and Harcup, 2009). The evidence is not conclusive; the nature of the international system means that many newsrooms have limited choice in terms of the availability of information. They have to accept what the international news agencies and major global broadcasters provide them with. The ability to select is curtailed – hence the international news agenda is similar in most media systems around the world. However, the treatment of news stories indicates that national perspectives, outlooks and loyalties still play a crucial role in shaping the reporting (for example, Nossek, 2004; Peng, 2008). It may be possible to talk about the universalisation of a US style of journalism, an increasing homogenisation of news structures and a standardisation of the international news agenda but the ways in which international stories are framed, interpreted and explained remain rooted in national cultures.

The national embeddedness of international journalism reflects the close connections between news organisations and the state and market, as well as the understanding they have of their audiences. Foreign correspondents have always been cosmopolitan in their disposition; most share John Simpson's assertion that 'we should be telling people more, not less, about the world around them' (Simpson, 2002: 203). They should also be telling them without fear or favour; but, as we have seen, this is not always possible. There are many ways in which foreign correspondents are locked into their national culture – their own cultural conditioning, their reliance on the state for information, the insistence of the market in satisfying particular audiences and clients, and the requirement to make the story clear and understandable to the folks back home. Much of the research into the emergence of global journalism has focused on how international news organisations such as CNN contribute to global interconnectedness, global citizenship, the sense of belonging to a global community or the building of a 'global sphere' (for example, Volkmer, 1999; Hannerz, 1996). Rather than examine what journalism does to the audience, we can postulate about the effect of audiences on the profession. With the mass of the people semi- or fully detached from the international media, national and local values predominate. It is elites who experience what is described as the 'compression of the world' and the 'intensification of consciousness'. Foreign correspondents are part of this 'transnational' class who, as a result of empire and international trade, have operated comfortably in a world of cultural difference since the earliest days of the print media. This class and their feelings of cosmopolitanism have extended with the development of international capital. However, their cosmopolitanism has always been anchored within national parameters of understanding. International journalism is devoted to the 'thematization of difference' (Cottle, 2009). This reflects their need to satisfy the audience which, in addition to getting a good story and bearing witness to events, is the primary driver of journalism. Reflecting difference is crucial to what international journalism does, telling international events from national and local perspectives.

The dilemma is whether today's foreign correspondents are able to do the job. There is an idealised notion of the specialised foreign correspondent put forward by the profession and promoted in the autobiographies and books of many foreign correspondents. We have identified in the previous chapters the variety of factors that impair the ability of international reporters to live up to this representation. From practical obstacles such as lack of language skills, limited cultural knowledge, vast territories to cover and short stays on the beat, to broader political, economic, cultural and organisational pressures, foreign correspondents have faced considerable challenges in reporting the world. In the era of globalisation these challenges have multiplied and the traditional correspondent now faces competition from other types of international news gatherer. This competition in some cases extends the range of coverage with the growth of non-western voices and perspectives such as Al-Jazeera in the international newsgathering process. However, it also highlights the limitations under which many correspondents today labour. They are more scrutinised, under greater editorial control, have less job security and exhibit fewer idiosyncrasies; they have less time to check stories and have to fight more for space and air time. Under these conditions, it is fair to ask whether even the most talented foreign correspondent can succeed in conveying the complexities of what is happening in the world today.

BIBLIOGRAPHY

Abbott, K (2009) 'Working together, NGOs and journalists can create stronger interna-
    tional reporting', www.niemanlab.org/2009/11/ngos-as-newsmakers-a-new-series-
    on-the-evolving-news-ecosystem/ (accessed 30/1/2010).

Adams, W (1982) *TV Coverage of International Affairs*. New Jersey: Ablex.

Adams, W (1986) 'Whose lives count? TV coverage of natural disasters', *Journal of
    Communication* 36(2): 113–22.

Adie, K (1988) 'Foreign bodies: part six', *The Listener*, 23 June.

Adie, K (2002) *The Kindness of Strangers*. London: Hodder

Ahern, T (1984) 'Determinants of Foreign News Coverage in Newspapers', in
    Stevenson, R and Shaw, D (eds) *Foreign News and the New World Information Order*.
    Ames: Iowa State University Press.

Alagiah, G (1999) 'New light on dark continent', *Guardian* Media Section, pp. 4–5.

Albritton, R and Manheim, J (1985) 'Public relations effort for the Third World: images
    in the news', *Journal of Communication* 35: 43–59.

Allan, S (2004) 'Conflicting Truths: Online News and the War in Iraq', in Paterson, C and
    Sreberny, A (eds) *International News in the Twenty-first Century* Luton: John Libbey.
    pp. 285–99.

Allan, S (2005) 'Introduction', in Allan, S (ed.) *Journalism: Critical Issues*. Milton
    Keynes: Open University Press.

Allan, S (2006) *Online News*. London: Sage.

Allan, S and Zelizer, B (2004) *Reporting War: Journalism in Wartime*. London:
    Routledge.

Allen, C and Hamilton, J Maxwell (2010) 'Normalcy and foreign news', *Journalism
    Studies* 11(53): 634–49.

Alleyne, M (1995) *International Power and International Communication*. London:
    Macmillan.

Alleyne, M (1997) *News Revolution: Political and Economic Decisions about Global
    Information*. London: Macmillan.

Alleyne, M (2003) *Global Lies? Propaganda, the UN and World Order*. London:
    Macmillan.

Alter, J (1990) 'Prime Time Revolution', *Newsweek*, 8 January.

Altschull, H (1995) *Agents of Power: The Media and Public Policy*. New York: Longman.

Anden-Papadopoulos, K (2008) 'The Abu Ghraib torture photographs: news frames,
    visual culture and the power of images', *Journalism Theory, Practice and Criticism*
    9(1): 5–30.

Anden-Papadopoulos, K (2009) 'US soldiers imaging the Iraq War on YouTube', *Popular Communication* 7: 17–27.

Anderson, B (1983) *Imagined Communities: Reflections on the Origins and Spread of Nationalism*. London: Verso.

Anderson, M and Richstad, J (1981) *Crisis in International News*. New York: Columbia University Press.

Anderson, P and Weymouth, A (1999) *Insulting the Public? The British Press and the European Union*. London: Longman.

Ankomah, B (2008) 'Reporting Africa', *Africa Files*, www.africafiles.org/printableversion.asp?id=18785 (accessed 4/11/2008).

Arblaster, P (2005) 'Posts, newsletters, newspapers: England in a European system of communications', *Media History* 11(1/2): 21–36.

Arlen, M (1968) *The Living Room War*. New York: Vintage Books.

Arlen, M (1982) 'The war: the Falklands, the Vietnam War and our collective memory', *The New Yorker*, 16 August.

Atwood, E and Murphy, S (1982) 'The "dialogue of the deaf": the new world information order debate', *International Communication Gazette* 30(13): 13–23.

Bagdikian, B (2004) *The New Media Monopoly*. Boston: Beacon Press.

Baines, G (1990) 'Beams fuel the flames', *The Guardian*, 8 January.

Baker, N (2004) 'Invisible Giants, Quiet Revolution', in Paterson, C and Sreberny, A (eds) *International News in the Twenty-first century*. Luton: John Libbey. pp. 63–78.

Baker, N (2009) 'Technology, Timelessness and Taste: The Battlefronts for the Twenty-first Century News Agency', in Owen, J and Purdey, H (eds) *International News Reporting: Frontlines and Deadlines*. London: Wiley-Blackwell. pp. 38–54.

Barnett, R and Cavanagh, J (1994) *Global Dreams: Imperial Corporations and the New World Order*. New York: Touchstone.

Barnet, R and Mueller, R (1974) *Global Reach*. New York: Simon & Schuster.

Barry, A (1988) 'Black Mythologies: Representation of Black People on British Television', in Twitchin, J (ed.) *The Black and White Media Book*. Stoke-on-Trent: Trentham Books.

Bartram, J (2003) 'News agency wars: the battle between Reuters and Bloomberg', *Journalism Studies* 4(3): 387–99.

Baum, S (2002) 'Sex, lies and war: how soft news brings foreign policy to the inattentive public', *The American Political Science Review* 96(1): 91–109.

Bauman, Z (1998) *Globalization – The Human Consequences*. London: Polity Press.

BBC (2003) *War Spin*, broadcast, 18 May.

BBC (2008) 'Does foreign news exist anymore?' News report, 21 November.

BBC (2010) *BBC's international news services attract record global audience*. Press release 24 May. www.bbc.co.uk/pressoffice/pressrelease/stories/2010/05-may/24wsn

BBC World Service (2001) *History's Witness: Ryszard Kapuściński*, http://www.bbc.co.uk/worldservice/people/highlights/010817_kapuscinski.shtml

Beattie, L, Miller, D, Miller, E and Philo, G (1999) 'The Media and Africa: Images of Disaster and Rebellion', in Philo, G (ed.) *Message Received*. London: Longman. pp. 229–68.

Beck, U (2006) *Cosmopolitan Vision*. Cambridge: Polity Press.

Beckett, C (2008) *SuperMedia: Saving Journalism So It Can Save the World*. Oxford: Blackwell Publishing.

Beer, A and Merrill, J (2004) *Global Journalism: Topical Issues and Media Systems*. London: Pearson.

Behr, E (1982) *Anyone Here Raped and Speaks English?* London: New English Library.

Bell, M (1995) *In Harm's Way: Reflections of a War Zone Thug*. London: Hamish Hamilton.

Bell, M (1998) 'The Journalism of Attachment', in Kiernan, M (ed.) *Media Ethics*. London: Routledge. pp. 16–22.

Bell, M (2008) 'The death of news', *Media, War and Conflict* 1(2): 221–31.

Benson, R (2010) 'Futures of the News: International Considerations and Further Reflections', in Fenton, N (ed.) *New Media, Old News: Journalism and Democracy in the Digital Age*. London: Sage. pp. 187–200.

Benthall, J (1993) *Disasters, Relief and the Media*. London: I.B. Taurus.

Berger, G (2009) 'How the internet impacts on international news: exploring paradoxes of the most global medium in a time of "hyperlocalism"', *The International Communication Gazette* 71(5): 355–71.

Berglez, P (2008) 'What is global journalism?', *Journalism Studies* 9(6): 845–58.

Bielsa, E (2008) 'The pivotal role of news agencies in the context of globalization: a historical approach', *Global Networks* 8(3): 347–66.

Bielsa, P and Bassett, S (2009) *Translation in Global News*. London: Routledge.

Billig, M (1995) *Banal Nationalism*. London: Sage.

Bilteryst, D (2001) 'Global News Research and Complex Citizenship. Towards an Agenda for Research on Foreign/International News and Audiences', in Hjarvard, S (ed.) *News in a Globalized Society*. Göteborg: Nordicom.

Bivens, R (2008) 'The internet, mobile phones and blogging', *Journalism Practice* 2(1): 113–29.

Boafo, S (1992) 'Mass media in Africa: constraints and possible solutions', *Media Development* 1(4): 49–52.

Bogart, L (1968) 'The overseas newsman: A 1967 profile study', *Journalism Quarterly* 45: 298–306.

Borrat, H (1992) 'Coverage of the Gulf War by the Spanish and Catalonian Media', in Mowlana, H, Gerbner, G and Schiller, H (eds) *Triumph of the Image: The Media's War in the Persian Gulf – A Global Perspective*. Boulder: Westview Press. pp. 152–63.

Boston, R (1990) *The Essential Fleet Street: Its History and Influence*. London: Blandford.

Boyd, D (2003) 'Sharq Al-Adna/The Voice of Britain: the UK's 'secret' Arabic radio station and Suez war propaganda disaster', *Gazette: The International Journal for Communication Studies* 65(6): 443–55.

Boyd-Barrett, O (1977) 'The Collection of Foreign News in the National Press: Organisation and Resources' (Working Paper 3), in Boyd-Barrett, O, Seymour-Ure, C and Tunstall, J (eds) *Studies on the Press*. London: HMSO. pp. 15–43.

Boyd-Barrett, O (1978) 'Market Control and Wholesale News: The Case of Reuters', in Boyce, G, Curran, J and Wingate, P (eds) *Newspaper History: From the 17th Century to the Present Day*. London: Constable. pp. 192–204.

Boyd-Barrett, O (1980) *The International News Agencies*. London: Constable.

Boyd-Barrett, O (1997) 'Global News Wholesalers as Agents of Globalisation', in Sreberny-Mohammadi, A, Wisbeck, D, McKenna, J and Boyd-Barrett, O (eds) *Media in a Global Context*. London: Arnold. pp. 131–44.

Boyd-Barrett, O (1998) 'Global News Agencies', in Boyd-Barrett, O and Rantanen, T (eds) *The Globalization of News*. London: Sage. pp. 19–34.

Boyd-Barrett, O (2000) 'National and international news agencies: issues of crisis and realignment', *International Communication Gazette* 62(1): 5–18.

Boyd-Barrett, O (2003) 'Globalizing the national news agency', *Journalism Studies* 4(3): 371–85.

Boyd-Barrett, O and Rantanen, T (1998) *The Globalization of News*. London: Sage.

Boyd-Barrett, O and Rantanen, T (2001) 'News Agency Correspondents', in Tunstall, J (ed.) *Media Occupations and Professions*. Oxford: Oxford University Press.

Boyd-Barrett, O and Rantanen, T (2004a) 'Global and National News Agencies: The Unstable Nexus', in de Beer, A and Merrill, J (eds) *Global Journalism: Topical Issues and Media Systems*. London: Pearson. pp. 35–49.

Boyd-Barrett, O and Rantanen, T (2004b) 'News Agencies as News Sources: A Re-evaluation', in Paterson, C and Sreberny, A (eds) *International News in the Twenty-first century*. Luton: John Libbey. pp. 31–46.

Boyd-Barrett, O and Thussu, D (1992) *Contra Flows in Global News: International and Regional News Exchange Mechanisms*. Luton: John Libbey.

Brayne, M (2004) 'Emotions, Trauma and Good Journalism', in Paterson, C and Sreberny, A (eds) *International News in the Twenty-first Century*. Luton: John Libbey. pp. 275–84.

Brittain, V (2007) 'Obiturary: Ryszard Kapuściński', *The Guardian*, 25 January.

Bromley, M (1997) 'The End of Journalism: Changes in Workplace Practices in the Press and Broadcasting in the 1990s', in Bromley, M and O'Malley, T (eds) *Journalism: A Reader*. London: Routledge. pp. 330–50.

Brook, T (2008) *Vermeer's Hat: The Seventeenth Century and the Dawn of the Global World*. London: Profile Books.

Brown, L (1977) 'The Treatment of News in Mid-Victorian Newspapers', in *Transactions of the Royal Historical Society* (Fifth Series).

Brown, L (1985) *Victorian News and Newspapers*. Oxford: Clarendon Press.

Brown, R (2003) 'Spinning the War', in Thussu, D and Freedman, D (eds) *War and the Media*. London: Sage. pp. 87–100.

Brownlees, N (2005) 'Spoken discourse in early English newspapers', *Media History* 11(1/2): 69–85.

Burman, T (2009) 'World Perspective: Ignoring the World at our Peril', in Owen, J and Purdey, H (eds) *International News Reporting*. London: Wiley-Blackwell. pp. 127–43.

Campbell, N, Davies, J and McKay, G (eds) (2004) *Issues in Americanisation and Culture*. Edinburgh: Edinburgh University Press.

Campbell, V (2004) *Journalism in the Information Age*. London: Arnold.

Cameron, J (1978) *Points of Departure: Experiments in Biography*. London: Panther.

Carlson, M (2007) 'Order versus access: news search engines and the challenges to traditional journalistic roles', *Media, Culture & Society* 29(6): 1014–30.

CARMA (2006) *The CARMA Report on Western Media Coverage of Humanitarian Disasters*. Carma, European Office, 2006. http://www.carma.com/images/white papers/CARMA%20Media%20Analysis%20%20Western%20Media%20 Coverage%20of%20Humanitarian%20Disasters.pdf

Carruthers, S (2000) *The Media at War*. London: Palgrave.

Carruthers, S (2004) 'Tribalism and Tribulation: Media Constructions of "African Savagery" and "Western Humanitarianism"', in Allan, S and Zelizer, B (eds) *Reporting War*. London: Routledge. pp. 155–73.

Carver, R (1982) 'Media and Zimbabwe', in Cohen, P and Gardner, C (eds) *It Ain't Half Racist, Mum: Fighting Racism in the Media*. London: Comedia. pp. 53–8.

Castells, M (1996) *The Rise of the Network Society*. London: Blackwell.

Chadwick, A (2006) *Internet Politics: State, Citizens and New Communication Technologies*. Oxford: Oxford University Press.

Chalkley, A (1970) *A Manual of Development Journalism*. New Delhi: Vikas.

Chambers, D, Steiner, L and Fleming, C (2004) *Women and Journalism*. London: Routledge.

Chang, T-K (1998) 'All countries are not created equal to be news: world system and international communication', *Communication Research* 25: 528–66.

Chang, T-K, Himelboim, I and Dong, D (2009) 'Open global networks, closed international flows: world system and political economy of hyperlinks in cyberspace', *International Communication Gazette* 71(3): 137–59.

Cheney, C (2010) 'Foreign Correspondence in Flux', *The Yale Globalist*, http://tyglobalist.org/index.php/20100404272/Focus/Foreign-Correspondence (accessed 26/7/10).

Chia, L (2007) 'Foreign news coverage in four online newspapers' BA thesis (unpublished) School of Journalism and Communication, University of Queensland, Brisbane, Australia, cited in Obijiofor, L and Hanush, F (forthcoming) *Journalism Across Cultures: An Introduction*. London: Palgrave.

Chibnall, S (1977) *Law and Order News*. London: Tavistock Press.

Chu, J and Gross, P (1988) 'Foreign Correspondents Covering Taiwan: A Preliminary Study of Attitudes, Perceptions and Processes', paper presented at International Association of Mass Communication research conference, Barcelona, Spain, July.

Clarke, B (2004) *From Grub Street to Fleet Street: An Illustrated History of English Newspapers to 1899*. Aldershot: Ashgate.

Clausen, L (2003) *Global News Production*. Copenhagen: Copenhagen Business School Press.

Cockburn, A (1987) *Corruptions of Empire*. London: Verso.

Cockett, R (1989) *The Twilight of Truth: Chamberlain, Appeasement and the Manipulation of the Press*. London: Weidenfeld and Nicholson.

Cohen, R and Kennedy, P (2000) *Global Sociology*. London: Palgrave.

Cohen, Y (1988) 'News media and the News Department of the Foreign and Commonwealth Office', *Review of International Studies* 14(2): 117–31.

Cohen, Y (n/d) Technological Change and Foreign News Reporting From Israel, http://cmsprod.bgu.ac.il/NR/rdonlyres/8676FECO-E297-4B96-BF2F-034487138388/12237/CohenY.pdf

Cole, J and Hamilton, JM (2008) 'The history of a surviving species: defining eras in the evolution of foreign correspondence', *Journalism Studies* 9(5): 798–812.

Collins, R (1990) *Television Policy and Culture*. London: Unwin Hyman.

Compaine, B (2002) 'Global Media', *Foreign Policy*, November/December: 20–8.

Constable, P (2007) 'Demise of the foreign correspondent', *The Washington Post* 18 February.

Constantine, S (1986) 'Bringing the Empire Alive: The Empire Marketing Board and Imperial Propaganda', in MacKenzie, J (ed.) *Imperialism and Popular Culture*. Manchester: Manchester University Press. pp. 192–231.

Consuming Hunger (1988) documentary produced by Maryknoll World Productions and directed by Ilan Ziv and Freke Vuijst.

Cook, J (2009) 'Internet warfare team unveiled: Twitters paid to spread Israeli propaganda', *Global Research*, 21 July, www.globalresearch.ca/PrintArticle.php@articleId=14465

Cooper, G (2007) '"Anyone here survived a wave, speak English and got a mobile?", Aid agencies, the Media and Reporting Disasters since the Tsunami', *The 14th Guardian Lecture*.

Cooper, G (2009) 'When lines between NGO and news organization blur', December 21www.niemanlab.org/2009/11/ngos-as-newsmakers-a-new-series-on-the-evolving-news-ecosystem/ (accessed 30/1/2010).

Cooper, K (1942) *Barriers Down*. New York: Farrer and Rinehart.

Constable, P (2007) 'Demise of the Foreign Correspondent', *The Washington Post*, 18 February.

Cottle, S (2009) *Global Crisis Reporting: Journalism in the Global Age*. Maidenhead: Open University Press.

Cottle, S and Nolan, D (2009) 'How the media's codes and rules influence the ways in which NGOs work', www.niemanlab.org/2009/11/ngos-as-newsmakers-a-new-series-on-the-evolving-news-ecosystem/ (accessed 30/1/2010).

Cozma, R and Hamilton, J (2009) 'Film portrayals of foreign correspondents: a content analysis of movies before World War II and after Vietnam', *Journalism Studies*, First article: 1–17.

Crouse, T (1972) *The Boys on the Bus*. New York: Ballantine Books.

Curran, J (1982) 'Communications, Power and Social Order', in Gurevitch, M, Bennett, T, Curran, J and Woollacott, J (eds) *Culture, Society and the Media*. London: Methuen. pp. 202–35.

Curran, J and Witschge, T (2010) 'Liberal Dreams and the Internet', in Fenton, N (ed.) *New Media, Old News: Journalism and Democracy in the Digital Age*. London: Sage.

Curran, J and Park, M-J (eds) (2000) *De-Westernising Media Studies*. London: Routledge.

Curran, J and Seaton, J (1997) *Power Without Responsibility*. London: Routledge.

Da Lage, O (2005) 'The Politics of Al-Jazeera or the Diplomacy of Doha', in Zayani, M (ed.) *The Al-Jazeera Phenomenon: Critical Perspective on New Arab Media*. London: Pluto Press. pp. 45–61.

Dahlgren, P and Chakrapani, S (1982) 'The Third World on TV News: Western Ways of Seeing the "Other"', in Adams, W (ed.) *Television Coverage of International Affairs*. New Jersey: Ablex. pp. 46–63.

Darwin, J (2007) *After Tamerlaine: The Rise and Fall of Global Empires, 1400–2000*. London: Penguin.

Deacon, D (2008) 'Elective and experiential affinities: British and American foreign correspondents and the Spanish Civil War', *Journalism Studies* 9(3): 392–408.

Deacon, D (2009) 'Going to Spain with the Boys: Women Correspondents and the Spanish Civil War', in Bailey, M (ed.) *Narrating Media History*. London: Routledge. pp. 66–78.

de Burgh, H (ed.) (2005) *Making Journalists*. London: Routledge.

de Moragas Spa, M, Garitaonandia, C and Lopez, B (1999) *Television On Your Doorstep: Decentralisation Experiences in the European Union*. Luton: John Libbey.

Deuze, M (2003) 'The web and its journalism. Considering the consequences of different types of news media online', *New Media & Society* 5: 203–30.

Deuze, M (2005) 'What is journalism? Professional identity and ideology of journalists reconsidered', *Journalism Theory, Practice & Criticism* 6(4): 443–65.

Dimitrova, D. and Strombeck, J (2008) 'Foreign policy and the framing of the 2003 Iraq war in elite Swedish and US newspapers', *Media, War and Conflict* 1(2): 203–20.

Dimitrova, D, Kaid, L, Williams, A and Trammell, K (2005) 'War on the web: the immediate news framing of Gulf War II', *The Harvard International Journal of Press/Politics* 10(1): 22–44.

D'Haenens, L and Blink, S (2007) 'Islam in the Dutch press: with special attention to the *Algemeen Dagblad*', *Media, Culture & Society* 29(1): 135–49.

D'Haenens, L and Verelst, C (2002) 'Portrayal of Indonesia's reform in the Dutch print media', *Gazette: The International Journal for Communication Studies* 64(2): 183–97.

Dorfman, A and Matterlart, A (1975) *How to Read Donald Duck: Imperialist Ideology in the Disney Comic.* New York: International General.

Dorman, W (1985) 'The media: playing the government's game', *Bulletin of Atomic Scientists* August: 118–24.

Dorman, W (1986) 'Peripheral vision: US journalism and the Third World', *World Policy* Summer: 419–45.

Dorman, W and Farhang, M (1987) *The US Press and Iran.* Berkeley: University of California Press.

Dover, C and Barnett, S (2004) *The World on the Box: International Issues in News and Factual Programmes on UK Television 1975–2003.* Third World and Environment Broadcasting Project.

Downing, J (1996) *International Media Theory.* London: Sage.

Elliott, P and Golding, P (1973a) 'The News Media and Foreign Affairs', in Boardman, R and Groom, AJR (eds) *The Management of Britain's External Relations.* London: Macmillan. pp. 305–30.

Elliott, P and Golding, P (1973b) 'Mass Communication and Social Change: The Imagery of Development and the Development of Imagery', in de Kadt, E (ed.) *The Sociology of Development.* London: Macmillan. pp. 229–52.

El-Nawawy, M and Iskandar, A (2003) *Al-Jazeera: The Story of the Network that is Rattling Governments and Redefining Modern Journalism.* Cambridge, MA: Westview Press.

El-Nawawy, M and Kelly, J (2001) 'Between the government and the press: the role of western correspondents and government public relations in Middle East coverage', *Press/Politics* 6(3): 90–109.

Elvestad, E (2009) 'Introverted locals or world citizens? A quantitative study of interest in local and foreign news in traditional media and on the internet', *Nordicom Review* 30(2): 105–23.

Emery, M (1989) 'An endangered species: The international news hole', *Gannett Center Journal* 3(4): 151–64.

Entman, R (2004) *Projections of Power: Framing News, Public Opinion and US Foreign Policy.* Chicago: University of Chicago Press.

Epstein, E (1973) *News from Nowhere.* New York: Vintage Books.

Erickson, E and Hamilton, J (2007) 'Happy Landings: A Defense of Parachute Journalism', in Perlmutter, D and Hamilton, JM (eds) *From Pigeons to News Portals.* Baton Rouge: Louisiana State University Press. pp. 130–49.

Fahmy, S (2010) 'How Could So Much Produce So Little? Foreign Affairs Reporting in the Wake of 9/11', in Golan, G, Johnson, TJ and Wanta, W (eds) *International Media Communication in a Global Age.* London: Routledge. pp. 147–59.

Fallows, J (1997) *Breaking the News: How the Media Undermine American Democracy.* New York: Vintage Books.

Fenby, J (1986) *The International News Services.* New York: Schocken Books.

Fenton, N (2009) 'Has the internet changed how NGOs work with established media? Not enough', www.niemanlab.org/2009/11/ngos-as-newsmakers-a-new-series-on-the-evolving-news-ecosystem/ (accessed 12/1/10).

Fenton, N (2010) 'NGOs, New Media and the Mainstream News: News from Everywhere', in Fenton, N (ed.) *New Media, Old News: Journalism and Democracy in the Digital Age.* London: Sage. pp. 153–68.

Ferguson, M (1992) 'The mythology about globalization', *European Journal of Communication* 7: 69–93.

First, A (2002) 'All women should cry: the presentation of women in foreign news', *Communications* 27(1): 35–61.

Fisk, R (1988) 'Press corps battles for Beirut headlines', *The Guardian*, May 28.

Flournoy, D and Stewart, R (1997) *CNN: Making News in the Global Market*. Luton: John Libbey.

Forbes, D, with Malan, M and Boyd-Barrett, O (1998) 'From Apartheid to Pluralism', in Boyd-Barrett, O and Rantanen, T (eds) *The Globalization of News*. London: Sage. pp. 154–72.

Fossato, F and Lloyd, J with Verkhovsky, A (2008) *The Web that Failed: How Opposition Politics and Independent Initiatives are Failing on the Internet in Russia*. Oxford: Reuters Institute for the Study of Journalism.

Fox, R (1988) 'Foreign bodies: part six', *The Listener*, 9 June.

Franks, S (2004) 'The world on the box: international issues in news and factual programmes', *The Political Quarterly* 75(X): 425–28.

Franks, S (2005) 'Lacking a clear narrative: foreign reporting after the Cold War', *The Political Quarterly* 76(51): 91–101.

Franks, S (2006) 'The CARMA report: western media coverage of humanitarian disasters', *The Political Quarterly* 77(2): 281–84.

Franks, S (2010) 'The neglect of Africa and the power of aid', *International Communication Gazette* 72(1): 71–84.

Franks, S and Seaton, J (2009) 'Is saving the world journalism's job?', *British Journalism Review* 20(2): 13–20.

Freedman, D (2010) 'The Political Economy of the "New" News Environment', in Fenton, N (ed.) *New Media, Old News: Journalism and Democracy in the Digital Age*. London: Sage. pp. 35–50.

Friedland, L (1992) *Covering the World: International Television News Services*. New York: Twentieth Century Fund Press.

Gaber, I, Seymour, E and Thomas, L (2009) 'Is the BBC biased? The Corporation and the coverage of the 2006 Israeli-Hezbollah war', *Journalism Theory and Practice* 10(2): 239–59.

Gallagher, M (1981) *Unequal Opportunities: The Case of Women and the Media*. Paris: UNESCO.

Galtung, J (2002) 'Peace Journalism – A Challenge', in Kempf, W and Luostarinen, H (eds) *Journalism and the New Order: Vol 2 Studying War and Media*. Göteborg: Nordicom.

Galtung, J and Ruge, M (1965) 'The structure of foreign news: the presentation of the Congo, Cuba and Cyprus crises in four Norwegian newspapers', *Journal of International Peace Research* 1: 64–91. Reprinted in Tumber, H (ed.) *News: A Reader*. Oxford: Oxford University Press. pp. 21–31.

Gans, H (1980) *Deciding What's News*. New York: Pantheon Books.

Gasher, M (2007) 'The view from here. A news-flow study of the on-line editions of Canada's national newspapers', *Journalism Studies* 8(2): 299–319.

Gasher, M and Gabriele, S (2004) 'Increasing circulation? A comparative news flow study of the *Montreal Gazette*'s hard copy and on-line editions', *Journalism Studies* 5(3): 311–23.

Gavin, N (2001) 'British journalists in the spotlight: Europe and media research', *Journalism Theory, Practice & Criticism* 2(3): 299–314.

Geertsema, M (2009) 'Women and news', *Feminist Media Studies* 9(2): 149–72.

Gellner, E (1983) *Nations and Nationalism*. Oxford: Blackwell.

Gerbner, G and Marvanyi, G (1983) 'The Many Worlds of International News?', in Richstad, J and Anderson, M (eds) *Crisis in International News: Policies and Prospects*. New York: Columbia University Press. pp. 184–96.

Ghorpade, S (1984) 'Foreign correspondents cover Washington for the world', *Journalism Quarterly* 61: 667–71.

Giffard, CA (1998) 'Alternative News Agencies', in Boyd-Barrett, O and Rataanen, T (eds) *The Globalisation of News*. London: Sage. pp. 191–201.

Giffard, CA (1999) 'The Beijing Conference on Women as seen by three international news agencies', *International Communication Gazette* 61(3–4): 327–41.

Giffard, CA and Rivenburgh, N (2000) 'News agencies, national images and global media events', *Journalism and Mass Communication Quarterly* 77(1): 8–21.

Gilboa, E (2005a) 'The CNN effect: the search for a communication theory of international relations', *Political Communication* 22(1): 27–44.

Gilboa, E (2005b) 'Media-broker diplomacy: when journalists become mediators', *Critical Studies in Media Communication* 22(2): 99–120.

Giridharadas, A (2009) 'These Days, No Reporting Behind a Nation's Back', *The New York Times* 15 March, www.nytimes.com/2009/03/15/weekinreview/15GIRIDHARADAS.html? (accessed 24/11/2009).

Gitlin, T (1980) *The World is Watching: Mass Media in the Making and Unmaking of the New Left*. Berkeley: University of California Press.

Glasgow Media Group (2000) *Viewing the World: News Content and Audience Studies*. London: DFID.

Golan, G (2008) 'Where in the world is Africa? Predicting coverage of Africa by US television networks', *International Communication Gazette* 70(1): 41–57.

Golding, P (1977) 'Media Professionalism in the Third World', in Curran, J, Gurevitch, M and Woollacott, J (eds) *Mass Communication and Society*. London: Edward Arnold. pp. 29–308.

Golding, P (1998) 'Global Village or Cultural Pillage? The Unequal Inheritance of the Communications Revolution', in McChesney, R, Meiksins Wood, E and Bellamy Foster, J (eds) *Capitalism and the Information Age: The Political Economy of the Global Communication Revolution*. New York: Monthly Review Press. pp. 69–85.

Golding, P and Elliott, P (1979) *Making the News*. London: Longman.

Golding, P and Harris, P (1997) *Beyond Cultural Imperialism: Globalisation, Communication and the New International Order*. London: Sage.

Goodman, A and Pollock, J (1997) *The World on a String: How to Become a Freelance Foreign Correspondent*. New York: Owl.

Gowing, N (2003) 'Journalists and War: the Troubling New Tensions Post 9/11', in Thussu, D and Freedman, D (eds) *War and the Media*. London: Routledge.

Gowing, N (2009) *'Skyful of Lies' and Black Swans: The New Tyranny of Shifting Information Power in Crises*. Oxford: Reuters Institute for the Study of Journalism.

Griffiths, D (2006) *Fleet Street: Five Hundred Years of the British Press*. London: The British Library.

Gurevitch, M, Levy, M and Roeh, I (1991) 'The global newsroom: convergences and diversities in the globalization of television news', in Dahlgren, P and Sparks, C (eds) *Communication and Citizenship: Journalism and the Public Sphere*. London: Routledge. pp. 195–217.

Gynnild, A (2005) 'Winner takes it all: freelance journalism on the global communication market', *Nordicom Review* 1(1): 111–20.

Hafez, K (2007) *The Myth of Media Globalization*. London: Polity.

Hafez, K (2009) 'Let's improve "global journalism"', *Journalism* 10(3): 329–31.

Hahn, O and Lonnendonker, J (2009) 'Transatlantic foreign reporting and foreign correspondents after 9/11: trends in reporting Europe in the United States', *International Journal of Press/Politics Online First*: 1–19.

Hall, J (2000) 'The first web war: bad things happen in unimportant places', *Journalism Studies* 1(3): 387–404.

Hallin, D (1986) *The Uncensored War: The Media and Vietnam*. Oxford: Oxford University Press.

Hallin, D and Mancini, P (2004) *Comparative Media Systems*. London: Sage.

Halonen, IK (1999) 'Images of war reporting: Mama, Mama, my hand is gone!', *Nordicom Review* 1(2): 5–18.

Halavais, A (2000) 'National borders on the world wide web', *New Media and Society* 2(1): 7–28.

Hamelink, C (1983) *Cultural Autonomy in Global Communications*. New York: Longman.

Hamelink, C (1995) *World Communication: Disempowerment and Self-Empowerment*. London: Zed Books.

Hamilton, JT and Lawrence, R (2010) 'Bridging past and future: using history and practice to inform social scientific study of foreign newsgathering', *Journalism Studies* 11(5): 683–99.

Hamilton, JM and Jenner, E (2002) *Redefining Foreign Correspondence*. The Joan Shorenstein Center on the Press, Politics and Public Policy Working Paper (Fall).

Hamilton, JM and Jenner, E (2003) 'The new foreign correspondence', *Foreign Affairs* September/October 82(5): 131–38.

Hamilton, JM and Jenner, E (2004) 'Redefining foreign correspondence', *Journalism* 5(3): 301–21.

Hamilton, JT (2010) 'The (many) markets for international news: how news from abroad sells at home', *Journalism Studies* 11(5): 650–66.

Hammersley, B (2009) 'Working at the Coalface of the New Media', in Owen, J and Purdey, H (eds) *International News Reporting: Frontlines and Deadlines*. London: Wiley-Blackwell. pp. 243–52.

Hammond, P (2007) *Media, War and Postmodernity*. London: Routledge.

Hampton, M (2004) *Visions of the Press in Britain, 1850–1950*. Urbana and Chicago: University of Illinois Press.

Hannerz, U (1992) *Global Complexity*. New York: Columbia University Press.

Hannerz, U (1996) *Transnational Connections: Culture, People and Places*. London: Routledge.

Hannerz, U (1998) 'Reporting from Jerusalem', *Cultural Anthropology* 13(4): 548–74.

Hannerz, U (2004) *Foreign News: Exploring the World of Foreign Correspondents*. Chicago: University of Chicago Press.

Hannerz, U (2007) 'Foreign correspondents and the varieties of cosmopolitanism', *Journal of Ethnic and Migration Studies* 33(2): 309.

Hanusch, F (2008) 'Valuing those close to us: a comparison of German and Australian quality newspapers' reporting of death in foreign news', *Journalism Studies* 9(3): 341–56.

Harcup, T and O'Neill, D (2001) 'What is news? Galtung and Ruge revisited', *Journalism Studies* 2(2): 261–80.

Harding, P (2009) *The Great Global Switch-off: International Coverage in UK Public Service Broadcasting*. A Report for POLIS/Oxfam.

Hardy, J (2008) *Western Media Systems*. London: Routledge.

Hargreaves, I (2000) 'Is there a future for foreign news?', *Historical Journal of Film, Radio and Television* 20(1): 55–61.

Harriman, E (1987) *Hack: Home Truths about Foreign News*. London: Zed Press.

Harris, P (1981) *Reporting Southern Africa: Western News Agencies Reporting from Southern Africa*. Paris: UNESCO.

Harrison, P (1986) 'An Independent View', talk at African Studies Association of the United Kingdom symposium, Royal Commonwealth Institute, London, 6 December.

Harrison, P and Palmer, R (1986) *News Out of Africa*. London: Hilary Shipman.

Hatchen, W (1971) *Muffled Drums: The News Media in Africa*. Ames: Iowa State University Press.

Hatchen, W (1996) *The World News Prism: Changing Media of International Communication* (4th edn). Ames: Iowa State University Press.

Hatchen, W (2001) *The Troubles of Journalism*. Mahwah, New Jersey: Lawrence Erlbaum Associates.

Headrick, D (1981) *The Tools of Empire*. Oxford: Oxford University Press.

Held, D (2000) *A Globalizing World? Culture, Economics, Politics*. London: Routledge.

Held, D, McGrew, A, Goldblatt, D and Perraton, J (1999) *Global Transformations: Politics, Economics and Culture*. Cambridge: Polity Press.

Herman, E and Chomsky, N (1988) *Manufacturing Consent: The Political Economy of the Mass Media*. New York: Pantheon Books.

Herman, E and McChesney, R (1997) *The Global Media: The New Missionaries of Global Capitalism*. London: Cassell.

Hess, S (1996) *International News and Foreign Correspondents*. Washington, DC: The Brookings Institute.

Hess, S (2005) *Through Their Eyes: Foreign Correspondents in the United States*. Washington, DC: The Brookings Institute.

Hiatt, F (2007) 'The vanishing foreign correspondent', *The Washington Post*, 29 January.

Hills, J (2002) *The Struggle for Global Communication: The Formative Century*. Chicago: Illinois Press.

Hirst, P and Thompson, G (1996) *Globalization in Question*. Cambridge: Polity Press.

Hoge, J (1997) 'Foreign news: who gives a damn?', *Columbia Journalism Review*, 11(12): 48–52.

Hoggart, S (1988) 'Foreign Bodies: Part Five', *The Listener*, 16 June.

Hogge, B (2007) 'Reporting Africa blog by blog', openDemocracy.net

Hohenberg, J (1993) *Foreign Correspondence: The Great Reporters and their Times*. New York: Syracuse University Press.

Hojer, B (2004) 'The discourse of global compassion: the audience and media reporting of human suffering', *Media, Culture & Society* 26(4): 513–31.

Holm, HH (2001) 'The Effect of Globalization on Media Structures and Norms: Globalization and the Choice of Foreign News', in Hjavard, S (ed.) *News in a Globalized Society*. Goteborg: Nordicom. pp. 113–28.

Holton, R (2009) *Cosmopolitanisms: New Thinking and New Directions*. London: Palgrave.

Horsman, M and Marshall, A (1995) *After the Nation-state: Citizens, Tribalism and the New World Disorder*. London: Harper Collins.

Horvit, B (2006) 'International News Agencies and the War Debate of 2003', *International Communication Gazette* 68(5–6): 427–47.

Ibrahim, D (2003) 'Individual perceptions of international correspondents in the Middle East: an obstacle to fair news?', *International Communication Gazette* 63(1): 87–101.

Ibrahim, D (2010) 'The framing of Islam on network news following the september 11th attacks', *International Communication Gazette* 72(1): 111–25.

Innis, H (1950) *Empire and Communication*. Toronto: University of Toronto Press.

James, J and Versteeg, M (2007) 'Mobile phones in Africa: how much do we really know?' *Social Indices Research* 84: 117–26.

Jessel, D (1982) *Trumpets and Typewriters*, BBC TV Documentary.

Joesphi, B (2005) 'Journalism in the global age: between the normative and empirical', *Gazette: The International Journal for Communication Studies* 67(6): 575–90.

Johnson, T and Fahmy, S (2010) 'See No Evil, Hear No Evil, Judge No Evil? Examining Whether Al-Jazeera English-language Website Users Transfer Their Belief in Its Credibility to its Satellite Network', in Golan, G, Johnson, TJ and Wanta, W (eds) *International Media Communication in a Global Age*. London: Routledge. pp. 241–60.

Jowett, G and O'Donnell, V (1999) *Propaganda and Persuasion* (3rd edn). London: Sage.

Kapuściński, R (1999) 'We live in a global media village. So why doesn't this woman give a damn what's on the news?', *The Guardian*, 16 August.

Kalb, M (1990) 'Foreword', in Serfaty, S (ed.) *The Media and Foreign Policy*. New York: St Martin's Press. pp. xiii–xix.

Kariithi, N (1994) 'The crisis facing development journalism in Africa', *Media Development* 4: 28–31.

Kaul, C (1997) 'Imperial Communications, Fleet Street and the Indian Empire c. 1850s–1920s', in Bromley, M and O'Malley, T (eds) *Journalism: A Reader*. London: Routledge. pp. 58–86.

Kaul, C (2000) 'Popular Press and Empire: Northcliffe, India and the *Daily Mail*, 1896–1922', in Catterall, P, Seymour-Ure, C and Smith, A (eds) *Northcliffe's Legacy: Aspects of the British Popular Press, 1896–1996*. London: Macmillan. pp. 45–70.

Kaul, C (2006) 'India, the Imperial Press Conferences and the Empire Press Union: The Diplomacy of News and the Politics of Empire, 1909–46', in Kaul, C (ed.) *Media and the British Empire*. London: Palgrave Macmillan. pp. 125–44.

Keeble, R (1998) 'The Myth of Saddam Hussein: New Militarism and the Propaganda Function of the Human Interest Story', in Kiernan, M (ed.) *Media Ethics*. London: Routledge. pp. 66–79.

Keen, A (2005) *The Cult of the Amateur: How blogs, MySpace, YouTube and the rest of today's user-generated media are killing our culture and economy*. London: Nicholas Brealey.

Keenan, T (1999) 'Looking like planes and falling like stars: Kosovo, "the first internet war"', *Social Identities* 7(4): 539–50.

Kendall, B (2009) 'Diplomacy and Journalism', in Owen, J and Purdey, H (eds) *International News Reporting: Frontlines and Deadlines*. London: Wiley-Blackwell. pp. 89–108.

Kennard, C and Murphy, S (2002) 'Characteristics of War Coverage by Female Correspondents', in Seib, P (ed.) *Media and Conflict in the Twenty-first Century*. London: Palgrave. pp. 127–40.

Kelly, S (1978) *Access Denied: The Politics of Press Censorship*. The Washington Papers, Georgetown University: Center for Strategic and International Studies.

Kester, B (2010) 'The art of balancing: foreign correspondence in non-democratic countries: the Russian case', *International Communication Gazette* 72(1): 51–69.

Kiernan, V (1995) *The Lords of Human Kind: European Attitudes to Other Cultures in the Imperial Age* (2nd edn). London: Serif.

Kiousis, S and Wu, X (2008) 'International agenda-building and agenda setting: exploring the influence of public relations counsel on US news media and public perceptions of foreign countries', *International Communication Gazette* 70(1): 58–75.

Kim, EG and Hamilton, JW (2006) 'Capitulation to capital? OhmyNews as alternative media', *Media Culture Society* 28(4): 541–60.

Kim, JY and Yang, SU (2008) 'Effects of government public relations on international news coverage', *Public Relations Review* 34: 51–3.

Kim, ST and Weaver, D (2003) 'Reporting on globalization', *Gazette* 65(2): 121–44.

Knightley, P (1975) *The First Casualty: The War Reporter as Hero, Propaganda and Myth Maker, from the Crimea to Iraq*. London: Andre Deutsch.

Knightley, P (1988) 'Foreign bodies part three', *The Listener*, 2 June.

Knightley, P (2003) *The First Casualty: The War Reporter as Hero, Propaganda and Myth Maker from the Crimea to Iraq* (2nd edn). London: Andre Deutsch.

Kumar, K (1996) 'International News on Indian Television', in French, D and Richards, M (eds) *Contemporary Television: Eastern Perspectives*. New Delhi: Sage.

Kung-Shankelman, L (2000) *Inside the BBC and CNN: Managing Media Organisations*. London: Routledge.

Laidi, Z (1998) *A World Without Meaning*. London: Routledge.

Lambert, P (1956) 'Foreign correspondents covering the United States', *Journalism Quarterly* 33: 349–56.

Latouche, S (1996) *The Westernisation of the World*. London: Polity Press.

Lawrenson, J and Barber, L (1986) *The Price of Truth: The Story of the Reuters millions*. London: Sphere Books.

Lee, CC (1982) 'How others see America', in Atwood, E, Bullion, SJ and Murphy, S (eds) *International Perspectives on News*. Carbondale: Southern Illinois University Press. pp. 53–76.

Lee, CC, Chan, J, Pan, Z and So, C (2002) *Global Media Spectacle: News War Over Hong Kong*. New York: State University of New York.

Lee, S (2007) 'International public relations as a predictor of prominence of US news coverage', *Public Relations Review* 33: 158–65.

Livingston, S (1997) 'Clarifying the CNN Effect: An Examination of Media Effects According to Type of Military Intervention', http://www.ksg.harvard.edu/presspol/research_publications/papers/research_papers/R18.pdf (accessed: 9/4/07).

Livingston, S (1998) 'Beyond the CNN Effect'. Talk at George Washington University, April.

Livingston, S (2007) 'The Nokia Effect: The Re-emergence of Amateur Journalism and What It Means for International Affairs', in Perlmutter, D and Hamilton, J (eds) *From Pigeons to News Portals: Foreign Reporting and the Challenge of New Technology*. Baton Rouge: Louisiana State University Press. pp. 47–69.

Livingston, S and Asmolov, G (2010) 'Networks and the future of foreign affairs reporting', *Journalism Studies* 11(5): 745–60.

Livingston, S and Van Belle, D (2005) 'The effects of satellite technology on newsgathering from remote locations', *Political Communication* 22: 45–62.

Llewellyn, T (2009) 'This cowardly decision betrays the values the corporation stands for', *The Observer*, 25 January.

Louw, E (2005) *The Media and Political Process.* London: Sage.

Loyn, D (2003) 'Witnessing the Truth', *Open Democracy,* www.opendemocracy.net (accessed 15/3/08).

Lynch, J (2004) 'Reporting the World: the Ethical Challenge to International News', in Paterson, C and Srerberny, A (eds) *International News in the Twenty-first Century.* Luton: John Libbey.

Lynch, J and McGoldrick, A (2005) *Peace Journalism.* Stroud: Hawthorn Press.

Luyendijk, J (2009) *Fit to Print: Misrepresenting the Middle East.* London: Scribe Publications.

Luyendijk, J (2010) 'Beyond orientalism', *International Communication Gazette* 72(1): 9–20.

MacBride, S (1980) *Many Voices, One World: Communication and Society, Today and Tomorrow.* Paris: UNESCO.

MacKenzie, J (1984) *Propaganda and Empire.* Manchester: Manchester University Press.

MacKenzie, J (1986) *Imperialism and Popular Culture.* Manchester: Manchester University Press.

MacKinnon, R (2008) 'Blogs and China correspondence: lessons about global information flows', *Chinese Journal of Communication* 1(2) online version, http://rconversation. blogs.com/about.html

Makunike, E (1993) 'Out of Africa! Western media stereotypes shape world's portrait', *Media & Values* 61(Winter): 10–12.

Mandaza, I (1986) 'News from the Third World: Crossing the Barrier', in Desbarts, P and Southerst, J (eds) *Information/Crisis/Development: News from the Third World.* Ontario: University of Western Ontario.

Mansfield, F (1936) *The Complete Journalist: A Study of the Principles and Practice of Newspaper Making.* London: Sir Isaac Pitman.

Marinovich, G and Silva, J (2001) *The Bang-Bang Club: Snapshots form a Hidden War.* London: Arrow Books.

Martin-Kratzer, R and Thorson, E (2010) 'Patterns of News Quality: International Stories Reported in American Media', in Golan, G, Johnson, TJ and Wanta, W (eds) *International Media Communication in a Global Age.* London: Routledge. pp. 160–76.

Marr, A (2004) *My Trade: A Short History of British Journalism.* London: Macmillan.

Massing, M (2009) 'The News about the internet', *The New York Review.* pp. 29–31.

Matheson, D (2004) 'Negotiating claims to journalism: webloggers' orientation to news genres', *Convergence* 10(4): 33–54.

Mattelart, A (1979) *Multinational Corporations and the Control of Culture.* Brighton: Harvester Press.

Mattelart, A (1994) *Mapping World Communication: War, Progress, Culture.* Minneapolis: University of Minnesota Press.

Mattelart, A (1996) *Networking the World 1794–2000.* Minneapolis: University of Minnesota Press.

McArthur, J (1992) *Second Front: Censorship and Propaganda in the Gulf War.* Berkeley: University of California Press.

McChesney, R (1999) *Rich Media, Poor Democracy: Communication Politics in Dubious Times.* Urbana, IL: University of Illinois Press.

McChesney, R and Schiller, D (2003) *The Political Economy of International Communication; Foundations for the Emerging Global Debate about Media Ownership and Regulation.* Technology, Business and Society Programme paper Number 11 October UNIRSD.

McGillivray, A (2006) *A Brief History of Globalization: The Untold Story of Our Incredible Shrinking Planet.* London: Robinson.

McGregor, B (1997) *Live, Direct and Biased? Making Television News in the Satellite Age*. London: Arnold.

McLuhan, M (1964) *Understanding Media: The Extensions of Man*. London: Ark Paperbacks.

McNair, B (1995) *An Introduction to Political Communication*. London: Routledge.

McNair, B (2006) *Cultural Chaos: Journalism, News and Power in a Globalised World*. London: Routledge.

McPhail, T (2006) *Global Communication: Theories, Stakeholders and Trends* (2nd edn). London: Blackwell.

McPhail, T (2010) *Global Communication: Theories, Stakeholders and Trends* (3rd edn). London: Blackwell.

Meisler, S (1978) 'Covering the Third World', *Columbia Journalism Review*, Nov/Dec: 34–7.

Melvern, L (2001) 'Missing the Story: the media and the Rwandan genocide', *Contemporary Security Policy* 22(3): 91–108.

Mercer, D, Mungham, G and Williams, K (1987) *The Fog of War*. London: Heinemann.

Messner, M and Distaso, M (2008) 'The source cycle: how traditional media and web logs use each other as sources', *Journalism Studies* 9(3): 447–63.

Miles, H (2005) *Al-Jazeera: How Arab TV News Challenged the World*. London: Abacus.

Miller, D (2004) 'Information Dominance: The Philosophy of Total Propaganda Control', in Kamalipour, Y and Snow, N (eds) *War, Media and Propaganda: A Global Perspective*. Lanham, MD: Rowman and Littlefield. pp.7–16.

Miller, D and Dinan, W (2008) *A Century of Spin: How Public Relations Became the Cutting Edge of Corporate Power*. London: Pluto Press.

Moeller, S (1999) *Compassion Fatigue: How the Media Sell Disease, Famine, War and Death*. New York: Routledge.

Monteiro, C (2002) 'Covering the lost empire: the Portuguese media and East Timor', *Journalism Studies* 3(2): 277–87.

Moorcraft, P and Taylor, P (2008) *Shooting the Messenger: The Political Impact of War Reporting*. Washington, DC: Potomac Books.

Morgan, D (1995) 'British Media and European Union News', *European Journal of Communication*, 10: 321–43.

Morley, D (2006) 'Globalisation and Cultural Imperialism Reconsidered: Old Questions in a New Guise', in Curran, J and Morley, D (eds) *Media and Cultural Theory*. London: Routledge. pp. 30–43.

Morris, AJ (1984) *The Scaremongers: The Advocacy of War and Re-armament 1896–1914*. London: Routledge and Kegan Paul.

Morrison, D and Tumber, H (1985) 'The foreign correspondent: dateline London', *Media, Culture and Society* 7: 445–70.

Mowlana, H (1975) 'Who covers America?', *Journal of Communication* 25: 85–91.

Mowlana, H (1996) *Global Communication in Transition: The End of Diversity?* London: Sage.

Mowlana, H (1997) *Global Information and World Communication* (2nd edn). London: Sage.

Moyo, D (2009) 'Citizen journalism and the parallel market of information in Zimbabwe's 2008 election', *Journalism Studies* 10(4): 551–67.

Mungham, G (1987) 'Israel: Fog Over Lebanon', in Mercer, D, Mungham, G and Williams, K. *The Fog of War: The Media on the Battlefield*. London: Heinemann. pp. 261–90.

Munnion, C (1999) 'Into Africa', in Glover, S (ed.) *The Secrets of the Press: Journalists on Journalism*. London: Allen Lane.

Musa, M (1997) 'From Optimism to Reality: An Overview of Third World News Agencies', in *Beyond Cultural Imperialism: Globalization, Communication and the New International Order*. London: Sage. pp. 117–46.

Mytton, G (1983) *Mass Communication in Africa*. London: Edward Arnold.

Ndangam, L (2008) 'Free lunch? Cameroon's diaspora and the online news publishing', *New Media & Society* 10(4): 585–604.

Neuman, J (1996) *Lights, Camera, War: Is Media Technology Driving International Politics?* New York: St Martin's Press.

Nkrumah, K (1965) *The African Journalist*. Dar-es-Salaam: Tanzania Publishers.

Norris, P (1999) 'Global communications and cultural identities', *Harvard International Journal of Press/Politics* 4(4): 1–7.

Nossek, H (2004) 'Our news and their news: the role of national identity in the coverage of foreign news', *Journalism Theory and Practice* 5(3): 343–68.

Nyaira, S (2009) 'Mugabe's Media War: How New Media Help Zimbabwean Journalists Tell Their Story', Working Paper, Joan Shorenstein Center on the Press, Politics and Public Policy, Harvard University.

Nyarota, G (2008) 'Africa through the eyes of African reporters', *The Zimbabwean Times,* http://www.thezimbabwetimes.com/?p=23356 (accessed 5/5/10).

Nye, J (2004) *Soft Power: The Means to Success in World Politics*. New York: Public Affairs.

Oates, S (2008) *Introduction to Media and Politics*. London: Sage.

Obijiofor, L and Hanusch, F (2003) 'Foreign News coverage in five African newspapers', *Australian Journalism Review* 23(1): 145–64.

O'Brien, C (1980) 'The best news there is', *Journalism Studies Review*. Cardiff, July.

Olsen, G, Carstensen, N and Hoyen, K (2002) 'Humanitarian Crises: What determines the level of emergency assistance? Media coverage, donor interests and the aid business', *Forgotten Humanitarian Crises Conference*, Copenhagen, 23 October.

O'Neill, D and Harcup, T (2009) 'News Values and Selectivity', in Wahl-Jorgensen, K and Hanitzsch, T (eds) *The Handbook of Journalism Studies*. London: Routledge. pp. 161–74.

Otte, J-T (2009) *Cyberspace and Propaganda: Israel and the War in Gaza*, www.princeton.edu/~lisd/archived/commentary_february2009.pdf

Owen, J and Purdey, H (2009) *International News Reporting*. London: John Wiley.

Painter, J (2008) *Counter-Hegemonic News: A Case Study of Al-Jazeera English and Telesur*. Oxford: Reuters Institute for the Study of Journalism.

Palmer, M (1978) 'The British press and international news, 1851–99', in Boyce, G, Curran, J and Wingate, P (eds) *Newspaper History: From the Seventeenth Century to the Present Day*. London: Constable. pp. 205–19.

Palmer, M (2008) 'International news from Paris- and London-based newsrooms', *Journalism Studies* 9(5): 813–21.

Palmer, M, Boyd-Barrett, O and Rantanen, T (1998) 'Global Financial News', in Boyd-Barrett, O and Rantanen, T (eds) *The Globalization of News*. London: Sage.

Parekh, B (1988) 'Reflections on ... the legacy of colonialism ...', in Twitchin, J (ed.) *The Black and White Media Show*. Stoke-on-Trent: Trentham Books. pp. 111–23.

Parenti, M (1986) *Inventing Reality: The Politics of the Mass Media*. New York: St Martin's Press.

Paterson, C (2001) 'Media Imperialism Revisited: The Global Public Sphere and the News Agency Agenda', in Hjarvard, S (ed.) *News in a Globalized Society*. Göteborg: Nordicom.

Paterson, C (2005) 'When global media don't play ball: the exportation of coercion', *International Journal of Media and Cultural Politics* 1(1): 53–58.

Paterson, C (2006) 'News Agency Dominance in International News on the Internet', *Papers in International and Global Communication* 01/06. Leicester: Centre for International Communication Research.

Paterson, C (2007) 'International news on the internet: why more is less', *Ethical Space: The International Journal of Communication Ethics* 4(1/2): 57–66.

Paterson, C and Sreberny, A (2004) *International News in the Twenty-first Century.* Luton: John Libbey.

Pavik, J (2000) 'The Impact of technology on journalism', *Journalism Studies* 1(2): 229–37.

Pavik, J (2005) 'Running the Technological Gauntlet: Journalism and New Media', in de Burgh, H (ed.) *Making Journalists.* London: Routledge. pp. 245–63.

Pedelty, M (1995) *War Stories.* New York: Routledge.

Peng, Z (2008) 'Framing the anti-war protests in the global village: a comparative study of newspaper coverage in three countries', *International Communication Gazette* 70(5): 316–77.

Perlmutter, D (1998) *Photojournalism and Foreign Policy. Icons of Outrage in International Crisis.* Westport, CT: Praeger.

Perlmutter, D and Hamilton, JM (2007) *From Pigeons to News Portals: Foreign Reporting and the Challenge of New Technology.* Baton Rouge: Louisiana State University Press.

Peterson, S (1979) 'Foreign news gatekeepers and criteria of newsworthiness', *Journalism Quarterly* 116–25.

Philo, G, Hilsum, L, Beattie, L and Holliman, R (1999) 'The Media and the Rwanda Crisis: Effects on Audiences and Public Policy', in Philo, G (ed.) *Message Received.* London: Longman. pp. 213–28.

Picard, R (1996) 'The rise and fall of communication empires', *The Journal of Media Economics* 9(4): 23–40.

Pieterse, J (1995) *White on Black: Images of Africa and Blacks in Western Popular Culture.* New Haven: Yale University Press.

Pieterse, J (2009) 'Representing the rise of the rest as threat', *Nordicom Review* 2: 57–70.

Pietilainen, J (2006) 'Foreign news and foreign trade: what kind of relationship?', *International Communication Gazette* 68(2): 217–28.

Pike, R and Winseck, D (2004) 'The politics of global media reform, 1907–23', *Media, Culture & Society* 26(5): 643–75.

Pilger, J (2001) *Heroes.* London: Vintage.

Pilger, J (2002) *The New Rulers of the World.* London: Verso.

Poole, S (2002) *Reporting Islam: The Media and Representations of Muslims in Britain.* London: IB Tauris.

Postman, N (2004) 'The information age: a blessing or a curse?', *Press/Politics* 9(2): 3–10.

Powers, S and el-Nawawy, M (2009) 'Al Jazeera English and global news networks: clash of civilisations or cross-cultural dialogue?', *Media, War & Conflict* 2(3): 263–84.

Preston, P (2007) 'Censorship and commitment: foreign correspondents in the Spanish Civil War', *Journal of Iberian Studies* 20(3): 231–41.

Preston, P (2008a) *Making the News: Journalism and News Cultures in Europe.* London: Routledge.

Preston, P (2008b) *We Saw Spain Die: Foreign Correspondents in the Spanish Civil War.* London: Constable.

Quist-Adade, C (2000) 'In the Shadow of the Kremlin: Africa's Media Image from Communism to Post-Communism', in Malak, A and Kavoori, AP (eds) *The Global*

Dynamics of News: Studies in International News Coverage and News Agencies. Stamford, Connecticut: Ablex. pp. 169–76.

Raeymaeckers, K, Cosijn, L and Deprez, A (2007) 'Reporting the European Union', *Journal Practice* 1(1): 102–19.

Rao, S (2009) 'Glocalization of Indian Journalism', *Journalism Studies* 10(4): 474–88.

Rantanen, T (1997) 'The Globalization of electronic news in the nineteenth century', *Media, Culture & Society* 19: 605–20.

Rantanen, T (2002) *The Global and the National: Media and Communications in Post-Communist Russia.* Lanham, MD: Rowman and Littlefield.

Rantanen, T (2004) 'European News Agencies and their Sources in the Iraq War Coverage', in Allen, S and Zelizer, B (eds) *Reporting War: Journalism in Wartime.* London: Routledge.

Rauch, J (2003) 'Rooted in nations, blossoming in globalization: a cultural perspective on the content of a "northern" mainstream and a "southern" alternative news agency', *Journal of Communication Inquiry* 27(1): 87–103.

Read, D (1992) *The Power of News: The History of Reuters.* Oxford: Oxford University Press.

Read, J (1941) *Atrocity Propaganda, 1914–1919.* New Haven, CT: Yale University Press.

Redden, J and Witschge, T (2010) 'A New News Order? Online News Content Examined', in Fenton, N (ed.) *New Media, Old News: Journalism and Democracy in the Digital Age.* London: Sage. pp. 171–86.

Reese, S (2004) 'Militarised Journalism', in Allan, S and Zelizer, B (eds) *Reporting War: Journalism in Wartime.* London: Routledge. pp. 247–65.

Reese, S (2008) 'Theorizing a Globalized Journalism', in Loffelholz, M and Weaver, D (eds) *Global Journalism Research.* London: Blackwell. pp. 240–52.

Reese, S, Rutigliano, L, Hyun, K and Jeong, J (2007) 'Mapping the blogosphere: professional and citizen based media in the global news arena', *Journalism Theory & Practice* 9(3): 235–61.

Richstad, J and Anderson, M (1981) *Crisis in International News: Policies and Perspectives.* New York: Columbia University Press.

Righter, R (1978) *Whose News? Politics, the Press and the Third World.* London: Burnet Books.

Rizvi, H (2009) 'Foreign News Channels Drawing US Viewers', 29 Jan IPS.

Roach, C (1987) 'The US position on the new world information and communication order', *Journal of Communication* 37(4): 36–51.

Roach, C (1997) 'The Western World and the NWICO: United We Stand?', in Golding, P and Harris, P (eds) *Beyond Cultural Imperialism: Globalisation, Communication and the New International Order.* London: Sage. pp. 94–116.

Roberts, M and Bantimaroudis, P (1997) 'Gatekeepers in international news: the Greek media', *Harvard International Journal of Press/Politics* 2(2): 62–76.

Robertson, R (1992) *Globalization: Social Theory and Global Culture.* London: Sage.

Robertson, R (1994) 'Globalization or glocalization?', *Journal of International Communication* 1: 33–52.

Robins, K (1997) 'What in the World is Going On?', in du Gay, P (ed.) *Production of Culture, Cultures of Production.* London: Sage. pp. 11–66.

Robinson, S (2006) 'Journalism and the internet', *New Media & Society* 8(5): 843–49.

Rodney, W (1988) *How Europe Underdeveloped Africa.* London: Bogle L'Overture Publications Ltd.

Rosenblum, M (1977) 'Reporting from the Third World', *Foreign Affairs* July 55(4): 814–35.

Rosenblum, M (1978) 'The Western Wire Services and the Third World', in Horton, P (ed.) *The Third World and Press Freedom.* New York: Praeger. pp. 104–31.

Rosenblum, M (1979) *Coups and Earthquakes: Reporting the World for America*. New York: Harper & Row.

Rosenblum, M (1993) *Who Stole the News? Why We Can't Keep Up With What Happens in the World*. New York: John Wiley and Sons.

Rosengren, K (1974) 'International news: methods, data and theory', *Journal of Peace Research* 11: 145–56.

Roy, I (2007) 'Worlds apart: nation-building on the National Geographic Channel', *Media, Culture & Society* 29(4): 569–92.

Said, E (1978) *Orientalism: Western Conceptions of the Orient*. London: Penguin.

Said, E (1981) *Covering Islam: How the Media and Experts Determine How We See the World*. London: Routledge & Kegan Paul.

Said, E (1997) *Covering Islam: How the Media and the Experts Determine How We See the Rest of the World* (2nd edn). London: Vintage.

Sakr, N (2004) 'Al-Jazeera Satellite Channel Global Newscasting in Arabic', in Paterson, C. and Sreberny, A (eds) *International News in the Twenty-first Century*. Eastleigh: John Libbey. pp. 147–68.

Schecter, D (2004) 'Selling the Iraq War: The Media Management Strategies We Never Saw', in Kamalipour, Y and Snow, N (eds) *War, Media and Propaganda: A Global Perspective*. Lanham, MD: Rowman & Littlefield Publishers. pp. 25–32.

Schiller, H (1969) *Mass Communications and the American Empire*. Boston: Beacon Press.

Schiller, H (1973) *The Mind Managers*. Boston: Beacon Press.

Schiller (1976) *Communication and Cultural Domination*. White Plains, NY: ME Sharpe Inc.

Schmemann, S (2010) 'Looking forward: the future of foreign correspondence', *Journalism Studies* 11(5): 761–63.

Schlesinger, D (2009) 'The Future of News Services', in Owen, J and Purdey, H (eds) *International News Reporting: Frontlines and Deadlines*. London: Wiley-Blackwell. pp. 15–37.

Scholte, J (2005) *Globalization: A Critical Introduction*. London: Palgrave.

Scott, B (2005) 'A contemporary history of digital journalism', *Television & New Media* 6(1): 89–126.

Seaga Shaw, I (2007) 'Historical frames and the politics of humanitarian intervention: from Ethiopia, Somalia to Rwanda', *Globalisation, Societies and Education* 5(3): 351–71.

Seib P (2002) *The Global Journalist: News and Conscience in a World of Conflict*. Lanham, MD: Rowman & Littlefield.

Seib P (2010) 'Transnational journalism, public diplomacy and virtual states', *Journalism Studies* 11(5): 734–44.

Shah, A (2007) 'Iraq War Media Reporting: Journalism and Propaganda', *Global Issues*, updated 1 August 2007, http://www.globalissues.org/article/461/media-reporting-journalism-and-propaganda (accessed 29/12/09).

Shanor, D (2003) *News from Abroad*. New York: Columbia University Press.

Shaw, D (2001) 'Foreign news shrinks in era of globalization', *Los Angeles Times*, 20 September.

Sheehy, M (2008) 'Foreign news stories more likely to include unnamed sources', *Newspaper Research Journal*, Summer.

Shuster, S (1988) 'Foreign competition hits the news', *Columbia Journalism Review* May/June: 43–5.

Sigal, L (1973) *Reporters and Officials: The Organisation and Politics of Newsmaking*. Lexington, MS: DC Heath.

Simpson, J (1988) 'Foreign bodies: part two', *The Listener*, 26 May.

Simpson, J (2002) *News From No Man's Land: Reporting the World*. London: Macmillan.

Simpson, J (2010) *Unreliable Sources: How the Twentieth Century was Reported*. London: Macmillan.

Sinclair, J (1982) 'From Modernization to Cultural Dependence: Mass Communication Studies and the Third World', in Martin, L and Hiebert, R (eds) *Current Issues in International Communication*. New York: Longman. pp. 286–93.

Sinclair, J, Jacka, E and Cunningham, S (1996) *New Patterns in Global Television: Peripheral Vision*. Oxford: Oxford University Press.

Sklair, L (1991) *Sociology of the Global System*. London: Harvester Wheatsheaf.

Sklair, L (2001) *The Transnational Capitalist Class*. London: Blackwell.

Skurnik, W (1981) 'A new look at foreign news coverage: external dependence or national interests?', *African Studies Review* 24(1): 99–112.

Smillie, D (1997) 'Foreign news finds niche on the net', *Christian Science Monitor*, 13 February.

Smith, A (1979) *The Newspaper: An International History*. London: Thames & Hudson.

Smith, A (1980) *The Geopolitics of Information: How Western Culture Dominates the World*. Oxford: Oxford University Press.

Smith, A (1983) 'Reflections and Refractions on the Flow of Information', in Alavi, H and Shanin, T (eds) *Introduction to the Sociology of 'Developing Societies'*. London: Macmillan Press.

Smith, J, Edge, L and Morris, V (2005) *Reflecting the Real World? How British TV Portrayed Developing Countries in 2005*. London: DFID, VSO and IBT.

Smith, V (2009) 'Freelance Journalism', in Owen, J and Purdey, H (eds) *International News Reporting: Frontlines and Deadlines*. London: Wiley-Blackwell. pp. 55–71.

Smyth, P (2009) 'On being an Irish foreign correspondent', *Studies: An Irish Quarterly Review*. http://www.studiesirishreview.ie/articles/2004/Smyth.htm (accessed 13/5/10).

Smythe, D (1981) *Dependency Road: Communications, Capitalism, Consciousness and Canada*. Norwood, NJ: Ablex.

Snow, N and Taylor, P (2006) 'The revival of the propaganda state: US propaganda at home and abroad since 9/11', *International Communication Gazette* 68(5–6): 389–407.

Sonaike, S (2004) 'The internet and the dilemma of Africa's development', *Gazette: The International Journal of Communication Studies* 66(1): 41–61.

Sontag, S (2003) *Regarding the Pain of Others*. New York: Farrar, Straus and Giroux.

Sonwalkar, P (2001) 'India: makings of little cultural imperialism', *International Communication Gazette* 63(6): 505–19.

Soo Lim, Y and Barnett, G (2010) 'The Impact of Global News Coverage on International Aid', in Golan, G, Johnson, TJ and Wanta, W (eds) *International Media Communication in a Global Age*. London: Routledge. pp. 89–108.

Sosale, S (2003) 'Envisioning a new word order through journalism: lessons from recent history', *Journalism Theory, Practice & Criticism*, 4(3): 377–92.

Sparks, C (2005) 'The problem of globalization', *Global Media and Communication* 1(1): 220–23.

Sparks, C (2008) *Globalization, Development and the Mass Media*. London: Sage.

Sparks, C with Reading, A (1998) *Communism, Capitalism and the Mass Media*. London: Sage.

Sreberny-Mohammdi, A (1984) 'The world of news', *Journal of Communication* (Winter): 121–34.

Sreberny-Mohammdi, A (1995) 'US Media Covers the World', in Downing, J Mohammadi, A and Sreberny-Mohammadi, A (eds) *Questioning the Media*. London: Sage. pp. 296–307.

Sreberny-Mohammadi, A (2000) 'The Global and Local in International Communications', in Curran, J and Gurevitch, M (eds) *Mass Media and Society* (3rd edn). London: Arnold. pp. 93–119.

Sreberny-Mohammadi, A, Wisbeck, D, McKenna, J and Boyd-Barrett, O (1997) *Media in a Global Context*. London: Arnold.

Sreberny, A and Paterson, C (2004) 'Introduction', in Paterson, C and Sreberny, A (eds) *International News in the Twenty-first Century*. Luton: John Libbey. pp. 3–27.

Sriramesh, K and Vercic, D (2007) 'The impact of globalization on public relations', *Public Relations Review* 33: 355–59.

Standard Techniques (1985) Documentary made for Channel 4 by Diverse Production, presenter Christopher Hird.

Standage, T (1999) *The Victorian Internet*. London: Phoenix.

Startt, J (1991) *Journalists for Empire*. Westport, CT: Greenwood Press.

Stead, WT (1886) 'Government by journalism', *The Contemporary Review*, May: 653–74.

Stephens, M (1997) *A History of News*. Fort Worth, TX: Harcourt Brace.

Stevenson, R and Cole, R (1984) 'Issues in Foreign News', in Stevenson, R and Shaw, D (eds) *Foreign News and the New World Information Order*. Ames: Iowa State University Press.

Stone, J (1980) 'The Picture from Abroad', in Barrett, M and Sklar, Z (eds) *The Eye of the Storm – the Alfred Du Pont-Columbia University Survey of Broadcast Journalism*. New York: Columbia University Press. pp. 215–25.

Strange, S (1994) *States and Markets* (2nd edn). London: Pinter Publishers.

Straubhaar, J (2007) *World Television: From Global to Local*. London: Sage.

Sussman, L (1981) 'The Western Media and the Third World's Challenge', in Anderson, M and Richstad, J (eds) *Crisis in International News*. New York: Columbia University Press. pp. 344–54.

Sutcliffe, J, Lee, M and Soderlund, W (2005) 'Women and crisis reporting: television news coverage of political crises in the Caribbean', *Press/Politics* 10(3): 99–124.

Sutherland, J (2004) *The Restoration Newspaper and its Development* (2nd edn). Cambridge: Cambridge University Press.

Tae Kim, S and Weaver, D (2003) 'Reporting globalization: a comparative analysis of sourcing patterns in five countries' newspapers', *Gazette: The International Journal of Communication Studies* 65(2): 121–44.

Tai, Z (2000) 'Media of the world and world of the media', *Gazette: The International Journal of Communication Studies* 62(5): 331–53.

Tai, Z and Chang, T-K (2002) 'The global news and the pictures in their heads: a comparative analysis of audience interest, editor perceptions and newspaper coverage', *Gazette: The International Journal of Communication Studies* 64(3): 251–65.

Taylor, P (1994) 'Back to the future: integrating the media into the history of international relations', *Historical Journal of Film, Radio and Television* 14(3): 321–29.

Taylor, P (1995) *Munitions of the Mind*. Manchester: Manchester University Press.

Taylor, P (1997) *Global Communications, International Affairs and the Media since 1945*. London: Routledge.

Taylor, P (1999) *British Propaganda in the Twentieth Century*. Edinburgh: Edinburgh University Press.

Taylor, P (2000) 'The World Wide Web goes to War, Kosovo 1999', in Gauntlett, D (ed.) *Web.Studies* London: Arnold. pp. 194–201.

Tenhunen, S (2008) 'Mobile technology in the village: ICTs, culture and logistics in India', *Journal of Royal Anthropological Institute* 14: 515–34.

Terrell, R (1986) 'Missing the beat of the revolution: the US press corps in South Africa', *Media Development* 3: 23–6.

The World is Watching (1988) Documentary directed by James Munro and Peter Raymount.

Third World and Environment Broadcasting Trust (2000) *Viewing the World: Production Study*. London: DIFD.

Thorsen, E (2008) 'Journalistic objectivity redefined? *Wikinews* and the neutral point of view', *New Media & Society* 10(6): 935–54.

Thurman, N (2007) 'The globalisation of journalism online: a transatlantic study of news websites and their international readers', *Journalism* 8(3): 285–307.

Thussu, D (2002) 'Managing the media in an era of round-the-clock news: notes from India's first tele-war', *Journalism Studies* 3(2): 203–12.

Thussu, D (2003) 'War, Infotainment and 24/7 News', in Thussu, D and Freedman, D (eds) *War and the Media*. London: Sage.

Thussu, D (2006) *International Communication: Continuity and Change* (2nd edn). London: Hodder.

Thussu, D (2007a) 'The "Murdochization" of news? The case of Star TV in India', *Media, Culture & Society* 29(4): 593–611.

Thussu, D (2007b) *News and Entertainment: The Rise of Global Infotainment*. London: Sage.

Tomlinson, J (1991) *Cultural Imperialism*. London: Pinter Publishers.

Townley, R (1984) 'The wars TV doesn't show you – and why', *TV Guide* 18 August. pp. 3–5.

Traber, M (1985) *Reporting Africa*. London: Thomson Foundation.

Traber, M and Nordenstreng, K (1992) *Few Voices, One World*. London: World Association of Christian Communication.

Tuinstra, F (2004) 'Caught Between the Cold War and the Internet', *Nieman Reports*, Fall, http://www.nieman.hardward.edu/reportsitem.aspx?id=100381 (accessed 29/12/09).

Tuinstra, F (2009) 'Internet Censorship: The Myth, Oft Told, and the Reality', *Nieman Reports*, http://www.nieman.hardward.edu/reportsitem.aspx?id=101905 (accessed 29/12/09).

Tumber, H and Palmer, J (2004) *Media at War: The Iraq Crisis*. London: Sage.

Tumber, H and Webster, F (2006) *Journalists Under Fire*. London: Sage.

Tunstall, J (1977) *The Media are American: Anglo-American Media in the World*. London: Constable.

Tunstall, J (1996) *Newspaper Power: The New National Press in Britain*. Oxford: Claredon Press.

Tunstall, J (2008) *The Media were American: US Mass Media in Decline*. Oxford: Oxford University Press.

Tunstall, J and Machin, D (1999) *The Anglo-American Media Connection*. Oxford: Oxford University Press.

Tunstall, J and Palmer, M (1991) *Media Moguls*. London: Routledge.

Twitchin, J (1988) *The Black and White Media Show Book*. Stoke-on-Trent: Trentham Books.

Uhlig, R (1999) 'Front line news now travels by email', *Daily Telegraph*, 27 March.

UNESCO (1978) *Mass Media Declaration*. Paris: UNESCO.

Utley, G (1997) 'The shrinking of foreign news: from broadcast to narrowcast', *Foreign Affairs* (March/April) 76(2): 2–10.

Van der Gaag, N and Nash, C (1988) *Images of Africa: the UK Report*. Oxford: Oxfam.

Van Ginnekin, J (1998) *Understanding Global News: A Critical Introduction*. London: Sage.

Vargas, L and Paulin, L (2007) 'Rethinking "Foreign News" from a Transnational Perspective', in Perlmutter, D and Hamilton, J (eds) *From Pigeons to News Portals: Foreign Reporting and the Challenge of New Technology*. Baton Rouge: Louisiana State University Press. pp. 20–46.

Vidyarthi, G (1988) *Cultural Neocolonialism*. New Delhi: Allied Press.

Vilanilam, J (1989) *Reporting a Revolution: The Iranian Revolution and the NIICO Debate*. New Delhi: Sage.

Viviano, F (2007) 'The Internet and Foreign News, Part 1: How We Report', http://cbs5.com/worldview/internet.news.viviano.2.937306.html (accessed 12/5/09).

Viviano, F (2008) 'The Internet and Foreign News, Part 2: The Perils of a Free Lunch', http://cbs5.com/worldview/television.literacy.viviano.2.937295.html (accessed 12/5/09).

Volkmer, I (1999) *CNN: News in the Global Sphere*. Luton: University of Luton Press.

Volkmer, I (2002) 'Towards a New World News Order: Journalism and Political Crises in the Global Network Society', in Allen, S and Zelizer, B (eds) *Journalism After September 11*, London: Routledge. pp. 235–46.

Vultee, F (2009) 'Jump back Jack, Mohammed's here', *Journalism Studies* 10(5): 623–38.

Wainaina, B (2005) 'How to write about Africa', *Granta*, Winter 92.

Walker, M (1982) *Powers of the Press: The World's Great Newspapers*. London: Quartet.

Wallis, R and Baran, S (1990) *The Known World of Broadcast News*. London: Routledge.

Wang, X (2010) 'An Exploration of the Determinants of International News Coverage in Australia's Online Media', in Glam, G, Johnson, T and Wanta, W (eds) *International Media Communication in a Global Age*. London: Routledge. pp. 261–76.

Weaver, D and Loffelholz, M (2008) *Global Journalism Research*. Oxford: Blackwell.

Wells, A (1972) *Picture Tube Imperialism*. New York: Orbis.

Wilke (1987) 'Foreign news coverage and international news flows over three centuries', *Gazette: The International Journal of Communication Studies* 39: 147–80.

Wilke, J (1998) 'Control of Domestic News Markets (2)', in Boyd-Barrett, O and Rantanen, T (eds) *The Globalization of News*. London: Sage. pp. 49–60.

Williston, S (2001) 'Global news and the vanishing American foreign correspondent', *Transnational Broadcasting Studies*, No. 6, Spring/Summer.

Wilnat, L and Weaver, D (2003) 'Through their eyes: the work of foreign correspondents in the United States', *Journalism* 4(4): 403–22.

Winseck, D (2008) 'Information operations "blowback": communication, propaganda and surveillance in the Global War on Terrorism', *International Communication Gazette* 70(6): 419–41.

Winseck, D and Pike, R (2007) *Communication and Empire: Media, Markets and Globalisation*. Durham, NC: Duke University Press.

Winseck, D and Pike, R (2009) 'The global media and the empire of liberal internationalism, circa 1910–30', *Media History* 15(1): 31–54.

Woollacott, M (1976) 'Western news-gathering – why the Third World has re-acted', *Journalism Studies Review* 1(1): 12–14.

Woollacott, M (2006) 'Morally engaged: reporters in crises', *The Political Quarterly* 76(August): 80–90.

Working, R (2004) 'Speaking in tongues: you're only as good as your translator', *Columbia Journalism Review* Jan/February.

Worsley, P (1984) *The Three Worlds: Culture and Development*. London: Weidenfeld & Nicholson.

Wu, H (2003) 'Homogeneity around the world? Comparing the systematic determinants of international news flows between developed and developing countries', *International Communication Gazette* 65(1): 9–24.

Wu, H (2007) 'A brave new world for international news? Exploring the determinants of the coverage of foreign news on US websites', *International Communication Gazette* 69(6): 539–51.

Wu, H and Hamilton, JM (2004) 'US foreign correspondents: changes and continuity at the turn of the century', *Gazette: International Journal for Communication Studies* 66(6): 517–32.

Xin Xin (2008) 'Structural change and journalism practice: Xinhua News Agency in the early 2000s', *Journalism Practice* 2(1): 46–63.

Zaharna, R and Villalobos, J (2000) 'A public relations tour of embassy row: the Latin diplomatic experience', *Public Relations Quarterly* 45(4): 33–7.

Zayani, M (2005) *The Al Jazeera Phenomenon: Critical Perspectives on New Arab Media*. London: Pluto Press.

Zelizer, B (2005) 'The Culture of Journalism', in Curran, J and Gurevitch, M (eds) *Mass Media and Society*. London: Hodder Arnold. pp. 198–214.

Zewe, C (2004) '"Infoganda" in uniform: The Bush administration creates media outlets to tell its story', http://www.nieman.harvard.edu/reportsitem.aspx?id=100788 (accessed 2/2/2010).

Zuckerman, E (2004) 'Using the Internet to Examine Patterns of Foreign Coverage', *Nieman Reports*. Fall: 51–52. http://www.nieman.harvard.edu/reportsitem.aspx?id=100530 (accessed 2/2/2010).

INDEX